国家重点研究基地
中国人民大学刑事法律科学研究中心编译委员会
主　任／赵秉志
总编译／谢望原

外 国 刑 法 典 译 丛

瑞典刑法典

陈 琴 译
谢望原 审校

外 国 刑 法 典 译 丛

北京大学出版社
PEKING UNIVERSITY PRESS

图书在版编目(CIP)数据

瑞典刑法典/陈琴译.—北京:北京大学出版社,2005.3
(外国刑法典译丛)
ISBN 978-7-301-08339-0

Ⅰ.瑞… Ⅱ.陈… Ⅲ.刑法-瑞典 Ⅳ.D953.24

中国版本图书馆 CIP 数据核字(2004)第 127112 号

书　　　名:瑞典刑法典
著作责任者:陈　琴　译
责 任 编 辑:孙战营
标 准 书 号:ISBN 978-7-301-08339-0/D·1027
出 版 发 行:北京大学出版社
地　　　址:北京市海淀区成府路 205 号　100871
网　　　址:http://www.pup.cn　电子邮箱:law@pup.pku.edu.cn
电　　　话:邮购部 62752015　发行部 62750672　编辑部 62752027
　　　　　　出版部 62754962
印 刷 者:河北三河新世纪印务有限公司
经 销 者:新华书店
　　　　　　650 毫米×980 毫米　16 开本　14.5 印张　230 千字
　　　　　　2005 年 3 月第 1 版　2008 年 1 月第 2 次印刷
定　　　价:22.00 元

未经许可,不得以任何方式复制或抄袭本书之部分或全部内容。
版权所有,侵权必究
举报电话:010-62752024　电子邮箱:fd@pup.pku.edu.cn

《外国刑法典译丛》编委会

编译委员会主任：中国人民大学赵秉志教授、法学博士，曾访学美国
总　　编　译：中国人民大学谢望原教授、法学博士，曾访学丹麦王国
编译审委会委员（排名不分先后）：
　　中国人民大学卢建平教授,法国法学博士,负责法文方面审译
　　中国人民大学冯军教授、法学博士,曾访学德国、日本,负责德文方面审译
　　清华大学张明楷教授,曾访学日本、德国,负责日文方面审译
　　清华大学黎宏教授,日本法学博士,负责日文方面审译
　　武汉大学莫洪宪教授、法学博士,曾访学俄罗斯、前南斯拉夫,负责俄文方面审译
　　武汉大学刘艳红教授、法学博士,曾访学德国,负责英文方面审译
　　西南政法大学陈忠林教授,意大利法学博士,负责意大利文方面审译
　　吉林大学张旭教授、法学博士,曾访学德国、比利时,负责英文方面审译
　　中南财经政法大学齐文远教授、法学博士,曾访学丹麦王国,负责英文方面审译
　　中南财经政法大学李希慧教授、法学博士,曾访学英国,负责英文方面审译
　　华东政法学院郑伟教授,德国法学博士,负责德文方面审译

《外国刑法典译丛》总序

译介外国刑法典是一项极其有意义的学术活动。早在20世纪中后期,美国法学界就曾经以《美国外国刑法典丛书》(The American Series of Foreign Penal Codes)形式译介过世界上数十个国家的刑事法典(包括西欧国家和东欧社会主义国家以及亚洲一些国家的刑法典),作为美国法学界比较研究或者立法借鉴用书出版。我国台湾地区也在20世纪70年代翻译出版过《各国刑法汇编》(包括欧洲和亚洲十余个国家的刑法典和刑法草案),作为台湾地区立法和法学教学研究的参考。我国虽然有一些译介外国刑事法典的著作零星出版,但并未形成规模。且20世纪80年代以后,世界范围内掀起了刑法改革的浪潮,两大法系很多国家进行了刑事法典或刑事制定法的修订。这些新的刑事立法只有极少数被介绍到中国来。考虑到我国刑事法学教学研究以及立法参考需要,并弥补译介外国刑事法典的不足,我们拟组织一批包括有海外访学经历且有较高外语水平和法律专业素养的中青年学者译介一批外国刑事法典。

考虑到世界上两大法系的刑事法各有优点,且我国急需吸收其立法优点和那些值得借鉴的先进刑法理论,尽快完善我国刑事立法,建立有中国特色的刑法学理论体系,因此我们拟用若干年时间,译介一批外国刑事法典(将包括大陆法系国家的刑事法典和英美法系国家的刑事制定法)。为了便于高明的读者完整地理解外国刑事法典且弥补翻译的失误,我们拟将译介之外国刑事法典的外文附录在后。

应当说明的是,由于各国刑法典一般以自己本民族语言为官方文本,而目前我国刑法学界很难找到通晓各国文字的人才,因此,一方面,我们力求从各国的本国语言文本翻译成中文,另一方面,我们在不能直接从其本民族语言译成中文的情况下,将以其英文本为根据译成中文。好在各国刑法典之译成英文,均为各国著名刑法学家所为,其专业水平与英文水平均有保障,虽然可能存在因为语文的转换出现难以避免的误差，但是对我们学习研究来说仍然是极具参考价值的。本译丛将首先考虑译介那些我国尚无中文本且在世界上具有重要影响的刑法典，同时，对于那些虽然曾经出版过中文本但年代已经久远且新近又有重大修订补充的具有重要影响的刑法典，我们也考虑将其纳入本译丛。即将翻译出版的刑事法典包括：丹麦刑法典与丹麦刑事执行法；瑞典刑法典；挪威刑法典；芬兰刑法典；荷兰刑法典；美国联邦刑法和三十多个州的刑法；澳大利亚刑事制定法；加拿大 2002 年修订刑事制定法；乌克兰刑法典；等等。

本刑法典译丛由国家重点研究基地中国人民大学刑事法律科学研究中心组织编译，由部分有海外留(访)学经历的知名刑事法学者组成编译委员会，以确保翻译质量。

我们热忱欢迎那些具有深厚专业素养和良好外文功底的刑事法学者加入到这个翻译外国刑法典的行列中来，也欢迎收集有我们尚缺的外国刑法典的同仁为我们提供译本原件并参与翻译。让我们共同携手为完善中国的刑事法制度、推进中国的刑法学研究作出自己的贡献！

国家重点研究基地
中国人民大学刑事法律科学研究中心
2004 年 10 月 16 日

中译者序

《瑞典刑法典》是瑞典关于犯罪与刑事责任的主要立法,于1962年通过并于1965年生效。刑法典的通过和生效标志着一个长期的刑事立法发展进程的终结,同时也意味着一个新的变革时期的开端。从刑事立法的正规化至现行刑法典的颁行,期间经历了近三百年。此前,在努力创造一个远离冲突的社会的过程中,瑞典一直在尝试新的立法方法和立法技术。

包含在《1734年大法典》中的《犯罪法》和《刑罚法》的出台,象征着曾在中世纪的瑞典以及瑞典强权时代盛行一时的立法技术寿终正寝。1809年,议会根据赫尔姆赫森(Holmhernsson)教授的提议,任命了一个委员会,为私法和刑法的彻底修改作准备。多数委员认为,应当根据社会的需要,参照国外立法,起草一部全新的刑法典。由于主张不同,莱本尼斯(Rabenius)教授(刑法的修订工作曾被授权给他)和他的一些同事退出了这个委员会。余下的成员当中,斯戴夫(Staaff)、里曲特(Richert)和阿夫则里斯(Afzelius)起草了1815年草案并呈递议会。由于该委员会非常忙碌,接下来的十年里倾心于私法的修改,直到1826年才重新回到刑法典的准备工作上来。1832年,刑法修改的准备工作完毕,新的草案以《巴伐利亚法典》、《汉诺威法典》、《奥地利法典》及各自的修正为蓝本。包括波塞斯(Boethius)、莱本尼斯(Rabenius)、格鲁布(Grubbe)、阿特本(Atterbom)和霍姆博森(Holmbergsson)在内的众多法学家都对这部草案提出了大量批评。为此,一个新的委员会于1839年出版了一部修订过的草案,并于1844年出版了自己的草案及其注释。这一修正版采取了激进的做法,只承认一种刑罚,即分成7个等级的简易监禁,因而没有被议会采纳。二十多年后,刑法改革采用了特殊的单行条例的形式,例如废除死刑,废除笞刑和教会苦役(适用于盗窃和抢劫),伪造罪和诈欺罪的惩处,谋杀、杀人以及人身伤害的惩处,单独监禁措施等方面的单行条例。1862年,政府提交了一部新的草案,这部草案获得通过并于 1864 年 2 月 16 日生效。人们普遍认为这部法案的改革力度极小。因此,尽管自从 1809 年的政治变革之后,瑞典就觉察到了制定新的刑法典的必要性,不过改革的车轮行进缓慢,新法典直到 1864 年才诞生,并在瑞典实施了整整一百年。

1909 年,为刑法改革和起草新刑法典设计原则的任务交到了当时最博学的学者、隆德大学刑法学教授约翰·塞伦(Johan Thyrén, 1861—1933 年)手中,其未尽的工作成为后续立法努力的基础。伟大的法律改革家和立法者卡尔·斯莱特(Minister Karl Schlyter, 1959 年至 1979 年期间担任法务大臣)分别于 1932 年和 1934 年为立法制定了指导方针。经过司法部的必要准备之后,为刑法改革和起草新刑法典设计原则的任务由刑法委员会以及刑法典委员会分别承担。刑法委员会成立于 1937 年,当时一家上诉法院的首席法官拜格·伊克博格(Biger Ekeberg, 1880—1968 年)被任命为刑法委员会的主席。刑法典委员会成立于 1938 年,被任命为主席的卡尔·斯莱特当时也是另一家上诉法院首席法官。刑法委员会主要研究犯罪问题,而刑法典委员会则主要关注刑罚问题。乌普萨拉大学刑法学教授伊万·斯特瑞尔(Ivar Strahl, 1899—1987 年)是这两个研究机构中最具影响力的人。根据斯莱特的方案,改革措施分步骤进行。研究完成之后,刑法委员会在一份关于刑法典的建议中概括其研究成果,而刑法典委员会也在一份关于立法和刑罚问题的建议中公布自己的成果。1962 年秋季,一部以刑法典为名的政府草案被提交给了议会。此后,在 1964 年又一部政府法案被提交给议会,目的是将这部刑法典颁布为制定法。这部法案的通过使得瑞典刑法典也即现行刑法典于 1965 年 1 月 1 日生效。此后,瑞典又对刑法典进行了数次修改,部分修改内容在本法典中有所反映。

如上所述,一部刑法典的制定、修改和解释,总是基于本国政治、经济、文化等形势发展和变化的需要,而且往往受到国际和国内刑法思潮及理论的影响。比如,1994 年瑞典在原刑法典重婚罪基础上增设的非法缔结婚姻罪和非法同性伴侣关系罪,就是基于国家和社会对同性恋的逐步认可,对于登记的同性恋伴侣与婚姻从刑法上给予同等保护。作为译者,当力求准确传达刑法典的原意,至于过多的评价,不仅为译者力不能及,亦有越权之嫌。不过,对于以下几个方面,译者认为有必要特别指出:

首先,瑞典非常注重对出版自由和表达自由的保护,对于针对二者的犯罪,必须以宪法的形式予以规定①。为此,瑞典特别限制涉及出版和表达自由的犯罪的立法权力。同时,根据《政府约法》的规定,法院必须根据议会制定的具体法律审理案件,不能直接以宪法文件作为审判的依据,所以判断行为是否构成有关出版和表达自由的犯罪仍然必须依据刑法的规定。值得注意的是,《表达自由法》和《出版自由法》规定了一个重要的原则——犯罪赔偿原则,即对于侵犯表达自由和出版自由的案件,只有行为被确定为犯罪,被害人才能向犯罪人提出赔偿,故在程序上表现为先刑事后民事②。至于表达自由的限度,依照刑法的规定,主要涉及以下几种犯罪:(1) 第五章第1条之诽谤罪及第2条之严重诽谤罪;(2) 第五章第3条之侮辱罪;(3) 第十九章第5条之间谍罪和第6条之重间谍罪;(4) 第十九章第7条之未经授权处理秘密信息罪、第8条之严重未经授权处理秘密信息罪及第10条的有关过失犯罪的规定;(5) 第十六章第5条之煽动叛乱罪;(6) 第十六章第8条之对民族、种族群体煽动罪;(7) 第十八章第1条之煽动罪;(8) 第十九章第10条之非法情报行为罪;(9) 第十九章第2条之煽动战争罪;(10) 第二十章第3条之泄漏职业秘密罪;(11) 第二十二章第1条之叛国罪和第2条之背叛罪;(12) 第二十二章第5条之散布谣言危及王国安全罪。

　　除《瑞典刑法典》以及宪法性的《出版自由法》和《表达自由法》外,数百个法律和条例都有关于犯罪和刑罚的规定。虽然瑞典称刑法典为"普通刑法",而称其他法律和条例为"特别刑法",但是宪法和法律都没有限制"普通刑法"和"特别刑法"对犯罪种类和程度的规范范围。在瑞典,最重要的特别刑法是《道路交通犯罪法》(1951年649号)、《走私货物处罚法》(1960年418号)、《麻醉品处罚法》(1968年64号)和《税收犯罪法》(1971年69号)。此外,还有大量主要不具有刑法性质但包含了许多刑法条款的法律,例如,《支票法》(1932年131号)第74条规定了支票诈欺罪。

---

① 瑞典的宪法文件目前有《政府约法》、《王位继承法》、《出版自由法》和《表达自由法》四部。参见《政府约法》第1章第3条和第2章第1条;《出版自由法》(1949年105号)第1章第1条;《表达自由法》(1991年1469号)第1章第1条的规定。

② 换言之,只有法院认定被告人的行为构成犯罪,受害人才能请求赔偿被侵犯表达自由的损失。这实际上是平衡保护公民的表达自由权和隐私权。而在我国,似乎更多考虑隐私权,更注重"表达"对他人造成的损害,而忽视对表达自由的保护。

其次,瑞典的刑事立法和司法实践都凸显轻刑化的理念。《瑞典刑法典》规定的对犯罪的制裁包括罚金和监禁之刑罚以及附条件之刑、缓刑和交付特别照管,监禁是最严重的制裁。瑞典于1921年废除了在和平时期犯罪的死刑,在1973年废除了在战争期间犯罪的死刑。刑法典第二十六章和《公共机构矫正待遇法》(1974年203号)规定了监禁的适用,监禁包括固定期限监禁和终身监禁。固定期限的监禁可以在14日至10年之间选择。终身监禁在一定条件下可以转化为固定期限的监禁。在一定条件下,可以对监禁适用附条件之刑和缓刑。瑞典刑事政策的一项基本原则是应最大限度地避免实施监禁,《瑞典刑法典》明确规定应当优先考虑监禁之外的其他制裁。在瑞典司法实践中,除谋杀罪和严重的麻醉品罪之外,往往对犯罪判处最低幅度的刑罚,而很少适用最高刑。例如,盗窃罪的最高刑可达2年监禁,但是瑞典目前对盗窃犯的处刑平均为2至3个月。司法实践中的这种量刑倾向导致了一种普遍的认识,即刑法典规定的刑度在很大程度上只是一种空置的威慑。在监禁的执行上,瑞典于2001年启动了一个以电子监测手段进行严密监督的项目,对于监禁刑期长的囚犯在服最后4个月之刑罚时可以通过电子监测手段进行,而不必在监狱服刑。

除刑罚和其他制裁外,法院可以对犯罪判处一项特殊法律后果,比如,根据刑法典第三十六章没收用于犯罪的财产;根据《侵权责任法》判处损害赔偿费;根据《外国人法》(1989年529号)驱逐犯严重罪的外国人;根据《驾驶证法》(1977年477号)吊销驾驶证;或者根据《禁止贸易法》(1986年436号)对严重不履行贸易义务的商人颁布限制贸易的禁令。对不能判处任何刑罚或其他制裁的法人,可以判处没收财产、法人罚金或惩罚性费用等特殊法律后果。

再次,瑞典的刑事立法体现了瑞典作为北欧一员的地域特色。北欧五国丹麦、挪威、瑞典、冰岛和芬兰由于地理、历史背景及文化渊源的缘故①,其刑事法律制度和规定存在许多相似及相同的地方。北欧刑法体系似乎具有双重立场,具有大陆法和普通法的典型混合性质。北

---

① 历史上,这五国的居民同源于诺连克-丘托尼克族。14世纪初,瑞典和芬兰同属一个王国,拥有共同的法律。1380年丹麦和挪威一度受一个君主的统治。1523年时,北欧只有两个国家,一个是包括丹麦、挪威、冰岛、法罗群岛和格陵兰岛的王国,另一个是包括瑞典和芬兰的王国。直到拿破仑战争之后,挪威和芬兰才成为独立国家。此后,这些国家间又经历了一些分合,最终形成今天的局面。

欧刑法虽然继受德国法的传统，但是也受到英美实用主义法律思想的影响。如果就制裁体系作为考察对象，瑞典与芬兰比丹麦和挪威更多受到传统价值的引导。简要地概括北欧刑法的特色，或许可以这样认为，北欧刑法的主旨是将犯罪看作一个社会问题，而不是应当消灭和打击的对象。因此，北欧刑法大都注重保护人权，在刑罚上不强调报应，偏重于一般预防。北欧对犯罪的一般预防思想实际上受斯堪的纳维亚的现实法律哲学的影响，不同于美国的实用主义和威慑观点。一般来说，北欧国家对犯罪制裁的标准比其他欧陆国家要低，更不用说美国。北欧刑事制度的这些特点在瑞典刑法中得到了鲜明的体现，比如，前述提及的瑞典对罪刑设置及制裁选择都彰显了轻刑化的理念。此外，瑞典刑事立法的北欧化特色，还表现在刑法典对北欧所缔结的一系列条约和协定的承认。北欧国家在刑事领域展开了广泛的合作。1948年3月18日北欧缔结了《关于承认和执行刑事判决公约》；1961年北欧国家制定了统一的引渡法；1962年北欧国家在赫尔辛基缔结了《丹麦、芬兰、冰岛、挪威、瑞典合作协定》，等等。《瑞典刑法典》对以上公约或协定都有细化的规定。例如，依照《瑞典刑法典》，瑞典法院根据属地主义和属人主义行使管辖权时不限于瑞典及其公民，而延伸至其他北欧国家及公民。

最后，有必要从比较法的视角予以简单阐释。一般来说，对他国刑法典的译介，不仅仅出于了解外国法律的兴趣，难免会有与本国法律相比较的意图。应当说，瑞典在地理、政治、经济和文化方面都与我国存在诸多差异①，仅从刑法典而言，也能很明显发现许多不同之处。比如，瑞典规定刑事责任年龄为15岁，对青少年犯罪有特殊的制裁制度；瑞典不承认法人的犯罪主体身份，对法人不适用刑法意义上的制裁措施②；瑞典只对刑法特别规定的犯罪才处罚预备、未遂和阴谋等犯罪的未完成形态；瑞典的刑罚只包括监禁和罚金，至于附条件之刑、缓刑和交付特别照管属于其他制裁，此外还规定了包括法人罚金在内的特殊法律后果，以及瑞典与我国对个罪的构成要件规定的差异，诸如此类，

---

① 瑞典位于北欧斯堪的纳维亚半岛东部，实行君主立宪制，实行发达的私营工商业与比较完善的国营公共服务部门相结合的"混合经济"，以高工资、高税收、高福利著称，国民文化素质较高。

② 如前所述，瑞典虽然不承认法人的犯罪主体身份，仍然可以依照刑法对其科处法人罚金或没收财产等，只是不将其视为刑罚或其他制裁。

不胜枚举。译者无意在此具体比较各项刑法制度的不同,况且,如果考虑各国的社会状况,并不存在孰优孰劣的问题。比如,我国没有实行瑞典的轻刑化,甚至没有废除死刑,应当说和我国的经济发展状况、社会文化传统以及国民法律素质等息息相关。再比如,我国地处东亚,不可能体会欧盟一体化和北欧合作所带给瑞典刑法的积极影响①。不过,瑞典刑法典的轻刑化所表达的价值取向,主要是保护人权的理念仍然是我国刑事法治不断追求的目标。

要说明的是,本法典依照英文版的《瑞典刑法典》翻译而来,因此只涉及至1999年5月1日的修改内容。关于此后的修改,有待进一步的整理和翻译。另外,《瑞典刑法典》不仅直接规定了犯罪的罪名,而且还根据犯罪的严重程度将犯罪划分为不同等级并赋予不同罪名,为了方便读者对罪名的查对,译本中一律使用黑体标出。

---

① 不过,西原春夫教授预言,随着亚洲经济的发展,欧洲所面临的事态迟早会在亚洲出现。参见西原春夫:《日本与德国的刑法与刑法学——现状和将来展望》,http://www.cass.net.cn/chinese/s07_fxs/s07_08_3.htm。

目 录

英译者序 ………………………………………………………（1）

第一编 总则 …………………………………………………（1）
  第一章 犯罪和对犯罪的制裁 ……………………………（1）
  第二章 瑞典法律的适用 …………………………………（2）

第二编 犯罪 …………………………………………………（5）
  第三章 对生命和健康的犯罪 ……………………………（5）
  第四章 对自由和安宁的犯罪 ……………………………（6）
  第五章 对名誉的犯罪 ……………………………………（8）
  第六章 性犯罪 ……………………………………………（9）
  第七章 对家庭的犯罪 ……………………………………（11）
  第八章 盗窃、抢劫和其他偷盗罪 ………………………（12）
  第九章 诈欺和其他不诚实罪 ……………………………（14）
  第十章 侵占和其他背信罪 ………………………………（16）
  第十一章 对债权人的犯罪 ………………………………（18）
  第十二章 损害罪 …………………………………………（20）
  第十三章 有关公共危险的犯罪 …………………………（20）
  第十四章 伪造罪 …………………………………………（23）
  第十五章 伪证、错误指控和其他不真实的陈述罪 ……（25）
  第十六章 对公共秩序的犯罪 ……………………………（27）
  第十七章 对行政行为的犯罪 ……………………………（31）
  第十八章 叛逆罪 …………………………………………（34）
  第十九章 对王国安全的犯罪 ……………………………（35）
  第二十章 滥用职位罪及其他 ……………………………（38）
  第二十一章 武装部队成员实施的犯罪 …………………（39）
  第二十二章 叛国罪及其他 ………………………………（41）
  第二十三章 未遂、预备、阴谋和共犯 …………………（45）

第二十四章　免除刑事责任的一般根据 …………… (46)

第三编　制裁 ………………………………………… (48)
 第二十五章　罚金及其他 ……………………………… (48)
 第二十六章　监禁 ……………………………………… (49)
 第二十七章　附条件之刑 ……………………………… (53)
 第二十八章　缓刑 ……………………………………… (54)
 第二十九章　刑罚的确定及制裁的免除 ……………… (57)
 第三十章　　制裁的选择 ……………………………… (59)
 第三十一章　交付特别照管 …………………………… (60)
 第三十二章　废除(1986 年 645 号法) ……………… (62)
 第三十三章　逮捕和还押候审期间的扣除 …………… (62)
 第三十四章　数罪并发和变更制裁的一般规定 ……… (63)
 第三十五章　制裁的限制 ……………………………… (66)
 第三十六章　没收财产、法人罚金以及犯罪
      的其他法律后果 …………………………… (68)
 第三十七章　监督委员会 ……………………………… (71)
 第三十八章　程序性规定及其他 ……………………… (74)

PART ONE　GENERAL PROVISIONS ………… (78)
 Chapter 1　On Crimes and Sanctions for Crime ……… (78)
 Chapter 2　On the Applicability of Swedish Law ……… (79)

PART TWO　ON CRIMES ………………………… (84)
 Chapter 3　On Crimes against Life and Health ……… (84)
 Chapter 4　On Crimes against Liberty and Peace …… (86)
 Chapter 5　On Defamation ……………………………… (90)
 Chapter 6　On Sexual Crimes ………………………… (92)
 Chapter 7　On Crimes against the Family …………… (96)
 Chapter 8　On Theft, Robbery and Other
      Crimes of Stealing ………………………… (97)

Chapter 9   On Fraud and Other Dishonesty .... (101)
Chapter 10 On Embezzlement and Other
            Breaches of Trust .... (105)
Chapter 11 On Crimes against Creditors .... (108)
Chapter 12 On Crimes Inflicting Damage .... (111)
Chapter 13 On Crimes Involving Public Danger .... (112)
Chapter 14 On Crimes of Falsification .... (117)
Chapter 15 On Perjury, False Prosecution and
            Other Untrue Statements .... (120)
Chapter 16 On Crimes against Public Order .... (125)
Chapter 17 On Crimes against Public Activity .... (133)
Chapter 18 On Crimes of Lese-majesty .... (137)
Chapter 19 On Crimes against the Security
            of the Realm .... (139)
Chapter 20 On Misuse of Office, etc. .... (144)
Chapter 21 On Crimes by Members
            of the Armed Forces .... (147)
Chapter 22 On Treason, etc. .... (151)
Chapter 23 On Attempt, Preparation,
            Conspiracy and Complicity .... (157)
Chapter 24 On General Grounds for Exemption from
            Criminal Responsibility .... (160)

PART THREE   ON SANCTIONS .... (163)
Chapter 25 On Fines, etc. .... (163)
Chapter 26 On Imprisonment .... (165)
Chapter 27 On Conditional Sentence .... (172)
Chapter 28 On Probation .... (174)
Chapter 29 On the Determination of Punishment and
            Exemption from Sanction .... (179)
Chapter 30 On Choice of Sanction .... (182)
Chapter 31 On Committal to Special Care .... (185)

Chapter 32	Repealed (Law 1986:645) .... (188)
Chapter 33	On Deduction of Period of Arrest and Remand in Custody .... (188)
Chapter 34	Certain Provisions on Concurrence of Crimes and Change of Sanction .... (190)
Chapter 35	On Limitations on Sanctions .... (196)
Chapter 36	On Forfeiture of Property, Corporate Fines and Other Special Legal Effects of Crime .... (200)
Chapter 37	On Supervision Boards .... (205)
Chapter 38	Certain Procedural Provisions, etc. .... (209)

后记 .... (215)

英译者序

《瑞典刑法典》于1962年通过,1965年1月1日生效。《瑞典刑法典》规定了瑞典绝大部分的犯罪行为。其他犯罪由特别立法规定。《瑞典刑法典》也包含了所有犯罪的一般规定、犯罪的制裁以及瑞典法律的适用。

将刑法典译成英文始于1972年。自此,考虑到立法的修改,进一步的翻译工作也一直在进行,最近一次是在1996年。现在的翻译由Norman Bishop完成,该翻译在详尽研究以前翻译的基础上,涉及直至1999年5月1日止对刑法典的修改内容。

采纳修正案的法律的编号标注在圆括号当中,并标明正在讨论之中的法律的编号。然而,并未涉及法律规定的变更安排或生效时间。

目前,仅仅使用中性术语书写法典的一部分内容。然而,法典其他部分使用的阳性术语应当理解为包括阴性。最终目的是将中性术语扩展至全文。

为对感兴趣的人提供帮助,司法部出版了该译文,但是司法部不承担翻译引起的法律后果以及由于使用引起的任何后果。

PREFACE

The Swedish Penal Code was adopted in 1962 and entered into force on 1 January 1965. It contains provisions on most of the acts that constitute crimes in Sweden. The provisions on other crimes are to be found in special legislation. It also contains general provisions on all crimes, the sanctions for crimes and the applicability of Swedish law.

The first translation of the Penal Code into English dates from 1972. Since then, several further translations have been made—the most recent in 1996—to take account of legislative amendments. The present translation, made by Norman Bishop, is based on a comprehensive review of earlier translations and takes account of amendments to the Penal Code up to 1 May 1999.

References to the laws adopting the amendments are given in parentheses and show the reference number of the law in question. However, laws regulating transitional arrangements or dates of entry into force have not been included.

At present only certain parts of the Code are written using gender neutral terminology. Nevertheless, male gender terminology in other parts of the Code is to be understood as including the female gender. The intention is ultimately to extend gender neutral terminology to the entire text.

The Ministry of Justice publishes the translation as a service to interested persons but takes no legal responsibility for the translation or for any consequences arising from its use.

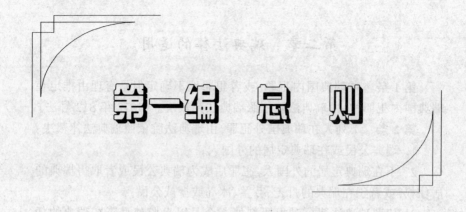

第一编 总 则

第一章 犯罪和对犯罪的制裁

第1条 本法典、其他法律和行政立法性文件规定的受本法典之刑罚处罚的行为是犯罪。(1994 年 458 号法)

第2条 故意实施的行为才能认定为犯罪,另有规定的除外。

在自愿引起的醉酒期间犯罪,或者犯罪人以其他方式使自己暂时丧失意识的,仍以犯罪论处。(1994 年 458 号法)

第3条 本法典中,制裁包括罚金和监禁之刑罚以及附条件之刑、缓刑和交付特别照管。(1988 年 942 号法)

第4条 按照有关个罪的规定和另外的特别规定适用刑罚。按照有关适用制裁的规定科处其他制裁,无论有关个罪的规定是否提及该制裁。(1988 年 942 号法)

第5条 监禁重于罚金。

与附条件之刑和缓刑有关的监禁的规定,见第三十章第 1 条。(1988 年 942 号法)

第6条 不满 15 岁的人犯罪,不科处制裁。(1988 年 942 号法)

第7条 废除。(1988 年 942 号法)

第8条 除制裁外,依照法律规定,犯罪可以导致没收财产、法人罚金或者其他法定特别后果以及损害赔偿责任。(1986 年 118 号法)

第二章 瑞典法律的适用

第1条 在瑞典国内犯罪,或者犯罪地不确定但是有理由推定在瑞典国内犯罪的,由瑞典法院依照瑞典法律裁决。(1972年812号法)

第2条 下列人在瑞典国外犯罪,由瑞典法院依照瑞典法律裁决:

1. 瑞典公民或在瑞典定居的外国人;
2. 不在瑞典定居的外国人,犯罪后成为瑞典公民或者取得瑞典的居住权,或者正在瑞典的丹麦、芬兰、冰岛或挪威公民;
3. 依照瑞典法律可对犯罪判处6个月以上监禁且正在瑞典的任何外国人。

犯罪地的法律认为行为不负刑事责任,或者犯罪地不属于任何国家,并且依照瑞典法律不可能处重于罚金之刑的,不适用前款规定。

对本条涉及之犯罪的制裁不应当重于犯罪地的法律对犯罪规定的最高刑罚。(1972年812号法)

第3条 除第2条规定外,在瑞典国外犯罪并有下列情形之一的,由瑞典法院依照瑞典法律裁决:

1. 在瑞典船舶或航空器内犯罪,或者在指挥官、船员或乘务员履行职务过程中犯罪;
2. 武装部队的成员在武装部队特遣队所处区域犯罪,或者其他人在此区域犯罪而该特遣队在此区域的目的不是训练;
3. 受雇于瑞典武装部队的国外特遣队的人在履行职务过程中在瑞典国外犯罪;
4. 针对瑞典国家、瑞典市政当局或议会或者瑞典公共机构犯罪;
5. 在不属于任何国家的区域针对瑞典公民、瑞典社团或私有机构、在瑞典定居的外国人犯罪;
6. 犯劫持罪,蓄意破坏海上、空中交通罪①,蓄意破坏航空港罪及犯上述罪之未遂,以及犯违反国际法罪、非法处理地雷罪、对国际法院虚假或过失陈述罪;
7. 依照瑞典法律,最低刑罚是4年或4年以上监禁的犯罪。

---

① 根据本条本项及第十三章5a条之规定,应为"蓄意破坏海上、空中交通罪",疑英文译本有误。——中文译者注

(1998 年 703 号法)

第 3a 条 除第 1 条至第 3 条的规定外,依照《关于刑事案件诉讼程序的国际合作法》(1975 年 19 号法)的规定应当由瑞典法院依照瑞典法律裁决的犯罪。(1976 年 20 号法)

第 4 条 犯罪行为实施地以及犯罪完成地或者在未遂情况下意图所犯之罪可能完成地,视为犯罪发生地。

第 5 条 处于瑞典国内的外国船舶或航空器内的外国人,包括指挥官、船员、飞行员或旅客,对其他外国人或外国犯罪的,未经瑞典政府或由瑞典政府指定的人授权,不受追诉。

对在瑞典国外实施的犯罪,仅在获得前款规定之授权后才可追诉。但是犯对国际法院虚假或过失陈述罪,或者具有下列情形之一构成犯罪的,不需要授权即可追诉:

1. 在瑞典船舶或航空器内犯罪或指挥官、船员、乘务员在履行职务过程中犯罪;

2. 武装部队的成员在武装部队的特遣队所处区域内犯罪;

3. 受雇于瑞典武装部队的国外特遣队的人在瑞典国外履行职务过程中犯罪;

4. 在丹麦、芬兰、冰岛或挪威犯罪,或者在位于瑞典或上述国家之一的地点之间从事正常贸易的船舶或航空器内犯罪;

5. 瑞典、丹麦、芬兰、爱尔兰或挪威公民对瑞典犯罪。(1993 年 350 号法)

第 5a 条 已生效的犯罪地所属的外国宣告的判决,或者已实施《1970 年 5 月 28 日关于刑事判决国际效力的欧洲公约》或《1972 年 5 月 15 日关于刑事诉讼移转的欧洲公约》的外国政府,对行为的责任作以下确定时,被告人不得因同一行为在瑞典被追诉:

1. 被告人被宣告无罪;

2. 被告人被宣告有罪但免除制裁;

3. 制裁已执行完毕或正在执行中;

4. 依照外国法律,制裁已经失效。

除外国政府应瑞典当局的请求启动法律程序外,前款不适用于第 1 条或第 3 条第 4 项、第 6 项、第 7 项所规定的犯罪。

外国宣告的判决已确定行为的责任,但是不存在本条前述的启动法律程序的障碍的,依照政府或政府授权的人的命令,可以在瑞典国内

再次追诉。(1987 年 761 号法)

第 6 条 在瑞典国内接受审判的行为人,因同一行为在国外受过刑罚处罚的,确定刑罚时应当适当考虑其已经在国外受过刑罚。对行为人应当处罚金或监禁,在国外已被判处剥夺自由的刑罚的,确定刑罚时应当充分考虑其已经在国外受过刑罚。

有前款规定之情形的,可以比照规定减轻或免除处罚。(1972 年 812 号法)

第 7 条 除本章关于瑞典法律的适用和瑞典法院的管辖权的规定外,还应当遵守获得普遍承认的国际公法的基本原则或与外国签订的协议的特别条款的限制。

第 7a 条 外国人在代表另一国家或国际组织执行一般职位的公务或职务时犯罪的,仅依政府的命令才受追诉。以误导性信息、隐瞒事实或其他手段意图隐匿犯罪时的身份的,不适用前述规定。(1985 年 518 号法)

第 7b 条 根据国际合作计划访问瑞典的外国军队的人在访问期间犯罪的,依政府的命令才受追诉。(1996 年 401 号法)

第 8 条 罪犯的引渡适用特别规定。

瑞典应当遵守有关从外国向瑞典引渡的条件的规定。

第二编 犯 罪

第三章 对生命和健康的犯罪

第1条 剥夺他人生命的,以**谋杀罪**处10年或终身监禁。

第2条 考虑导致犯罪的环境因素或其他理由,犯第1条之罪不太严重的,以**非预谋杀人罪**处6年以上10年以下监禁。

第3条 妇女杀死自己刚出生的婴儿,或者因被禁锢而在精神紊乱或极度悲伤状态下杀死自己孩子的,以**杀婴罪**处6年以下监禁。

第4条 废除。(1974年596号法)

第5条 对他人身体施以伤害、疾病或疼痛,或者致使他人丧失体力或处于类似的无助状态的,以**伤害罪**处2年以下监禁;犯罪轻微的,处罚金或6个月以下监禁。(1998年393号法)

第6条 犯第5条之罪严重的,以**重伤害罪**处1年以上10年以下监禁。

判断犯罪是否严重,应当特别考虑以下因素:是否使他人有生命危险,或者造成严重的身体伤害、严重疾病或具有其他明显特别残忍或野蛮的情况。(1988年2号法)

第7条 过失致人死亡的,以**致人死亡罪**处2年以下监禁;犯罪轻微的,处罚金。

犯罪严重的,处6个月以上6年以下监禁。驾驶机动车实施犯罪的,判断犯罪是否严重,应当特别考虑被告人是否受酒精或其他物质的影响。(1993年1462号法)

第8条 过失致人身体伤害或并不轻微的疾病的,以**致人伤害或**

疾病罪处罚金或6个月以下监禁。

犯罪严重的,处4年以下监禁。驾驶机动车实施犯罪的,判断犯罪是否严重,应当特别考虑被告人是否受酒精或其他物质的影响。(1993年1462号法)

第9条 重大过失致使他人有生命、严重身体伤害或严重疾病的危险,以**对他人制造危险罪**处罚金或2年以下监禁。

第10条 故意或过失违反《工作环境法》(1977年1160号)规定的预防疾病和事故的职责,犯第7条至第9条规定之罪的,应当依照《工作环境法》的规定以**对环境的犯罪**之一处罚。(1991年679号法)

第11条 谋杀罪、非预谋杀人罪、杀婴罪或不轻微的伤害罪的未遂、预备,谋杀罪、非预谋杀人罪或重伤害罪的阴谋,以及没有揭露重伤害罪的,依照第二十三章的规定处罚。(1991年679号法)

第12条 引起身体伤害或疾病,犯罪不太严重的,仅受害方告诉或为公共利益,公诉人才提起诉讼。(1991年679号法)

第四章 对自由和安宁的犯罪

第1条 意图伤害他人身体或健康,或者迫使他人服务,或者勒索他人,劫持并带走或者禁锢儿童或其他人的,以**绑架罪**处4年以上10年以下或终身监禁。

犯罪不太严重的,处6年以下监禁。(1998年393号法)

第2条 除第1条规定的情形外,绑架或禁锢他人,或者以其他方式剥夺他人自由的,以**非法剥夺自由罪**处1年以上10年以下监禁。

犯罪不太严重的,处罚金或2年以下监禁。(1998年393号法)

第3条 除第1条、第2条之规定外,非法胁迫或欺骗某人,使其进入军队、工作部门或其他类似限制状态,或者引诱某人前往或留在具有被迫害或因随意性关系被剥削的危险的国外某个地方,或者陷入其他困境的,以**使人陷入危险处境罪**处1年以上10年以下监禁。

犯罪不太严重的,处罚金或2年以下监禁。(1998年393号法)

第4条 以殴打或其他暴力,或者以犯罪相威胁,迫使他人做、服从或不做某事的,以**非法胁迫罪**处罚金或2年以下监禁。威胁告发、揭发他人的犯罪或者公布有关他人的有害信息,实施这类胁迫如果属不正当的,也以非法胁迫罪论处。

犯前款之罪严重的，处 6 个月以上 6 年以下监禁。判断犯罪是否严重，应当特别考虑是否具有使人痛苦以逼取供述或者使用其他酷刑的行为。

第 4a 条　对与自己有或曾经有密切关系的人实施第三章、第四章或第六章规定之罪，如果行为之部分要素反复侵犯他人尊严并严重损害他人自信的，以**严重侵犯尊严罪**处 6 个月以上 6 年以下监禁。

男子对与其有或曾经有婚姻关系或者可视为婚姻的同居关系的妇女犯前款之罪的，以**严重侵犯妇女尊严罪**依照前款处罚。（1998 年 393 号法）

第 5 条　对他人使用武器或者以实施犯罪相威胁，引起被威胁的人对自己或他人的人身或财产安全产生严重恐惧的，以**非法威胁罪**处罚金或 1 年以下监禁。

犯罪严重的，处 6 个月以上 4 年以下监禁。（1993 年 207 号法）

第 6 条　非法侵入或停留于他人的生活寓所的，无论是房间、房屋、院子或船舶，以**侵犯住宅安宁罪**处罚金。

未经授权侵入或停留于办公室、工厂、其他建筑或船舶、储藏区或其他类似场所的，以**非法侵入罪**处罚金。

犯前两款之罪严重的，处 2 年以下监禁。

第 7 条　骚扰他人身体，或者开枪、扔石块、制造大的噪音或以其他轻率的行为骚扰他人的，以**骚扰罪**处罚金或 1 年以下监禁。（1993 年 207 号法）

第 8 条　非法获取邮政、电信公司以邮件或电信传递、传送的交流信息的，以**侵犯邮政、电信秘密罪**处罚金或 2 年以下监禁。（1993 年 601 号法）

第 9 条　除第 8 条之规定外，非法开拆信件、电报或者取得被封缄、上锁或封闭保藏之物的，以**侵入安全保管处罪**处罚金或 2 年以下监禁。

第 9a 条　除第 8 条之规定外，对室内讲话、他人之间的谈话或者不允许公众进入且行为人没有参加或行为人以不正当手段进入的协商会或其他会议的讨论，非法秘密窃听或者为复制声音以技术手段录音的，以**窃听罪**处罚金或 2 年以下监禁。（1975 年 239 号法）

第 9b 条　意图以第 8 条规定的方式犯侵犯电信秘密罪或第 9a 条之罪，使用技术手段，对犯罪的既遂不负责任的，以犯罪的预备处罚金

或2年以下监禁。(1975年239号法)

第9c条 除第8条、第9条之规定外,非法获取自动数据处理记录,或者在记录器中非法改变、删除或插入记录的,以**侵犯数据秘密罪**处罚金或2年以下监禁。本条中所指记录还包括为使用自动数据程序以电子或类似方式正在处理的信息。(1998年206号法)

第10条 绑架罪、非法剥夺自由罪或使人陷入危险处境罪的预备、阴谋,以及没有揭露上述犯罪的,依照第二十三章的规定处罚。严重非法胁迫罪或侵犯数据秘密罪的未遂、预备,如果既遂也不能被认为轻微的,同样适用本规定。(1998年206号法)

第11条 侵犯住宅安宁罪、不太严重的非法侵入罪、非在公共场所实施的非法窃听罪或该罪的预备、非在公共场所实施的骚扰罪、侵入安全保管处罪,仅受害方告诉,或为公共利益公诉人才提起诉讼。威胁告发、揭发他人的犯罪或者公布有关他人的有害信息,犯非法胁迫罪或者该罪的未遂、预备的,同样适用本规定。(1975年239号法)

第五章　对名誉的犯罪

第1条 意图使他人受到其他人的不尊重,指摘他人是罪犯或拥有应当受指责的生活方式,或者以其他方式发布信息的,以**诽谤罪**处罚金。

有义务表达自己的想法,或者考虑到环境因素就事项发布信息是可辩解的,或者行为人能证明信息真实或有合理根据的,不处罚。

第2条 犯第1条之罪严重的,以**重诽谤罪**处罚金或2年以下监禁。

判断犯罪是否严重,应当特别考虑信息是否因为内容或散播的范围等被认为导致严重的损害。

第3条 以侮辱性的言词或指控,或者以其他无耻的行为侮辱他人,依照第1条或第2条不受处罚的,以**侮辱罪**处罚金。

犯罪严重的,处罚金或6个月以下监禁。

第4条 诋毁死者名誉,冒犯了生者或者考虑自死者在世之时和其他情况可以被认为扰乱了死者应当享有之安宁的,依照第1条或第2条处罚。

第5条 第1条至第3条之罪,仅受害方可以提起诉讼。如果受

害方告诉,并且基于特别理由为公共利益提起诉讼是必要的,公诉人也可以对下列行为提起诉讼:

1. 诽谤或重诽谤;
2. 侮辱正履行公务或即将行使公职的人;
3. 影射他人的种族、肤色、国籍、民族起源或宗教信仰,侮辱他人;
4. 影射他人有同性恋倾向,侮辱他人。

直接针对死者诽谤的,死者尚健在的配偶、直系继承人、父亲、母亲或兄弟姐妹可以提起诉讼,公诉人考虑特别理由也可以为公共利益提起诉讼。

犯第1条至第3条之罪,侮辱当时正身处瑞典的外国政府首脑或外国派驻瑞典的代表,并因此侮辱了外国政府的,公诉人无需考虑前款规定可以提起诉讼,但必须有政府或政府授权的人的命令。(1998年393号法)

第六章 性 犯 罪

第1条 以暴力或威胁,该威胁包含迫近的危险或被威胁者认为包含迫近的危险,强迫他人性交或者从事类似的性行为,考虑侵害的性质和一般情况该性行为与强迫性交类似的,以**强奸罪**处2年以上6年以下监禁。致使陷入无助或类似无能力状态的,应当视为与暴力相同。

考虑暴力或威胁的性质以及一般情况,犯罪不太严重的,处4年以下监禁。

犯罪严重的,以**重强奸罪**处4年以上10年以下监禁。判断犯罪是否严重,应当特别考虑暴力是否危及生命,或者行为是否导致了严重伤害或严重疾病,或者考虑使用的方法、被害人很年轻或其他情形,行为是否特别残忍或野蛮。(1998年393号法)

第2条 除第1条之规定外,非法胁迫他人使从事性行为的,以**性胁迫罪**处2年以下监禁。

行为特别残忍或有其他情形,犯罪严重的,以**严重性胁迫罪**处6个月以上4年以下监禁。(1992年147号法)

第3条 明显妄用他人所处的从属状态,诱使他人从事性行为的,以**性剥削罪**处2年以下监禁。不恰当地利用他人无助、其他无能力状态或正遭受精神困扰的处境,与他人发生性行为的,同样适用本规定。

行为特别残忍或有其他情形,犯罪严重的,以**严重性剥削罪**处 6 年以下监禁。(1998 年 393 号法)

第 4 条 与不满 18 岁的后代、有责任抚养的人或者公共机构决定其有责任照顾或监管的人发生性行为的,以**对未成年人性剥削罪**处 4 年以下监禁。除本章前述规定的情形外,与不满 15 岁的人发生性行为的,同样适用本规定。

行为人特别缺乏对未成年人的考虑、未成年人年幼或有其他情形,犯罪严重的,以**对未成年人严重性剥削罪**处 2 年以上 8 年以下监禁。(1998 年 393 号法)

第 5 条 废除。(1994 年 1499 号法)

第 6 条 除本章前述规定外,与自己的子女或后代性交的,以**与后代性交罪**处 2 年以下监禁。

与和自己有血缘关系的兄弟姐妹性交的,以**与兄弟姐妹性交罪**处 1 年以下监禁。

受非法胁迫或其他不适当手段,被强迫犯罪的,不适用本条规定。(1992 年 147 号法)

第 7 条 除本章前述规定外,与不满 15 岁的儿童发生性接触,或者诱使儿童实施或参与有性意味的行为的,以**性骚扰罪**处罚金或 2 年以下监禁。

以胁迫、引诱或其他不当影响诱使已满 15 岁但不满 18 岁的人实施或参与有性意味的行为,如果行为被用于制作淫秽图片,或者与制作淫秽图片无关但是构成淫秽姿势的,以性骚扰罪处罚。

以冒犯他人的方式暴露自己,或者恣意违反礼仪观念以言词或行为明显猥亵他人的,同样适用本条规定。(1994 年 1499 号法)

第 8 条 帮助或在经济上不当利用他人卖淫的,以淫媒罪处 4 年以下监禁。

对房屋有使用权的人,明知房屋的全部或部分空间被用于卖淫,仍然授予他人房屋的使用权,怠于采取合理期待其终止授权的措施,致使卖淫行为在该房屋持续进行或重新开始的,应当认定为帮助卖淫,依照前款规定处罚。

第 9 条 犯第 8 条之罪严重的,以重淫媒罪处 2 年以上 6 年以下监禁。

判断犯罪是否严重,应当特别考虑被告人是否帮助大规模卖淫或

残忍地利用他人。(1984年393号法)

第10条 许诺或支付报酬,与或试图与不满18岁的人发生性关系的,以**诱奸未成年人罪**处罚金或6个月以下监禁。(1984年399号法)

第11条 本章规定的针对不满法定年龄者犯罪负刑事责任,要求没有实际认识到被害人真实年龄之行为人有合理根据推定其被害人没有达到该年龄。(1998年393号法)

第12条 实施强奸罪、重强奸罪、性胁迫罪、严重性胁迫罪、性剥削罪、严重性剥削罪、对未成年人性剥削罪、对未成年人严重性剥削罪、淫媒罪以及重淫媒罪未遂的,依照第二十三章的规定处罚。共同预备、阴谋实施强奸罪、重强奸罪、对未成年人严重性剥削罪和重淫媒罪而不举发这些犯罪的,也依照第二十三章的规定处罚。(1998年393号法)

第13条 犯第4条第1款第2句对未成年人性剥削罪或未遂,或者犯第7条第1款性骚扰罪,犯罪人与未成年的被害人在年龄和发育上差别不大的,为公共利益才提起公诉。(1994年1499号法)

第七章 对家庭的犯罪

第1条 已婚的人缔结新的婚姻,或未婚的人与已婚的人结婚的,以**重婚罪**处罚金或2年以下监禁。

已登记的同性伴侣关系①的一方缔结婚姻的,以**非法缔结婚姻罪**处罚金或2年以下监禁。(1994年1119号法)

第1a条 已结婚的人登记同性伴侣关系,或已登记的同性伴侣关系的一方登记同性伴侣关系的,以**非法同性伴侣关系罪**处罚金或2年以下监禁。其他人登记同性伴侣关系,其同性伴侣已结婚或是已登记的同性伴侣关系之一方的,同样适用本规定。

第2条 废除。(1994年1119号法)

第3条 以告知当局错误信息或者不告知当局信息为手段,隐瞒或交换儿童,非法为自己或为他人提供虚假家庭身份,或者剥夺他人正

---

① 根据1995年生效的瑞典《同性伴侣关系法》(1994年1117号),同性恋配偶可以通过登记程序成为同性伴侣关系,原则上与婚姻关系相同。但是,适用于夫妻的规定对同性伴侣存在一些例外,主要是共同父母身份或对子女的共同监护权。——中文译者注

确家庭身份的,以**擅自变更家庭身份罪**处罚金或 2 年以下监禁。

第 4 条 未经授权使不满 15 岁的儿童脱离监护人监管的,以**对儿童任意行为罪**处罚金或 1 年以下监禁,针对个人自由的犯罪除外。与他人共同拥有对不满 15 岁的儿童的监护权,欠缺适当理由任意带走儿童,或者即将获得对儿童监护权的人未经授权实际占有儿童,如此不顾法律擅自处理的,同样适用本规定。

未经授权使不满 15 岁的儿童脱离依照《保护青年特别条款法》(1990 年 52 号)对该儿童拥有监护权的人的监管的,依照前款规定负刑事责任,针对个人自由或帮助逃匿的犯罪除外。

犯前两款之罪严重的,处 6 个月以上 2 年以下监禁。(1993 年 207 号法)

第 5 条 擅自变更家庭身份罪或严重的对儿童任意行为罪的未遂,依照第二十三章的规定处罚。(1993 年 207 号法)

第 6 条 对儿童任意行为罪,公诉人为公共利益才提起诉讼。(1973 年 648 号法)

第八章 盗窃、抢劫和其他偷盗罪

第 1 条 意图获得而非法取走属于他人之物,该盗用行为涉及财产损失的,以**盗窃罪**处 2 年以下监禁。

第 2 条 考虑被盗物的价值和犯罪的其他情况,犯第 1 条之罪轻微的,以**轻盗窃罪**处罚金或 6 个月以下监禁。

第 3 条 废除。(1987 年 791 号法)

第 4 条 犯第 1 条之罪严重的,以**重盗窃罪**处 6 个月以上 6 年以下监禁。

判断犯罪是否严重,应当特别考虑非法盗用是否发生在侵入住宅后,或者是否盗用他人携带的财产,或者被告人是否携带武器、爆炸物或类似帮助性之物,或者行为是否具有其他特别危险或残忍的性质,或者涉案财产是否具有重大价值或蒙受能被敏锐察觉的损失。(1988 年 2 号法)

第 5 条 以暴力或威胁窃取他人财物,该威胁包含迫近的危险或者被威胁者认为包含迫近的危险,或者在盗窃后或盗窃时被抓住,以该暴力或威胁抵抗试图重获被盗财物之人的,以**抢劫罪**处 1 年以上 6 年以下监禁。以该暴力或威胁强迫他人为或不为某行为,致使被告人获利而被强迫的人或其代表的人遭受损失的,同样适用本规定。致使他人陷入无助或类似无能力的状态的,应当认为与暴力相当。

考虑到暴力、威胁或其他情况,前款规定的行为性质不太严重的,不以抢劫罪论处而以行为触犯的其他罪名处罚。(1975 年 1395 号法)

第 6 条 犯第 5 条之罪严重的,以**重抢劫罪**处 4 年以上 10 年以下监禁。

判断犯罪是否严重,应当特别考虑暴力是否危及生命,或者行为是否导致严重身体伤害或严重疾病,或使用其他非常野蛮的手段,或残忍地利用被害人无防御或无遮蔽之状况。

第 7 条 非法获取或使用他人的机动车或其他机动交通工具的,以**盗窃交通工具罪**处 2 年以下监禁;犯罪轻微的,处罚金,依照本章前述规定犯罪可罚的除外。

犯罪严重的,处 6 个月以上 4 年以下监禁。

第 8 条 除本章有特别规定外,非法获取并使用或以其他方式盗用某物的,以**非法剥夺占有罪**处罚金或 6 个月以下监禁。安装或破坏锁或以其他手段非法妨碍他人的占有,或者以暴力或暴力威胁阻止他人行使保留或取走某物的权利,但是没有盗用的,同样适用本规定。

犯罪严重的,处 2 年以下监禁。

第 9 条 为回复个人的权利,非法妨碍他人占有的,以**自行回复占有罪**处罚金或 6 个月以下监禁。

第 10 条 非法转移电能的,以**非法转移电能罪**处罚金或 1 年以下监禁。

犯罪严重的,处 6 个月以上 4 年以下监禁。(1993 年 207 号法)

第 11 条 从森林或田野非法获取第十二章第 2 条第 2 款规定的物体,不构成非法侵入罪的,适用本章关于盗用财产的规定。

非法建造或毁坏栅栏、建筑、挖掘、犁耕、筑路、放牧或以其他方式妨碍他人对不动产的占有,或者未经授权剥夺他人对不动产或其中一部分的占有的,适用第 8 条和第 9 条关于非法剥夺占有和非法回复占有的规定。

第 12 条 盗窃罪、重盗窃罪、抢劫罪、重抢劫罪、盗窃交通工具罪或非法转移电能罪的未遂、预备、阴谋或没有揭露抢劫罪、重抢劫罪的,依照第二十三章的规定处罚。盗窃交通工具罪的既遂可能被认为轻微的,不处罚其未遂。

第 13 条 除重盗窃罪、抢劫罪和重抢劫罪外,对下列人犯本章规定的其他罪的,仅受害方告诉或为公共利益,公诉人才提起诉讼:

1. 与被告人共同生活的人,临时性居住的除外;
2. 配偶、直系血亲、姻亲、兄弟姐妹、姻兄弟、姻姐妹;
3. 与被告人有类似密切关系的任何其他人。

适用本条规定时,对犯罪的从犯和犯收受赃物罪、轻收受赃物罪的人,视为与被告人相同。(1987 年 791 号法)

第九章 诈欺和其他不诚实罪

第 1 条 欺骗某人为或不为某行为,致使被告人获利而被欺骗者或其代表的人受损的,以**诈欺罪**处 2 年以下监禁。

输入不正确或不完整的信息,或者修改程序或记录,或者使用其他手段非法影响自动数据处理或其他类似自动处理的结果,致使行为人获利而他人受损的,也以诈欺罪论处。(1986 年 123 号法)

第 2 条 考虑损失程度和第 1 条规定之罪的其他情形,犯罪轻微的,以**诈欺性行为罪**处罚金或 6 个月以下监禁。

利用住宿、饮食、交通、观看表演或类似以支付现金为对价之事获取利益,没有履行债务的,无论是否有人被欺骗,以诈欺性行为罪处罚。行为涉及的价值微不足道且具有第 1 条规定的其他情况的,不适用本规定。(1976 年 1139 号法)

第 3 条 犯第 1 条之罪严重的,以**重诈欺罪**处 6 个月以上 6 年以下监禁。

判断犯罪是否严重,应当特别考虑行为人是否滥用公众信任或者使用虚假文件或令人误解的簿记,或者犯罪是否具有其他特别危险的性质、涉及重大价值或导致可敏锐察觉的损失。(1976 年 1139 号法)

第 4 条 非法胁迫某人为或不为某事,致使行为人获利而被胁迫者或其代表的人遭受损失,不构成抢劫罪或重抢劫罪的,以**勒索罪**处 2 年以下监禁;犯罪轻微的,处罚金。

犯罪严重的,处 6 个月以上 6 年以下监禁。

第 5 条 依据合同或其他法律交易,意图获取与对价明显不成比例或不给付对价的利益,利用他人的困境、愚钝、思虑不周或对行为人的依赖的,以**高利剥削罪**处罚金或 2 年以下监禁。

依据商业行为或者其他常规或大规模经营行为中的信用授权,获取与相对债务明显不成比例的利润或其他财产利益的,也以高利剥削罪处罚。

犯罪严重的,处 6 个月以上 4 年以下监禁。(1986 年 123 号法)

第 6 条 有下列行为之一的,以**收受赃物罪**处 2 年以下监禁:

1. 以使财产难以归还予他人的方式,占有他人被犯罪剥夺之财产的;

2. 从他人的犯罪收益中获取不当利益的;

3. 不当为他人提供利用来自犯罪收益的财产或者该财产的价值的机会的;

4. 意图隐瞒财产的来历,帮助搬运、转移或变卖源自犯罪收益的财产,或者采取类似措施的;

5. 以要求、转移或其他类似手段主张由于犯罪引起的财产所有权的。

在商业活动或部分常规或大规模经营的商业活动中,以使财产难以归还予他人的方式,获取或收受可以合理推定为是从他人处盗用之物的,以收受赃物罪处罚。

犯前两款之罪严重的,处 6 个月以上 6 年以下监禁。(1993 年 207 号法)

第 7 条 犯第 6 条之罪轻微的,以**轻收受赃物罪**处 6 个月以下监禁或罚金。

有下列情形之一的,以轻收受赃物罪处:

1. 除第 6 条第 2 款之规定外,以使财产难以归还予他人的方式,获取或收受可以合理推定为是从他人处盗用之物的;

2. 第 6 条第 1 款规定的情形,没有认识到但有合理理由推定涉及犯罪的;

3. 以第 6 条第 1 款第 1 项规定的方式参与从他人处盗用财产的犯罪,没有认识到但有合理理由推定已经实施犯罪的。(1991 年 451 号法)

第 8 条 除本章前 7 条之规定外,不诚实地误导他人并诱导其为或不为某事,由此损害他人或其代表的人的利益的,以**不诚实行为罪**处罚金或 2 年以下监禁。(1970 年 414 号法)

第 9 条 以影响商品、证券或其他财产的价格为目的,向公众公布或散播误导性信息的,以**阴谋欺诈罪**处 2 年以下监禁,犯罪轻微的,处罚金或 6 个月以下监禁。

帮助组织股份公司或其他公司的人,或者因其职位应当特别熟悉公司的人,故意或重大过失向公众或持有公司股份能以财务意见影响公司评估的人公布或散播误导性信息,造成损害的,依照前款处罚。

犯罪严重的,处 6 个月以上 6 年以下监禁。(1993 年 207 号法)

第 10 条 为了用作对相关民事诉讼施加压力之手段,接收他人为出庭或其他不正当目的而制作的虚假文件或他人开出的资金不足之支票的,以**高利剥削取财罪**处罚金或 2 年以下监禁。

第 11 条 诈欺罪、重诈欺罪、勒索罪或高利剥削罪的未遂、预备,依照第二十三章的规定处罚。勒索罪的未遂不适用第二十三章第 3 条的规定。

意图欺骗承保人或具有其他欺骗性意图,造成自己或他人的人身或财产损害的,以诈欺罪或重诈欺罪的预备处罚。具有前述意图竭力引起该损害的,适用本规定。在造成损害前主动避免完成行为的,应当免除刑事责任。

第 12 条 第八章第 13 条关于限制公诉人起诉权的规定,适用于除重诈欺罪之外的本章其他犯罪。

违反协议撤回个人的存款数额或储蓄账户构成诈欺罪或诈欺性行为罪,以及第 2 条第 2 款规定的诈欺性行为罪,公诉人为公共利益才提起诉讼。(1994 年 141 号法)

第十章 侵占和其他背信罪

第 1 条 通过合同、公共或私人服务或者类似情形,代表他人占有财产,对财产有移交和负责义务的人,侵占财产或者不顾其履行义务必须遵守的事项,导致自己获利而财产所有人受损的,以**侵占罪**处 2 年以下监禁。

第 2 条 考虑财产的价值和其他情况,犯第 1 条之罪轻微的,以**扣留财产罪**处罚金或 6 个月以下监禁。

第 3 条 犯第 1 条之罪严重的,以**重侵占罪**处 6 个月以上 6 年以下监禁。

判断犯罪是否严重,应当特别考虑行为人是否滥用要职,是否使用虚假的证明或令人误解的簿记,或者行为是否具有其他特别危险的性质,是否涉及相当数量的财产或导致可特别敏锐察觉的损失。

第 4 条 除本章前 3 条规定外,占有财产的人对自己占有的他人所保留、保证或其他属于他人的所有权或法定担保权的财产采取任何措施,剥夺了他人的财产或其他权利的,以**非法处分罪**处罚金或 2 年以下监禁。

第 5 条 基于信托地位被授权管理他人的金融事务、独立处理需要合格技术知识的任务或者对前述事务或任务的管理进行监督的人,滥用信托地位损害被代理人利益的,以**代理人对被代理人背信罪**处罚金或 2 年以下监禁。依照第 1 条至第 3 条的规定,犯罪可罚的,不适用前述规定。

犯罪严重的,处 6 个月以上 6 年以下监禁。判断犯罪是否严重,应当特别考虑罪犯是否使用虚假的证明或令人误解的簿记,是否导致被代理人重大或可被特别敏锐察觉的损失。

受托管理他人法律事务,滥用信托地位损害被代理人利益的,无论该事务是否具有金融或技术性质,应当依照第 1 款的规定处罚。(1986 年 123 号法)

第 6 条 除本章前 5 条规定外,滥用代理权代表他人采取法律措施损害被代理人的利益,或者滥用代理权收回本票或类似票据,对属于他人之物主张权利的,以**滥用代理权罪**处罚金或 2 年以下监禁。依据尚未签发的文书要求给付,或者要求给付已经清偿的债务,或者要求交付已收讫的货物,或者在被提出要求时提供尚未给付的收据的,同样适用本规定。

第 7 条 非法使用属于他人之物引起损害或不便的,以**非法使用罪**处罚金或 6 个月以下监禁。

财产所有人采取非法建筑、挖掘、犁耕、筑路、放牧或其他类似行为使用财产,损害他人对该财产的权利的,同样适用前款规定。

犯第 1 款之罪严重的,处 6 个月以上 4 年以下监禁。(1993 年 207 号法)

第 8 条 基于过错或偶然占有财产,没有履行法律规定的对被发现或属于他人的财产的通知义务的,以**未归还遗失财产罪**处罚金。不顾该义务意图盗用财产,或者以第 4 条规定的方式处分财产的,适用第

4 条规定。

第 9 条 侵占罪、重侵占罪或代理人对被代理人背信罪的未遂,依照第二十三章的规定处罚。

第 10 条 除重侵占罪和严重的代理人对被代理人背信罪外,第八章第 13 条关于限制公诉人起诉权的规定也适用于本章规定的犯罪。

非法侵占被告通过财产租赁协议或给付发生后才转移产权之协议取得之财产,或者非法侵占被告借助于追索权之信用购买主体而获得的其他财产的,公诉人仅因特别理由为公共利益才可以提起诉讼。(1994 年 1411 号法)

第十一章 对债权人的犯罪

第 1 条 无清偿能力或有明显危险变成无清偿能力的人,毁损、赠与或者以其他类似行为处置有重大价值的财产的,以**对债权人不诚实罪**处 2 年以下监禁。通过一项或系列类似行为使自己无清偿能力或引起变成无清偿能力的明显危险的,同样适用本规定。

与依照《重订还债期法》(1994 年 334 号法)重订还债期、破产或和债权人协商和解有关的债务人,隐瞒资产、报告不存在的债务或提供其他类似性质的错误信息的,也以对债权人不诚实罪处罚,在陈述被宣誓接受验证或者被作为诉讼的根据之前予以更正的除外。与其他执行程序有关的债务人援用错误的文书或虚假的合同,妨碍根据程序扣押必须向债权人支付或担保的财产的,同样适用本规定。

即将破产的债务人从瑞典王国转移有重大价值的资产,意图从破产财产中扣留该资产,或者已经破产的债务人从破产管理人处扣留资产的,以对债权人不诚实罪处罚。(1994 年 335 号法)

第 2 条 犯第 1 条之罪严重的,以**严重对债权人不诚实罪**处 6 个月以上 6 年以下监禁。

判断犯罪是否严重,应当特别考虑罪犯是否证明虚假的陈述,或者是否使用虚假的文件或令人误解的簿记,或者犯罪是否具有相当大的规模。

第 3 条 无清偿能力或有明显危险变成无清偿能力的人,利用没有获得相应利润的手段继续经营企业,或者生活方式浪费奢侈,或者从事有风险的事业,或者欠考虑地承担繁重的义务,或者从事类似的行为,故意或重大过失严重损害其经济状况的,以**过失不考虑债权人罪**处2年以下监禁。行为人没有认识到,但有合理理由推定自己无清偿能力或有明显危险变成无清偿能力的,同样适用本规定。

与依照《重订还债期法》(1994年334号法)重订还债期、破产或和债权人协商和解有关的债务人,重大过失隐瞒资产、报告不存在的债务或提供其他类似性质的错误信息的,也以过失不考虑债权人罪处罚,在陈述被宣誓接受验证或者被作为诉讼的根据之前予以更正的除外。(1994年335号法)

第4条 无清偿能力或有明显危险变成无清偿能力的人,通过清偿未到期的债务,或者不以通常方式支付,或者债发生时未达成担保协议却提供担保,或者采取其他行为偏袒特定的债权人,明显减少其他债权人的权利的,以**偏袒债权人罪**处2年以下监禁。无清偿能力的人为不适当的目的,以前述规定之外的其他手段偏袒某一债权人,引起大量减少其他债权人的权利的明显危险的,同样适用本规定。

债务人为促成和解,秘密提供支付或其他利益,或者许诺提供支付或其他利益的,也以偏袒债权人罪处罚。(1986年43号法)

第5条 没有将商业交易记入账目或保留账单资料,或者将虚假信息记入账目,或者以其他方式故意或重大过失不履行依据《簿记法》(1976年125号法)、《基金法》(1994年1220号法)或《津贴债务保护法》(1967年531号)规定的维持账目之义务,导致不能主要从账目评估交易过程或者财务结果或状况的,以**簿记罪**处2年以下监禁;犯罪轻微的,处罚金;犯罪严重的,处6个月以上4年以下监禁。(1994年1220号法)

第6条 第1条第1款的对债权人不诚实罪的未遂、第1条第3款的从瑞典王国转移资产的对债权人不诚实罪的未遂,依照第二十三章的规定处罚。(1986年43号法)

第7条 代表债务人的人,实施依照本章规定债务人应当负刑事责任的行为,将其视为债务人处罚。

在第4条规定的情形,债权人使用不适当的威胁,或者不适当地许诺利益,或者与行为人串通,接受或者容许债务人向自己许诺提供支付、担保或其他利益的,以共犯处罚。(1986年43号法)

第8条 犯第3条第1款的过失不考虑债权人罪,公诉人为公共利益才提起诉讼。(1982年150号法)

第十二章 损害罪

第1条 毁坏、损伤不动产、动产,损害他人权利的,以**损害罪**处罚金或6个月以下监禁。

第2条 考虑损害的财产无价值及其他情节,犯第1条之罪轻微的,以**侵害罪**处罚金。

从森林、田野非法取走正在生长的树、草,或者从正在生长的树上取走嫩枝、树枝、树皮、叶子、韧皮、橡实、果仁或树脂,或者取走被风吹倒的树、石头、砂砾、草皮或类似不准备使用之物,考虑被取走财物的价值及其他情节,犯罪轻微的,以侵害罪处罚。

第3条 犯第1条之罪严重的,以**重损害罪**处4年以下监禁。

判断犯罪是否严重,应当特别考虑行为是否对他人生命或健康产生极端的危险,或者是否损害具有重大文化或经济价值之物,或者损害能否被特别敏锐察觉。

第4条 非法穿过建筑地、种植园或其他可能被损害之地行走的,以**非法路径罪**处罚金。

第5条 重损害罪的未遂、预备以及没有揭露该罪的,依据第二十三章规定处罚。

第6条 犯侵害罪、非法路径罪,侵害私人权利的,公诉人为公共利益才提起诉讼。

第十三章 有关公共危险的犯罪

第1条 放火危及他人生命或健康,或者使他人财产遭受重大毁坏的,以**纵火罪**处2年以上8年以下监禁。

犯罪不太严重的,处1年以上3年以下监禁。(1993年207号法)

第2条 犯第1条之罪严重的,以**重纵火罪**处6年以上10年以下固定期限的监禁或终身监禁。

判断犯罪是否严重,应当特别考虑是否在火势容易蔓延的人口密集的居住区放火,或者是否对许多人或者特别重要的财产构成危险。

第3条 引起爆炸、洪水、塌方、海难、航空器或火车事故或其他类似灾难,危及他人生命或健康,或者使他人财产遭受重大毁坏的,以**危及公众的毁灭罪处2年以上8年以下监禁。

犯罪不太严重的,处1年以上3年以下监禁。

犯罪严重的,处6年以上10年以下固定期限的监禁或终身监禁。(1993年207号法)

第4条 毁损对瑞典国防、公众生存、司法管理、公共管理或维持瑞典国内公共秩序和安全相当重要之财产,或者以其他方式实施不限于妨害劳动或鼓励此类行为,严重扰乱或阻碍使用前述财产的,以**蓄意破坏罪**处4年以下监禁。损害或以前述规定的其他方式,严重扰乱或阻碍公共交通或电信、电话、电台或其他类似公共设施正常使用,或者严重扰乱或妨害供水、照明、供热、动力的供应装置的,同样适用本规定。

第5条 犯第4条之罪严重的,以**重蓄意破坏罪**处2年以上10年以下监禁或终身监禁。

判断犯罪是否严重,应当特别考虑是否对瑞典王国的安全、许多人的生命或特别重要的财产引起危险。

第5a条 以非法胁迫手段,强占、妨碍为运输货物或乘客、拖行、救助、捕鱼或其他捕捞在民事贸易海上交通中使用的航空器或船舶的运行的,以**劫持罪**处4年以下监禁。以非法胁迫手段强占海上平台,意图实施与勘探、开发自然资源有关的行为或具有其他经济目的的,同样适用本规定。

有下列情形之一的,以**蓄意破坏海上、空中交通罪**处4年以下监禁:

1. 毁坏、严重损伤第1款规定的船舶、平台或者运行中的航空器的;

2. 采取行动危害第1款规定的船舶、平台或者飞行中的航空器的安全的。

犯第1款、第2款之罪严重的,处2年以上10年以下固定期限的监禁或终身监禁。判断犯罪是否严重,应当特别考虑是否对许多人引起危险,或者行为是否具有其他特别危险的性质。(1990年416号法)

第5b条 有下列情形之一,并且行为的性质危及航空港的运行或安全的,以**蓄意破坏航空港罪**处4年以下监禁:

1. 对处于向国际交通开放的航空港内的人使用严重暴力或严重暴力威胁的;

2．毁坏、严重损伤属于航空港或用于航空港交通的装置，或者没有运行但停泊在航空港的航空器的；

3．使用暴力或暴力威胁妨碍该航空港的运行的。

犯罪严重的，处 2 年以上 10 年以下固定期限的监禁或终身监禁。判断犯罪是否严重，应当特别考虑行为是否对许多人的生命造成危险或具有其他特别危险的性质。（1990 年 416 号法）

第 6 条 不谨慎地处理火、爆炸或者以其他方式过失导致下列结果之一的，以**过失危及公众罪**处罚金或 6 个月以下监禁：

1．火灾或第 1 条、第 2 条或第 3 条规定的灾难或发生灾难的危险；

2．第 4 条规定的损害或阻碍；

3．第 5a 条第 2 款或第 5b 条第 1 款第 2 项规定的损害。

犯罪严重的，处 2 年以下监禁。（1990 年 416 号法）

第 7 条 投毒或污染食物、水或类似物，或者以其他方式传播有毒物质或类似物，或者传染、传播严重疾病，对人的生命或健康造成普遍危险的，以**传播有毒、污染物质罪**处 6 年以下监禁。

犯罪严重的，处 4 年以上 10 年以下监禁或终身监禁。判断犯罪是否严重，应当特别考虑行为是否意图危害他人的生命或健康，或者是否使许多人处于危险中。

第 8 条 投毒，或者传染、传播恶性疾病，或者传播有害的动物、杂草，或者以其他类似手段对动物、植物造成普遍危险的，以**引致毁坏罪**处罚金或 2 年以下监禁。

犯罪严重的，处 6 个月以上 6 年以下监禁。判断犯罪是否严重，应当特别考虑是否意图造成毁坏，或者是否使重大价值的财产处于危险中。

第 8a 条 废除。（1998 年 809 号法）

第 9 条 过失犯第 7 条、第 8 条之罪的，以**过失处理有毒、污染物质罪**处罚金或 2 年以下监禁。（1998 年 809 号法）

第 10 条 处理火、爆炸物或有毒物质，或者以其他方式引起第 1 条、第 2 条或第 3 条规定的火灾或灾难的危险或者第 7 条、第 8 条规定的普遍的危险，并且意识到危险后，没有采取合理期待的避免危险的措施，依照本章前述规定不负刑事责任的，以**怠于避免公共危险罪**处罚金或 1 年以下监禁。

第 11 条 依照第 1 条、第 2 条、第 3 条、第 6 条、第 7 条、第 8 条、第 9 条或第 10 条,或者依照第 5a 条第 2 款第 2 项或第 5b 条第 1 款第 2 项、第 3 项的规定应当负刑事责任,在重大的不便或妨害出现前主动避免其中规定的危险或结果的,可以比照规定减轻处罚。引起的危险轻微且规定的刑罚不超过 1 年监禁的,不处罚。(1998 年 809 号法)

第 12 条 纵火罪、重纵火罪、危及公众的毁灭罪、蓄意破坏罪、重蓄意破坏罪、劫持罪、蓄意破坏海上、空中交通罪、破坏航空港罪、传播有毒、污染物质罪或者引致毁坏罪的未遂、预备或阴谋,以及没有揭露上述犯罪的,依照第二十三章的规定处罚。(1990 年 416 号法)

第十四章 伪 造 罪

第 1 条 冒写他人真名或假名或者以欺骗获得他人的签名或者以其他方式制作虚假的文书,或者对真实的文书作欺骗性更改或添加,危及证明的,以**伪造文书罪**处 2 年以下监禁。

文书包括议定书、合同、承诺性便条、证书、作为证据或其他与证据同等重要的其他记录以及身份证、票据或类似的证明标志。

第 2 条 犯第 1 条之罪轻微的,以**伪造文书罪**处罚金或 6 个月以下监禁。

判断犯罪是否轻微,应当特别考虑文书是否不太重要,例如兑付登记收据、副券或类似的证明收据,或者是否为帮助他人获得权利而犯罪。

第 3 条 犯第 1 条之罪严重的,以**重伪造文书罪**处 6 个月以上 6 年以下监禁。

判断犯罪是否严重,应当特别考虑伪造是否涉及政府机构的重要档案或普通贸易中特别重要的文书,例如证券、股票或抵押契据,或者是否具有其他特别有害的性质。

第 4 条 毁坏文书,呈递无法使用的文书或者移送文书,当时无权以此方式处分,危及证明且不构成簿记罪的,以**隐匿文书罪**处 2 年以下监禁;犯罪轻微的,处罚金或 6 个月以下监禁。

犯罪严重的,处 6 个月以上 4 年以下监禁。(1982 年 150 号法)

第 5 条 未经许可,在艺术品、实用艺术品或其他类似作品上附加或伪造他人的姓名或签名,因而使人认为被仿冒者确认其为该作品之原始作者的,以**伪造签名罪**处 2 年以下监禁;犯罪轻微的,处罚金或 6 个月以下监禁。

犯罪严重的,处 6 个月以上 4 年以下监禁。(1970 年 489 号法)

第 6 条 伪造在瑞典国内、国外有效的纸币、硬币,或者有其他伪造纸币、硬币行为的,以**伪造货币罪**处 2 年以下监禁;犯罪轻微的,处罚金或 6 个月以下监禁。

犯罪严重的,处 2 年以上 8 年以下监禁。

第 7 条 伪造有效的邮票、封戳或其他在国内、国外有价值的印记,无论是官方或大众使用,或者伪造在尺寸、重量、商品、文书或其他之物上国内、国外官方管制的印记,或者粘贴伪造的印记或虚假地粘贴真实的印记,或者伪造其他印记或贴有印记之物,危及证明的,以**伪造印记罪**处 2 年以下监禁;犯罪轻微的,处罚金或 6 个月以下监禁。

犯罪严重的,处 6 个月以上 4 年以下监禁。

第 8 条 虚假地附加标志或其他能被当作有效的界标、水标、固定点或其他测量表面或高度标志之物,或者移动、取走、毁坏或损伤该标志,危及证明的,以**伪造固定标志罪**处 4 年以下监禁;犯罪轻微的,处罚金或 6 个月以下监禁。

第 9 条 援用伪造的文书,为出售提供或保留有伪造签名的作品,使伪造的纸币或硬币流通,使用伪造的具有价值的标志或伪造的管制印记,援用伪造的固定标志或者使用其他以上述方式伪造的任何物,危及证明的,因使用伪造物与伪造的处罚相同。①

第 10 条 除第 9 条的规定外,广泛经销容易被误认为有效的纸币、硬币或其他有价值的官方金属代币的,以**非法经销伪造物罪**处罚金。

第 11 条 依照本章前述规定应当承担刑事责任,在任何重大的不便出现之前主动避免行为造成的证明危险的,可以比照规定减轻处罚。引起的危险轻微且刑罚在 1 年监禁以下的,不处罚。

第 12 条 伪造文书罪、重伪造文书罪、隐匿文书罪、伪造签名罪、伪造货币罪、伪造印记罪、伪造固定标志罪或使用伪造物罪的未遂、预备,以及没有揭露伪造货币罪的,依照第二十三章处罚。犯罪的既遂如

---

① 英译本之本条没有以斜体标注的罪名,如果不存有疏漏和错误,"使用伪造物"的应构成与使用对象相应的伪造罪。——中文译者注

果被认为轻微的,不处罚。

第十五章 伪证、错误指控和其他不真实的陈述罪

第1条 依法宣誓的人提供不真实的信息或隐瞒真相的,以**伪证罪**处4年以下监禁;犯罪轻微的,处罚金或6个月以下监禁。

犯罪严重的,处2年以上8年以下监禁。判断犯罪是否严重,应当特别考虑是否意图使无辜的人被宣判犯重罪,或者意图对某人造成重大伤害。(1975年1292号法)

第2条 在法庭审理期间,宣称将如实陈述,但是提供不真实的信息或隐瞒真相的,以**当事人不真实陈述罪**处罚金或2年以下监禁;犯罪轻微的,处罚金或6个月以下监禁。

第3条 重大过失犯第1条、第2条之罪的,以**过失陈述罪**处罚金或6个月以下监禁。

第4条 前3条规定的陈述被证明对争议点没有意义的,不处罚。

有权拒绝表达自己的意见,并且依照情况存在合理理由,但是提供不真实的信息或隐瞒真相的,同样适用前款规定。

第4a条 应当受刑罚处罚的人向丹麦、芬兰、冰岛或挪威的法院提供不真实的信息或隐瞒真相,如果应当在瑞典国内宣誓后陈述,并且依照第2条的规定由当事人在民事案件中陈述的,以**对北欧法院虚假陈述罪**依照第1条的规定处罚。重大过失犯罪的,以**对北欧法院过失陈述罪**依照第3条的规定处罚。

前款规定的行为也相应适用第4条、第14条和第15条的规定。(1975年1292号法)

第4b条 证人、专家在欧共体法院、该法院的初审法院或欧洲自由贸易区法院宣誓后提供不真实的信息或隐瞒真相,如果应当在瑞典国内经宣誓陈述,以**对国际法院虚假陈述罪**依照第1条的规定处罚。重大过失犯罪的,以**对国际法院过失陈述罪**依照第3条的规定处罚。

前款规定的行为也适用第4条、第14条和第15条的相应规定。(1995年316号法)

第5条 起诉无辜的人,意图使其被宣判有罪的,以**虚假起诉罪**处2年以下监禁;犯罪轻微的,处罚金或6个月以下监禁。

犯罪严重的,处 6 个月以上 4 年以下监禁。判断犯罪是否严重,应当特别考虑起诉是否与重罪有关,或是是否涉及滥用行政职位。

没有起诉的可成立理由而起诉的,以**不正当起诉罪**处罚金或 6 个月以下监禁。

第 6 条 告发无辜的人,意图使其被宣判有罪的,以**诬告罪**处 2 年以下监禁;犯罪轻微的,处罚金或 6 个月以下监禁。

没有认识到但有合理根据推定被告发的人是无辜的,以**不正当控告罪**处罚金或 6 个月以下监禁。

第 7 条 除第 6 条的规定外,向公诉人、警察机关或其他机关不诚实地指控他人有犯罪行为,宣称损害情节或者否认无罪或减轻情节,如果该机关有义务接受此类报告的,以**虚假控罪罪**对行为人处 2 年以下监禁;犯罪轻微的,处罚金或 6 个月以下监禁。

没有认识到但有合理根据推定信息是虚假的,以**过失控罪罪**处罚金或 6 个月以下监禁。

第 8 条 意图使无辜的人被宣判有罪,妨碍、销毁证据或援用虚假证据的,以**妨碍证据罪**处 2 年以下监禁;犯罪轻微的,处罚金或 6 个月以下监禁。

犯罪严重的,处 6 个月以上 4 年以下监禁。

第 9 条 实施了本章前述规定的行为,依照前述规定不负刑事责任,但是引起他人无法定原因却遭受刑罚或其他重大损害的危险,并且认识到危险后怠于实施合理要求其避免损害的行为的,以**怠于避免司法错误罪**处罚金或 6 个月以下监禁。

第 10 条 在依照法律或法规以誓言、信仰、荣誉或类似确认而制作的书面证词中,提供虚假的信息或隐瞒真相,危及证明的,以**虚假确认罪**处罚金或 6 个月以下监禁;犯罪严重的,处 2 年以下监禁。

重大过失犯罪的,以**过失确认罪**处罚金或 6 个月以下监禁。

第 11 条 在证书或其他文书上,就其身份或个人事务之外的其他事务提供不真实的信息,或者为出庭而准备与法律文书有关的文书,危及证明的,以**虚假证明罪**处罚金或 6 个月以下监禁。涉及滥用官方职位或有其他原因,犯罪严重的,处 2 年以下监禁。

援用或以其他方式使用第 1 款涉及的虚假文书,危及证明的,以**使用虚假文书罪**依照第 1 款的规定处罚。

第 12 条 滥用护照、证书或类似签署了特定个人姓名的文书,声称自己或他人是那个人,或者传授如此滥用文书,或者传授将副本、摄像复制品或其他虚假文书作为某文书的正确版本,危及证明的,以**滥用文书罪**处罚金或 6 个月以下监禁;犯罪严重的,处 2 年以下监禁。

第 13 条 否认自己在文书上的签名,危及证明的,以**否认签名罪**处罚金或 6 个月以下监禁;犯罪严重的,处 2 年以下监禁。

第 14 条 依照本章前述规定应当负刑事责任,在引起重大不便前主动更正错误,或者以其他手段避免产生更多不便的危险的,可以比照规定从轻处罚。危险轻微且法定刑罚不超过 6 个月监禁的,不处罚。

第 15 条 伪证罪的预备,或者涉及尽力教唆伪证的伪证罪的阴谋,或者妨碍证据罪的未遂,依照第二十三章的规定处罚。犯罪如果既遂被认为轻微的,不处罚。

第十六章 对公共秩序的犯罪

第 1 条 一群人扰乱公共秩序,意图使用集体暴力反对公共机构或者强迫、阻碍采取一定的措施,经机构命令解散而不解散的,对教唆者和领导者以**暴乱罪**处 4 年以下监禁,对其他参与群众行动的人处罚金或 2 年以下监禁。

服从公共机构的命令解散的,对教唆者和领导者以暴乱罪处罚金或 2 年以下监禁。

第 2 条 具有第 1 条规定的意图,一群人对个人或财产使用集体暴力的,无论公共机构是否在场,以**暴力骚乱罪**对教唆者和领导者处 10 年以下监禁,对参与群众行动的人处罚金或 4 年以下监禁。

第 3 条 人群中的许多人怠于遵守旨在维持秩序的命令,扰乱公共秩序,或者为此目的侵入被围住或已用栅栏隔开的地区,没有发生暴乱的,以**违反警察命令罪**处罚金或 6 个月以下监禁。

第 4 条 以暴力行为、大噪音或其他类似手段,扰乱或试图妨碍公众宗教仪式、其他公众祈祷活动、婚礼、葬礼或类似仪式、法院的开庭、其他的国家或市政官方典礼或者为商议、讲授或听讲演举行的公众集会的,以**扰乱仪式、公众集会罪**处罚金或 6 个月以下监禁。

第 5 条 在人群或集会前,或者在散布或为散布而发行的出版物中,或者在其他对公众的通告中,言词怂恿或以其他方式试图诱使人们实施犯罪行为,规避公民义务或违抗公共机构的,以**煽动叛乱罪**处罚金或6个月以下监禁。

在武装部队成员的集会前,以言词或以与武装部队成员的其他交流方式怂恿,或者以其他方式试图诱使他们实施某行为或疏于履行其服役职责的,依照煽动叛乱罪的规定处罚。

犯罪轻微的,不处罚。判断犯罪是否轻微,应当特别考虑诱使或试图诱使是否事实上只会招致无关紧要的危险。

考虑罪犯试图教唆犯重罪或其他情节,犯罪必须被认为严重的,处4年以下监禁。(1986年645号法)

第6条 武装部队成员聚会,集体威胁推翻或反抗部队的合法机构的,以**叛变罪**处罚金或4年以下监禁;对叛变的教唆者和领导者,处6年以下监禁。

叛变的参与者对个人或财产使用集体武力、暴力的,处6年以下监禁;对教唆者和领导者,处10年以下监禁或终身监禁。

犯罪严重的,处10年以下监禁或终身监禁。判断犯罪是否严重,应当特别考虑是否在战时或在其他违反军事纪律将造成特别危险的时间实施犯罪行为。(1986年645号法)

第7条 废除。(1970年225号法)

第8条 在散布的言论或消息中,暗指种族、肤色、民族或种族起源或者宗教信仰,威胁或蔑视民族、种族或其他类似群体的,以**对民族、种族群体煽动罪**处2年以下监禁;犯罪轻微的,处罚金。(1988年835号法)

第9条 商人在商业行为中根据种族、肤色、民族或种族起源或者宗教信仰歧视他人,违反与其他人的商业往来中通常适用的条款或条件,不与他人交易的,以**非法歧视罪**处罚金或1年以下监禁。

前款关于商人歧视的规定,也适用于在商业中受雇的人或其他代表商人的人,以及受雇于公用事业或有公共职责的人。

公众集会、聚会的组织者和该组织者的合作者,根据种族、肤色、民族或种族起源或者宗教信仰歧视他人,违反通常适用于其他人的条款或条件,拒绝他人进入公众集会、聚会的,也以非法歧视罪处罚。

上述第1款至第3款规定的人,以规定的方式,由于他人有同性恋倾向而歧视他人的,也以非法歧视罪处罚。(1987年610号法)

第10条 未经授权,移动、损害或粗暴对待尸体或死者的骨灰,掘开坟墓或以其他方式损害坟墓,或者滥用棺材、骨灰盒、坟墓或死者的

其他安息场所或者墓碑的,以**破坏坟墓安宁罪**处罚金或6个月以下监禁。(1993年207号法)

第10a条 有下列情形之一的,以**儿童淫秽物品罪**处2年以下监禁;犯罪轻微的,处罚金或6个月以下监禁:

1. 在淫秽图片中描绘儿童的;
2. 散布、转移、许可使用、展出或以其他方式使其他人获得该儿童图片的;
3. 取得或提供该儿童图片的;
4. 撮合该儿童图片的买方和卖方订立合同,或者采取其他类似措施帮助经营该图片的;
5. 占有该儿童图片的。

儿童是指没有完成发育的人,或者从图片和图片的附带情况来看明显不满18岁的人。

在商业或其他以营利为目的的活动中,过失散布第1款规定的该类图片的,依照第1款的规定处罚。

犯第1款之罪严重的,以**严重儿童淫秽物品罪**处6个月以上4年以下监禁。判断犯罪是否严重,应当特别考虑是否在商业或其他营利活动中实施犯罪,或者是否系统地或大规模地实施一部分犯罪,或者是否涉及特别大数量的图片,或者图片中儿童是否遭受特别残酷的对待。

画、涂或以其他类似的手工方式,制作第1款规定的该类图片,没有散布、转移、许可使用、展出或以其他方式使其他人获得的意图,不适用禁止描绘和占有的规定。在其他情形下,如果考虑情况行为是正当的,不构成犯罪。(1998年1444号法)

第10b条 在图片中描绘性暴力或性胁迫,意图散布该图片或描绘的,除考虑情况行为是正当的外,以**非法描绘暴力罪**处罚金或2年以下监禁。在活动图像中插入或大量描绘对人、动物的极端暴力,意图散布该图像或描绘的,处罚与前同。

在商业或其他以营利为目的的活动中,过失散布第1款提及的描绘的,依照第1款的规定处罚。

国家电影审查委员会批准公开放映的电影或录像,不适用第1款和第2款的规定。活动图像的技术录制品的内容与委员会批准的电影或录像的内容相同的,也不适用第1款和第2款的规定。此外,第1款和第 2 款的规定不适用于公开放映的电影或录像。

提供证书证实国家电影审查委员会已经批准与活动图像的技术录制品具有相同内容的电影或录像,散布录制品的,不依照第 1 款和第 2 款的规定负刑事责任,证书是虚假的并且散布录制品的人认识到或应当认识到证书是虚假的除外。(1998 年 1444 号法)

第 10c 条 在商业或其他以营利为目的的活动中,故意或重大过失向 15 岁以下的人供应详尽描绘对人、动物的暴力或暴力威胁的电影、录像或其他活动图像的技术录制品的,以**非法供应技术录制品罪**处罚金或 6 个月以下监禁。

国家电影审查委员会批准向 15 岁以下儿童放映的电影或录像,不适用第 1 款的规定。与电影审查国家委员会批准的电影或录像具有相同内容的活动图像的技术录制品,也不适用第 1 款的规定。此外,第 1 款的规定不适用于公开放映的电影或录像。

提供证书证实国家电影审查委员会已经批准向 15 岁以下儿童放映与具有相同内容的电影或录像的,不依照第 1 款的规定负刑事责任,证书是虚假的并且供应录制品的人认识到或应当认识到证书是虚假的除外。(1998 年 1444 号法)

第 11 条 在公共场所陈列或以类似容易招致公众厌烦的方式展览淫秽图片的,以**非法展览淫秽图片罪**处罚金或 6 个月以下监禁。通过邮件向他人寄送,或者以其他方式向他人主动提供淫秽图片的,同样适用本规定。(1970 年 225 号法)

第 12 条 在儿童或年青人中散布可能使其变残忍或对培养其道德具有其他严重危险的文章、图片或技术录制品的,以**引青少年入歧途罪**处罚金或 6 个月以下监禁。(1998 年 1444 号法)

第 13 条 虐待、使过度劳累、忽视或以其他方式,故意或重大过失不正当地使动物遭受痛苦的,以**残酷对待动物罪**处罚金或 2 年以下监禁。(1972 年 629 号法)

第 14 条 为公众非法组织赌博或者其他类似的完全或基本随机会而定结果的活动,并且考虑行为的性质、赌注的经济价值和其他情况,明显具有危险或者具有为组织者带来重大经济收益的性质的,对组织者以**非法赌博罪**处罚金或 2 年以下监禁。在其向公众开放的公寓或其他场所内,准许实施该行为的,同样适用本规定。(1986 年 1007 号法)

第 14a 条 犯第 14 条第 1 款之罪严重的,以**重非法赌博罪**处 6 个月以上 4 年以下监禁。

判断犯罪是否严重,应当特别考虑行为是否职业化,或者是否涉及重大金额,或者是否具有其他特别危险的性质。(1982 年 1061 号法)

第 15 条 对一人或多人的生命、健康危险或财产重大毁坏之危险的存在,提供虚假陈述,引起采取不必要的安全措施的,以**虚假警报罪**处罚金或 1 年以下监禁。

犯第 1 款之罪严重的,处 6 个月以上 4 年以下监禁。

不恰当地使用警报、紧急信号或其他类似装置,引起警察、营救部门、消防队、救护部门、军队、海上营救部门或其他公共安全部门不必要的出动的,以**不恰当使用警报罪**处罚金或 6 个月以下监禁。(1993 年 207 号法)

第 16 条 在公共场所喧哗或公然实施易于引起公众愤慨的其他行为的,以**妨害治安行为罪**处固定罚金。(1991 年 240 号法)

第 17 条 叛变罪的预备、阴谋或者没有揭露叛变罪的,依照第二十三章的规定处罚。重非法赌博罪的未遂或预备、并不轻微的第 10a 条第 1 款儿童淫秽物品罪的未遂以及严重儿童淫秽物品罪的未遂或预备,同样适用本规定。(1998 年 1444 号法)

第 18 条 授予他人对住处的用益权,明知财产的全部或者很大部分被用于犯非法赌博罪、重非法赌博罪,或者犯严重非法赌博罪的未遂、预备,没有采取合理要求其终止授权的措施,致使犯罪行为持续或重新占用财产的,应当视为帮助实施犯罪,依照第二十三章关于共犯的规定处罚。(1980 年 892 号法)

第 19 条 对第 10c 条规定的犯罪提起公诉,必须获得国家电影审查委员会的事先同意。对第 10b 条规定之罪就相关电影和录像提起公诉前,国家电影审查委员会应当发表意见。(1991 年 1560 号法)

第十七章 对行政行为的犯罪

第 1 条 以暴力或暴力威胁,在他人行使行政职权时攻击他人,或者强迫他人执行或不执行职务行为或为报复强迫他人的,以**对公务员实施暴力、威胁罪**处 4 年以下监禁;犯罪轻微的,处罚金或 6 个月以下监禁。因为以前行使行政职权的人在职期间为或不为某事,攻击此人

的,同样适用本规定。(1975 年 667 号法)

第2条 除第 1 条之规定外,以强迫或阻止他人行使行政职权为目的,或以报复职务行为为目的,非法实施引起他人痛苦、损伤或不便的行为,或者以该后果相威胁,以**对公务员暴行罪**处罚金或 6 个月以下监禁。

犯罪严重的,处 4 年以下监禁。(1975 年 667 号法)

第3条 废除。(1975 年 667 号法)

第4条 除本章前述规定的情形外,抵抗或以其他方式企图阻止他人行使行政职权的,以**暴力抵抗罪**处罚金或 6 个月以下监禁。(1975 年 667 号法)

第5条 对依照特别命令应当享有与行使行政职权同等保护的人,或者正在或已经被征召帮助公务员因而应当享有该类保护的人,实施暴行反抗或阻碍的,适用第 1 条、第 2 条和第 4 条的规定。(1975 年 667 号法)

第6条 废除。(1976 年 509 号法)

第7条 向第二十章第 2 条规定的雇员或其他人给予、承诺给予或提供贿赂或其他不当报酬,使其行使行政职责的,以**贿赂罪**处罚金或 2 年以下监禁。(1977 年 103 号法)

第8条 在公职或其他有关就行政事务投票的选举中,企图阻止投票、篡改投票结果或以其他方式不当影响投票的,以**选举不当行为罪**处罚金或 6 个月以下监禁。

犯罪严重的,处 4 年以下监禁。判断犯罪是否严重,应当特别考虑是否使用暴力或暴力威胁,或者是否涉及滥用行政职务。

就按照既定方式投票或放弃就行政事务投票之事项,收受他人给予或承诺给予的不当利益,或者向他人索取不当利益,不构成受贿罪的,以**为投票收受不当报酬罪**处罚金或 6 个月以下监禁。(1977 年 103 号法)

第9条 未经授权,企图获取应当保密的有关就公共问题行使选举权的事务的信息的,以**侵犯选举隐私罪**处罚金或 6 个月以下监禁。

第10条 因为他人向法庭或其他机构申诉、应诉、作证或在听证时作其他陈述,或者为了阻止他人这么做,以暴力或暴力威胁恐吓他人的,以**干涉司法事务罪**处罚金或 2 年以下监禁。因为他人在行政听证时作证或作其他陈述,或者为了阻止他人作该陈述,实施其他行为引起痛苦、损害或不便,或者以实施该行为相威胁,恐吓他人的,同样适用本条规定。

犯罪严重的,处 6 个月以上 6 年以下监禁。(1997 年 389 号法)

第 11 条 隐匿罪犯,帮助罪犯脱逃,毁灭犯罪证据或以其他类似方式阻挠犯罪被发现或被起诉的,以**保护罪犯罪**处罚金或 1 年以下监禁。

犯罪严重的,处 6 个月以上 4 年以下监禁。

没有认识到但有合理根据推定他人是罪犯的,处罚金。

考虑被告人与罪犯的关系以及其他情况,犯罪轻微的,不处罚。(1993 年 207 号法)

第 12 条 帮助同监犯、被还押候审者、被逮捕者或其他被合法剥夺自由的人获得自由,或者在如此脱逃后,藏匿或以其他类似行为帮助该人的,以**帮助脱逃罪**处罚金或 1 年以下监禁。

犯罪严重的,处 6 个月以上 4 年以下监禁。

考虑剥夺自由的性质和目的、行为人采用的手段以及行为人与其帮助脱逃的人的关系,犯罪轻微的,不处罚。(1993 年 207 号法)

第 13 条 非法移动、损坏或以其他方式处理被扣押、被临时扣押、被担保、被没收或被采取其他类似手段的财产,损坏或移动官方的告示、封印或者以其他方式非法开启官方封闭之物,或者违反类似的官方宣布的命令的,以**违反官方命令罪**处罚金或 1 年以下监禁。

拒绝承认官员有权命令的,以**妨碍官员罪**处罚金。(1981 年 827 号法)

第 14 条 废除。(1975 年 667 号法)

第 15 条 未经授权,声称正在行使行政职权的,以**假冒公职罪**处罚金或 6 个月以下监禁。未经授权,穿着制服,佩戴象征标记或其他公务象征标记,使其看来属于武装部队或其他行政部门,或者属于处理公共通讯的部门或供给水、照明、热或动力的公共部门的,同样适用本规定。

对公众或任何个人造成重大损害,或者有其他情况,犯罪严重的,处 2 年以下监禁。

未经授权,声称自己是辩护律师的,以**假冒辩护律师罪**处罚金。(1975 年 667 号法)

第 16 条 对公务员实施暴力、威胁罪的未遂或预备,依照第二十三章的规定处罚,犯罪如果既遂被认为轻微的除外。帮助脱逃罪的未遂或预备,也依照第二十三章的规定处罚。(1981 年 463 号法)

第 17 条 被给予贿赂的人既不是国家、地方机构的雇员,也不是第二十章第 2 条第 2 款第 1 项至第 4 项规定的人的,仅雇主或行贿者的负责人告诉或者为公共利益,公诉人才提起诉讼。(1977 年 103 号法)

第十八章 叛 逆 罪

第 1 条 意图以武力或其他暴力手段推翻政体,或者意图因此强制或阻碍国家元首、政府、议会或最高司法机关的措施或决定,采取有实现该意图的危险的行动,不构成重叛逆罪的,以**煽动罪**处 10 年或终身监禁;危险微小的,处 4 年以上 10 年以下监禁。(1974 年 565 号法)

第 2 条 攻击国王、其他王室成员或代表国王的摄政者,犯第三章至第五章规定之罪,原法定刑为 6 个月以下监禁的,应当处 4 年以下监禁;原法定刑为 6 个月以上 4 年以下监禁的,应当处 6 年以下监禁。(1974 年 565 号法)

第 3 条 意图对公众安全或公民自由实施犯罪,聚集或领导武装部队,维持武装部队的聚集,为武装部队提供武器、弹药或其他类似装备或者训练武装部队使用武器的,以**武装威胁法律秩序罪**处 6 年以上 10 年以下监禁。

第 4 条 创建或参加一个社团,该社团成为一个类似军队或警察部门的武力工具,或者考虑社团的特征及组织目的,很可能发展成为一个类似军队或警察部门的武力工具,并且该社团不是经正当授权以增强国防和警力,或者代表该社团经营武器、弹药或其他类似装备,为该社团的活动提供建筑或土地,或以金钱或其他方式为该社团提供支持的,以**非法军事活动罪**处罚金或 2 年以下监禁。

第 5 条 意图影响公众意见的形成或者侵犯政府组织或贸易、工业协会的行动自由,使用非法胁迫或非法威胁,危及言论、集会或结社自由的,以**妨碍公民自由罪**处 6 年以下监禁。

第 6 条 自残或以其他方式,使自己不能履行在武装部队的军事义务或保卫王国,或者装病或以其他欺骗手段逃避该义务的,以**逃避国防义务罪**处罚金或 2 年以下监禁;王国正处于战争状态的,处罚金或 4

年以下监禁。

第7条 煽动罪或武装威胁法律秩序罪的未遂、预备或阴谋以及没有揭露上述犯罪,以及妨碍公民自由罪或逃避国防义务罪的未遂,依照第二十三章的规定处罚。

第8条 犯第三章至第五章之罪,侵害国王或第2条规定的其他人,除导致发生死亡外,没有政府的命令公诉人不得提起诉讼。本条规定之罪的未遂、预备或阴谋,以及没有揭露该罪的,同样适用本规定。(1974年565号法)

第十九章 对王国安全的犯罪

第1条 意图以暴力或其他非法手段或接受外国帮助,使王国或其中一部分置于外国的统治下或依附于外国政权,或者使王国的一部分因而被分裂出去,并且采取有实现该意图之危险的行动的,以**重叛逆罪**处10年或终身监禁;危险微小的,处4年以上10年以下监禁。

意图在外国的帮助下胁迫或阻碍国家元首、政府、议会或最高司法机关的措施或决定,实施会发生该危险的行为的,以重叛逆罪处罚。(1974年565号法)

第2条 以暴力手段或受外国帮助,导致王国有陷入战争或其他敌对状态的危险,不构成重叛逆罪的,以**煽动战争罪**处2年以上8年以下监禁。

第3条 被任命代表王国与外国政权谈判的人,或者被任命在与代表外国政权利益的人交易时保护王国利益的人,滥用代表王国的权力或其他受托地位,对王国造成重大损害的,以**与外国政权谈判不忠诚罪**处2年以上10年以下固定期限的监禁或终身监禁。

第4条 瑞典公民未经政府或政府指定的人的许可,在关系王国的外交事务中允许自己成为外国政权的代理人,或者任何具有所谓的被授权的代理人身份的人就该事务与代表外国政权利益的人谈判的,以**任意与外国政权谈判罪**处2年以下监禁;王国正处于战争状态的,处4年以下监禁。

犯罪危及王国的自决权或与外国政权的和平关系的,处1年以上6年以下监禁;王国正处于战争状态的,处4年以上10年以下固定刑期的监禁或终身监禁。(1976年509号法)

第5条 以帮助外国政权为目的,未经授权获取、传送、给予或以其他方式泄漏关于国防设施、部队、供给、进口、出口、生产方式、谈判、决定或其他情况的信息,向外国政权泄漏该信息会危害王国的整体防御或其他安全的,无论信息正确与否,以**间谍罪**处 6 年以下监禁。以该条规定的目的,未经授权制作或占有包含上述信息的文章、图画或其他物的,同样适用本规定。(1981 年 1165 号法)

第6条 犯第 5 条之罪严重的,以**重间谍罪**处 4 年以上 10 年以下固定刑期的监禁或终身监禁。

判断犯罪是否严重,应当特别注意:考虑到战争正在进行,行为是否具有特别危险的性质,或者行为是否涉及重大事务,或者行为人是否泄漏基于他的政府或私人部门的职位而委托给他的事务。

第7条 没有帮助外国政权为目的,未经授权获取、传送、给予或泄漏有关秘密事务的信息,向外国政权泄漏该信息会危害王国的国防,或危害在战争或战争引起的特别状况期间对人民的必要供给的维持,或危害王国的其他安全的,无论信息正确与否,以**未经授权处理秘密信息罪**处罚金或 2 年以下监禁。(1981 年 1165 号法)

第8条 犯第 7 条之罪严重的,以**严重未经授权处理秘密信息罪**处 4 年以下监禁。

判断犯罪是否严重,应当特别注意:考虑到战争正在进行,行为是否涉及外国政权的帮助或具有特别危险的性质,或者行为是否涉及具有重大意义的事务,或者被告人是否泄漏基于其政府或私人部门的职位而向其告知的信息。(1976 年 509 号法)

第9条 重大过失传送、给予或泄漏第 7 条规定的信息的,处罚金或 6 个月以下监禁;王国正处于战争状态的,处罚金或 2 年以下监禁。(1981 年 1165 号法)

第10条 以帮助外国政权为目的,实施行为企图获取有关军事或其他事务的信息,向外国政权泄漏该信息会危害另一外国政权的安全,或者在王国内并非偶然性的帮助实施该行为的,以**非法情报行为罪**处罚金或 1 年以下监禁。

以帮助外国政权为目的,秘密或以欺骗手段在王国内实施行为企图获取有关他人个人情况的信息,或者并非偶然性的帮助实施该行为的,同样以非法情报行为罪处罚。

犯本条之罪严重的,处 6 个月以上 4 年以下监禁。(1993 年 207

号法）

第 11 条 侵害外国政权的国家元首或派驻本王国的代表，因而侮辱该外国政权，构成第三章或第四章之罪的，原法定刑为 6 个月以下监禁的，应当处 2 年以下监禁；原法定刑为 6 个月以上 2 年以下监禁的，应当处 4 年以下监禁。侵入外国政权的代表占有的房屋，损害房屋或房屋里面的财产，因而侮辱该外国政权的，同样适用本规定。（1970 年 225 号法）

第 12 条 未经政府授权，在王国内为外国军事部门或类似部门招募人员，或者诱使他人非法离开本国以图加入该部门的，以**非法招募罪**处罚金或 6 个月以下监禁；王国正处于战争状态的，处 2 年以下监禁。（1974 年 565 号法）

第 13 条 收受外国政权或代表外国政权利益的任何外国人的金钱或其他财产，对影响王国政体之根基的事务，或对由议会、政府权力决定的对王国安全具有意义的任何问题，意图通过出版、散播作品或以其他方式影响公众意见的，以**接受外国帮助罪**处 2 年以下监禁。（1981 年 1165 号法）

第 14 条 重叛逆罪、与外国政权谈判不忠诚罪、间谍罪、严重间谍罪、严重未经授权处理秘密信息罪或非法情报行为罪的未遂、预备或阴谋，以及未经授权处理秘密信息罪的未遂、预备，依照第二十三章的规定处罚。为了预备、可能或帮助犯严重叛逆罪，与外国政权建立联系的，也属于重叛逆罪的阴谋。

没有揭露重叛逆罪、与外国政权谈判不忠诚罪、间谍罪、重间谍罪、严重未经授权处理秘密信息罪的，依照第二十三章的规定处罚。没有认识到但应当认识到正在实施犯罪的，也应当据此承担刑事责任。（1976 年 509 号法）

第 15 条 考虑由于发出警告或其他原因，行为人应当认识到正在实施重叛逆罪、与外国政权谈判不忠诚罪、间谍罪、重间谍罪或严重未经授权处理秘密信息罪，帮助犯该罪的，应当作为从犯处罚，不应当超过 2 年监禁。（1976 年 509 号法）

第 16 条 非法情报活动罪、接受外国帮助罪或非法招募罪，或者非法情报行为罪的未遂、预备或阴谋，未经政府授权公诉人不得提起诉讼。

犯第三章、第四章之罪，侮辱第 11 条规定的外国政权，以及该罪的

未遂、预备、阴谋和没有揭露该罪的,未经政府或政府指定的人授权,公诉人不得提起诉讼。(1981年1165号法)

第二十章 滥用职位罪及其他

第1条 在行使行政职权时,以作为或不作为,故意或过失不履行职责的,以**滥用职位罪**处罚金或2年以下监禁。考虑行为人的职权、在其他方面行使行政权力的职位的性质或其他情况,犯罪轻微的,不处罚。

故意犯第1款之罪严重的,以**重滥用职位罪**处6个月以上6年以下监禁。判断犯罪是否严重,应当特别考虑罪犯是否严重滥用职位,或者犯罪是否对个人或公共部门造成严重损害或重大不正当利益。

参与国家、市决策会议的成员以该身份采取的任何行动,不适用本条第1款、第2款的规定追究责任。

依照本法或其他法律应当受处罚的犯罪,不适用本条第1款和第2款的规定。(1989年608号法)

第2条 雇员就履行职责之事项收受他人给予或承诺给予的贿赂或其他不当报酬,或者向他人索取贿赂或其他不当报酬,以**受贿罪**处罚金或2年以下监禁。雇员在获得职位前或离开职位后实施该行为的,同样适用本规定。犯罪严重的,处6年以下监禁。

第1款关于雇员的规定,也适用于下列人:

1. 董事会、行政部门、理事会、委员会或其他属于国家、市、郡议会、地方机构协会、教区、宗教团体或社会保险机关等类似机构的成员;

2. 执行法定任务的人;

3. 《武装部队成员违反纪律法》等(1986年644号法)法律中规定的武装部队的成员或者履行法定职责的其他人;

4. 没有如前所述的任命或指派,行使行政职权的人;

5. 除第1项至第4项规定的情形外,基于受托地位被赋予任务的人。任务是指管理他人的法律或经济事务,或者独立完成要求合格技术知识的工作,或者监督管理该事务或工作。(1993年207号法)

第3条 违反法律、行政立法性文件或者依照法律、行政立法性文件签发的命令、条文规定的保守秘密的义务,泄漏或非法使用秘密,依照其他规定不处罚的,以**泄漏职业秘密罪**处罚金或1年以下监禁。

过失犯第 1 款之罪的,处罚金;犯罪轻微的,不处罚。(1980 年 102 号法)

第 4 条 被选举担任国家、地方政府有关行使行政职权的职位的人,犯应当处 2 年以上监禁之罪,通过犯罪证明其明显不胜任该职位的,法院可以撤职。

第 2 条第 2 款第 1 项规定的其他雇主分配的职位,应当被认为与国家、地方政府的职位一样。(1988 年 942 号法)

第 5 条 国家、地方政府的雇员或者第 2 条第 2 款第 1 项至第 4 项规定的其他人,在执行任命或指派的任务时不履行义务,构成犯罪的,如果没有其他规定的阻碍,公诉人可以提起诉讼。

虽然有第 1 款的规定,仍然应当适用下列规定:

1．本法载明未经政府或政府指定的人的授权不得提起诉讼的规定;

2．其他法律、行政立法性文件对第 1 款阐述的执行任命或指派的任务的人犯可处刑罚之罪提起诉讼的规定。

第 1 款规定之外的人收受贿赂,仅雇主、负责人告诉或为公共利益,公诉人才提起诉讼。

除对特定案件有其他规定外,仅被害人告诉或为公共利益,并且有利于被害人的公诉人才对泄漏职业秘密罪提起诉讼。

议会成员、部长、最高法院的法官、最高行政法院的法官或者执行议会及其下属机构任命或指派的任务的人,在执行任命或指派的任务时犯罪的,对犯罪的起诉由单独条文规定。(1977 年 103 号法)

第 6 条至第 15 条 废除。(1975 年 667 号法)

第二十一章　武装部队成员实施的犯罪

第 1 条 当王国处于战争状态时,应当适用本章的规定。

王国有进入战争状态的危险,或者王国普遍存在非常的状态或情况,诸如战争或者王国可能发现自己陷于战争危险所引发的状态或情况的,政府可以命令适用本章规定。(1986 年 645 号法)

第 2 条 一旦第 1 条规定的状态或情况停止,政府应当命令不再适用本章规定。(1986 年 645 号法)

第 3 条 在本章规定中,所有有义务在武装部队服役的人都应当被认为是武装部队的成员。

"武装部队"也应当被理解为包括：

1. 没有义务在武装部队服役但是有义务保卫王国的警官；

2. 依照《重要设施保护法》(1990年217号法)任命的卫队和被保护区的卫队；

3. 隶属于正在战场上或处于类似情况的武装部队分遣队的所有其他人；

4. 有组织抵抗运动的成员。(1990年218号法)

第4条 本章关于武装部队的成员的规定也适用于：

1. 战俘；

2. 在王国保持中立的战争期间被拘留的参战者；

3. 为执行医疗或精神照顾的目的，与战俘或被拘留的参战者一起居住或停留的外国人。(1986年645号法)

第5条 武装部队成员拒绝或没有服从上级的命令，或者过度迟延执行该命令的，以**违抗上级命令罪**处罚金或2年以下监禁；命令显然与行为人的职责没有任何联系的，不处罚。(1986年645号法)

第6条 犯前条之罪严重的，以**严重违抗上级命令罪**处10年以下或终身监禁。判断犯罪是否严重，应当特别注意是否在战斗期间或在违反军事纪律会造成特别危险的时期犯罪。(1986年645号法)

第7条 武装部队成员逃匿或非法擅离职责的，以**擅离军职罪**处罚金或2年以下监禁。

犯罪严重的，处10年以下或终身监禁。判断犯罪是否严重，应当特别注意罪犯是否在战斗或协同战斗期间逃匿，或者是否参加敌军或自愿向敌军投降。(1986年645号法)

第8条 武装部队的成员以暴力或暴力威胁，在上级履行职责时袭击上级的，无论是迫使还是阻止其履行职责或者有源自其职位性质的其他原因，以**对上级实施暴力、威胁罪**处罚金或2年以下监禁。

哨兵和武装部队维持秩序的其他守卫应当被给予上级的身份。

犯罪严重的，处6年以下监禁。判断犯罪是否严重，应当特别注意是否在战斗期间或违反军事纪律会造成危险的时期犯罪。(1986年645号法)

第9条 武装部队成员向敌军成员或居住在敌方领地的人非法传递消息，或者与其建立联系的，以**通敌罪**处罚金或2年以下监禁。

(1986 年 645 号法)

第 10 条 在战斗期间或违反军事纪律会造成严重危险的时期,武装部队成员建议该武装部队的其他成员向敌人投降,或者在武装部队的其他成员面前,擅自鼓励不忠或者涣散军心的,以**削弱战斗意志罪**处 10 年以下或终身监禁。(1986 年 645 号法)

第 11 条 武装部队成员在履行职责时,没有为战斗做好防御准备,为行动准备分遣队,获得财产或物资,或者以其他方式为军事行动做准备的,以**怠于军事准备罪**处 10 年以下或终身监禁。(1986 年 645 号法)

第 12 条 武装部队的成员在指挥武装部队的分遣队时,未经授权将战斗阵地、军用物资或与对敌战争具有重大意义的任何物品交给敌人,或者率领自己及分遣队向敌人投降的,以**未经授权投降罪**处 10 年以下或终身监禁。(1986 年 645 号法)

第 13 条 武装部队的成员在战斗或协同战斗期间,没有履行职责竭尽所能帮助开展战争的,以**战斗渎职罪**处 10 年以下或终身监禁。(1986 年 645 号法)

第 14 条 武装部队成员故意或重大过失忽视所承担的职责,并且过错严重的,以**违反职责罪**处 2 年以下监禁。

本章其他条款规定处罚行为的,不适用前款规定。(1986 年 645 号法)

第 15 条 擅离军职罪的未遂、预备或阴谋以及没有揭露该罪,以及对上级实施暴力或威胁罪的预备、阴谋,依照第二十三章的规定处罚。

帮助或教唆犯违反职责罪的,仅因此忽视职责的人应当受处罚。(1986 年 645 号法)

第 16 条 第 7 条、第 9 条、第 10 条和第 12 条规定的"敌人"应当包括不与王国处在战争状态,但可能与王国发生战争的外国政权。(1986 年 645 号法)

第二十二章 叛国罪及其他

第 1 条 当王国处于战争状态时,有下列行为之一,对王国任何方面的防御造成重大损害,或者为敌人提供大量帮助的,以**叛国罪**处 4 年以上 10 年以下或终身监禁：

1. 阻碍、误导或背叛从事王国防御的人，或者诱使他们叛变、不忠或丧失斗志的；

2. 出卖、毁坏或损害对王国防御的任何方面很重要的物资或财产的；

3. 为敌人获取军事人力、物资、财产或服务的；

4. 实施任何其他犯罪行为的。(1986 年 645 号法)

第 2 条 第 1 条规定之行为对防御的任何方面造成的损害可能小于该条的规定，或者为敌人提供帮助所导致的后果小于该条的规定的，以**背叛罪**处 6 年以下监禁。(1986 年 645 号法)

第 3 条 过失犯第 1 条、第 2 条之罪的，以**过失损害国家罪**处 4 年以下监禁。(1986 年 645 号法)

第 4 条 在敌占区为敌人获取物资、财产或服务，符合第 1 条至第 3 条的规定，如果考虑人的需要、行为人的生计或其他特殊情况，不能被认为不适当的，不处罚。(1986 年 645 号法)

第 5 条 当王国处于战争状态时，在公众中散布、引致散布危害王国安全的虚假传闻或其他不真实的声明，或者向敌人传递、引致传递该虚假传闻或其他不真实的声明的，以**散布谣言危及王国安全罪**处罚金或 2 年以下监禁。

当王国处于战争状态时，在武装部队成员中散布鼓励不忠或丧失斗志的虚假传闻或其他不真实的声明的，也适用前款规定。(1986 年 645 号法)

第 6 条 严重违反与外国政权的条约、协定，或者违反普遍认可的关于处理武装冲突的国际人道主义法的原则、信念的，以**违反国际法罪**处 4 年以下监禁。严重违反是指：

1. 使用国际法禁止的任何武器；

2. 滥用联合国的徽章、《保护特定国际医疗徽章法》(1953 年 771 号法)规定的徽章、议会的旗帜或其他国际认可的徽章，或者以其他奸诈行为杀害或伤害敌手；

3. 攻击平民或者受伤或残疾的人；

4. 明知攻击会对平民的人身、财产造成特别严重的伤亡、损失，仍然不加选择地发动攻击；

5. 对依照国际法享受特别保护的机构、设施发动攻击；

6. 使依照国际法享受特别保护的人遭受剧烈的痛苦,胁迫战俘、平民在其敌人的武装部队服务,或者违反国际法剥夺平民的自由;

7. 除上述第1项至第6项规定的情形外,任意大肆损害、侵占依照国际法享受特别保护的财产。

犯罪严重的,处10年以下或终身监禁。判断犯罪是否严重,应当特别考虑犯罪是否包括大量的单独行为,或者是否许多人被杀害或伤害,或者犯罪是否导致重大的财产损失。

武装部队成员违反国际法犯罪的,其合法上级能够预见犯罪会发生,没有履行职责防止犯罪的,对该上级也应当处罚。(1994年1721号法)

第6a条 有下列情形之一,不构成违反国际法罪的,以**非法处理化学武器罪**处4年以下监禁:

1. 开发、生产或以其他方法获取、储藏或持有化学武器,或者直接、间接把化学武器转移给他人的;

2. 使用化学武器的;

3. 参加为使用化学武器而进行的军事准备的;

4. 将使用暴乱控制物资作为战争手段的。

第1款第1项至第3项规定的"化学武器"是指《联合国关于开发、生产、占有、使用和销毁化学武器公约》所界定的化学武器。

犯罪严重的,处10年以下或终身监禁。判断犯罪是否严重,应当特别注意犯罪是否可能极大促进化学武器的开发、生产、扩散或对人使用。(1994年119号法)

第6b条 使用、开发、生产、获取、占有或转移杀伤性的地雷的,以**非法处理地雷罪**处4年以下监禁,构成违反国际法罪的除外。

第1款仅适用于《1997年9月18日关于禁止使用、储存、生产、运输和销毁杀伤性地雷公约》所规定的地雷。

以第2款的公约所允许的方式处理地雷的,不构成犯罪。

犯罪严重的,处10年以下或终身监禁。判断犯罪是否严重,应当特别考虑犯罪是否极大促进以危及许多人的生命和健康的方式使用地雷。(1998年1703号法)

第6c条 违反联合国关于完全禁止核爆炸条约,参加或者以任何其他方式协作实行核武器试验或其他形式的核爆炸,以**实行非法核爆炸罪**处4年以下监禁,构成违反国际法罪的除外。

犯罪严重的,处 10 年以下或终身监禁。判断犯罪是否严重,应当特别考虑犯罪是否对核爆炸特别重要,或者对许多人或特别重要的财产构成危险。(1998 年 1703 号法。生效时间由政府决定)

第 7 条 叛国罪、背叛罪的未遂、预备或阴谋,依照第二十三章的规定处罚。叛国罪、背叛罪的阴谋,包括为准备、促成或帮助实施该罪而与敌人联络。在王国陷入战争、占领或其他敌对状态的危险时,即使战争没有实际爆发,对叛国罪、背叛罪的预备、阴谋,也应当处罚。

没有揭露叛国罪、背叛罪的,也依照第二十三章的规定处罚。即使没有认识到但应当认识到正在实施犯罪的,也应当处罚。(1986 年 645 号法。废除时间由政府决定)

第 7 条 叛国罪、背叛罪的未遂、预备或阴谋,依照第二十三章的规定处罚。叛国罪、背叛罪的阴谋,包括为准备、促成或帮助实施该罪而与敌人联络。在王国有陷入战争、占领或其他敌对状态的危险时,即使战争没有实际爆发,对预备、阴谋,也应当处罚。

没有揭露叛国罪、背叛罪的,也依照第二十三章的规定处罚。即使没有认识到但应当认识到正在实施犯罪的,也应当处罚。

实行非法核爆炸罪的未遂、预备,依照第二十三章的规定处罚。(1998 年 1703 号法。生效时间由政府决定)

第 8 条 在战争期间,有理由推定战争的习惯法允许实施犯罪的,比照犯罪的规定减轻处罚;有特别减轻情节的,不处罚。(1986 年 645 号法)

第 9 条 对与王国结盟的国家、该国的武装部队或该国武装部队的成员,犯第二十一章或本章之罪的,应当适用法律关于对王国、王国的武装部队或王国武装部队成员犯罪的规定。(1986 年 645 号法)

第 10 条 王国有进入战争状态的危险,或者王国普遍存在非常的状态或情况,如同战争或者王国可能发现自己处于战争危险所激起的状态或情况的,政府可以命令适用第十九章和本章关于王国处于战争状态时的规定。前述情形不复存在时,政府应当废除命令。

王国被外国政权完全或部分占领,不存在军事敌对的,前述各章和第二十一章关于王国防御的规定适用于抵抗行为,关于敌人的规定适用于占领政权。(1986 年 645 号法)

第 11 条 本章的"敌人"也应当包括不与王国处在战争状态,但可能与王国发生战争的外国政权。(1986 年 645 号法)

第二十三章 未遂、预备、阴谋和共犯

第1条 开始实施犯罪未达既遂,有导致犯罪既遂的危险或者因偶然情况排除该危险,如果法律有明确规定处罚未遂的,以犯罪未遂处罚。

对未遂犯的刑罚,不高于既遂犯的最高刑罚;既遂犯的最低刑是2年或2年以上监禁的,不低于监禁。

第2条 意图犯罪或帮助犯罪,给予、收受金钱或其他财物,作为犯罪的事前、事后报酬,或者获取、建造、给予、收受、保存或转移毒药、爆炸物、武器、撬锁工具、伪造工具或其他类似工具,或者实施其他类似行为的,法律有明确规定处罚预备的,以犯罪预备处罚,犯罪既遂或未遂的除外。

法律有明确规定的,处罚阴谋。阴谋是指某人决定与他人共同犯罪,以及某人同意、提议犯罪或企图诱使他人犯罪。

对预备犯、阴谋犯的刑罚,应当低于既遂犯的最高刑罚,也可以低于最低刑罚。除可以对既遂犯判处8年或8年以上监禁之外,对预备犯和阴谋犯的处罚不超过2年监禁。犯罪达至既遂的危险微小的,不处罚犯罪的预备、阴谋。

第3条 自愿中止实施犯罪,或以其他方式防止犯罪既遂的,不负未遂、预备或阴谋的责任。犯罪即使既遂,如果具有必须非法利用才达到目的的方法,自愿防止利用该方法犯罪的,可以不负犯罪既遂的刑事责任。

第4条 本法典对犯罪规定的处罚,不仅适用于实施犯罪的人,而且也适用于对以建议或行为帮助犯罪的人。依照其他法律、行政立法性文件应当处监禁的任何其他犯罪,同样适用本规定。

诱使他人犯罪,自己没有实行的,以教唆犯罪或帮助犯罪处罚。

每一共犯应当根据可归于其故意或过失来评判。法律对经理、债务人或其他具有特殊身份的人犯罪规定的刑罚也适用于犯罪的共犯。

法律有特别规定的,不适用本款规定。(1994年458号法)

第5条 对被胁迫、欺骗或者滥用其年轻、单纯或从属状态以致犯罪的共犯,或者处于次要地位的共犯,比照为犯罪规定的其他情形,减轻处罚;对案件轻微的情形,不处罚。对具有特殊身份的共犯科处刑罚的,同样适用本规定。

第6条 除对自己或与自己有密切关系的人有危险外,没有及时告发或以其他方式揭露正在实施的犯罪,法律有特别规定的,以没有揭露该犯罪处罚,适用对该犯罪中仅处于次要地位的共犯相同的规定;然而,在任何情况下不得处重于2年监禁之刑。在适用特别规定的案件中,对没有认识到但应当认识到犯罪正在实施的,同样适用本规定有关没有揭露犯罪的刑罚。

在第1款规定之外的案件中,除阻止犯罪对其或与其有密切关系的人有危险外,父母、其他抚养儿童的人或监护人没有阻止处于其照顾、监管之下的人犯罪,并且没有向某机关告发的,依照第1款的规定处罚。

没有揭露、阻止犯罪的,除正在实施的行为已经发展到能对其处罚之外,不处罚。

第7条 本法典对通过犯罪亲自获取收益或盗用某物所规定的刑罚,同样适用于故意为他人获取收益或盗用某物。

第二十四章 免除刑事责任的一般根据

第1条 仅在考虑侵害的性质、对象的重要性和总体情况,行为明显不正当时,基于自我防卫而实施的行为才构成犯罪。

自我防卫权针对下列情形行使:

1. 对人身、财产实施或即将实施的犯罪侵害;
2. 因犯罪被抓住时以暴力、暴力威胁或者其他方式阻碍财产的重新占有的人;
3. 已经非法强行进入或正试图强行进入房间、住宅、庭院或者船舶的人;
4. 被命令离开住所时予以拒绝的人。(1994年458号法)

第2条 监狱的囚犯、被还押候审的人、被逮捕的人或者其他被剥夺自由的人,逃跑或者以暴力或暴力威胁进行抵抗,或者以其他方式对照管并有义务监视其行为的人进行抵抗,可以根据环境使用正当的武力阻止逃跑以维持秩序。在涉及本款规定的案件中,上述之外的其他人进行抵抗,同样适用本规定。

警察和特定的其他人员使用武力的权力,由《警察法》(1984年387

号法)另行规定。(1994年458号法)

第3条 在兵变或战斗期间,以及违反军事纪律的犯罪造成了特别危险之时,面对违抗上级命令的下级,军队上级可以使用必要的武力以获取服从。(1994年458号法)

第4条 除本章先前规定的情形外,仅在考虑危险的性质、对他人的损害以及总体情况,超出必要性而实施的行为是不可辩护的,才构成犯罪。

必要性存在于危险威胁生命、健康、财产或法律所保护的其他重大利益之时。(1994年458号法)

第5条 依照本章第1条至第4条或《警察法》(1984年387号法)第10条的规定,某人被授权实施在其他情况下应当受处罚的行为的,任何帮助他的人也同样被授权。(1994年458号法)

第6条 在适用本章第1条至第5条或《警察法》(1984年387号法)第10条的案件中,依照当时的情形行为人很难停下来思考,以致行为超出被允许的限度的,不应当因此承担责任。(1994年458号法)

第7条 经他人同意而对他人实施犯罪行为,仅在考虑行为造成的伤害、侵犯或危险,以及行为目的和其他情形,行为不可辩护的,才构成犯罪。(1994年458号法)

第8条 依照行为人应当服从之人的命令实施犯罪行为,如果考虑服从的正当性、行为的性质以及总体情况,行为人有义务遵守命令的,不处罚。(1994年458号法)

第9条 误解行为被允许而实施犯罪行为,由于在宣布刑法规定时的错误而引起误解,或者由于其他原因,行为明显可原谅的,不处罚。(1994年458号法)

第三编 制 裁

第二十五章 罚金及其他

第1条 根据对有待判决之罪的规定,可科处的罚金包括日罚金、概括罚金和标准罚金。没有规定特定形式的罚金的,应当处日罚金;可处少于30日罚金的,应当处概括罚金。(1993年201号法)

第2条 日罚金的天数应当为30日以上150日以下。

考虑被告人的收入、财产、抚养或赡养义务和其他经济情况,判处日罚金的数额是合理的,每日的罚金应当为30以上1000以下瑞典克朗的固定数额,包括1000瑞典克朗。存在特殊理由的,日罚金的数额可以调整。

日罚金的最低总额是450瑞典克朗。(1991年240号法)

第3条 概括罚金的数额为100以上2000以下瑞典克朗。如果明确规定了较低的最高数额的,适用该规定。(1991年240号法)

第4条 根据对犯罪的规定,标准罚金是指应当依照特殊的计算依据来确定的罚金。

标准罚金的最低数额是100瑞典克朗。(1991年240号法)

第5条 数罪之每一罪均可处罚金的,对数罪可以并处罚金。

存在特殊理由的,法院可以对规定了概括罚金的一罪或数罪处概括罚金,同时对其他罪处另一种形式的罚金。

对规定应当处标准罚金或不可能转化为监禁的罚金之罪,不可以并处罚金。(1991年240号法)

第6条 数罪之任一罪可处日罚金的,作为数罪并罚的罚金以日罚金处。

作为数罪并罚的日罚金，可处至多 200 日，概括罚金可处至多 5000 瑞典克朗。

任一犯罪规定了确定的最低罚金的，不应当处更低的罚金。（1993 年 201 号法）

第 7 条 罚金收归国家所有。（1991 年 240 号法）

第 8 条 《罚金执行法》（1979 年 189 号法）规定了罚金的收缴和执行。

不支付罚金的，可以根据《罚金执行法》的规定将罚金转化为 14 天以上 3 个月以下监禁，另有规定的除外。（1991 年 240 号法）

第 9 条 法院或其他行政机构对个案判处的附条件之罚金，应当比照第 7 条和第 8 条的规定适用。

至于其他附条件之罚金，应当适用本章关于罚金的规定。（1991 年 240 号法）

第二十六章 监　　禁

第 1 条 根据对犯罪的规定，监禁分为固定期限监禁和终身监禁。监禁的固定期限不超过 10 年，不少于 14 天，第 2 条或第 3 条另有规定除外。依照第二十八章第 3 条的规定，监禁并处缓刑的，监禁的期限依照该规定。

作为未支付罚金的替代刑处监禁的，适用单独的规定。（1981 年 331 号法）

第 2 条 任一罪可处监禁的，监禁可以作为数罪的合并刑罚科处。

固定期限的监禁可以高于数罪中的最高刑期，但应当低于各罪的最高刑期的总和。高于最高刑期的不能超过以下限制：

1. 规定的最高刑低于 4 年监禁的，不超过 1 年；
2. 规定的最高刑为 4 年或 4 年以上 8 年以下监禁的，不超过 2 年；
3. 规定的最高刑为 8 年或者 8 年以上监禁的，不超过 4 年。

依照第 2 款科处的罚金应当视为相当于 14 天监禁。

不能科处低于规定的最低刑中的最长刑期的监禁。（1988 年 942 号法）

第3条 被处至少2年监禁的人,在判决获得终局法律效力后,再犯6年以上监禁之罪的,可处比该罪最高刑期延长4年的监禁;在数罪的情形下,处第2条为数罪规定的最高刑期。

不满21岁的人犯罪,不适用第1款的规定延长监禁期限。

外国判决与瑞典判决具有同样效果。(1981年211号法)

第4条 废除。(1988年942号法)

第5条 应当在监狱执行监禁,另有规定除外。(1998年604号法)

第6条 被判处固定期限监禁的人,执行刑罚的2/3,至少执行1个月之时,应当假释,第2款、第3款或第7条另有规定的除外。

依照第二十八章第3条科处的监禁,以及替代罚金的监禁,不得假释。

经已决犯请求,可以比第1款、第7条规定的时间延缓至以后的时间假释。(1998年604号法)

第6a条 废除。(1998年604号法)

第7条 已决犯严重违反在监狱服刑应当遵守的条件的,可以延期假释。

每次适用延期,最多为15天。

决定延期时,应当考虑决定是否会对已决犯产生其他负面后果。(1998年604号法)

第8条 同时科处几项监禁时,应当考虑适用第2条①确定监禁的合并刑期。然而,这一规定不适用于依照第二十八章第3条科处监禁,或未支付罚金而转为科处监禁的情形。

服刑期应当包含依照第三十三章第5条、第6条规定的法庭命令执行刑罚的期间。(1993年201号法)

第9条 国家监狱与缓刑管理局根据第6条第3款决定延缓假释,根据第7条决定延期假释。

政府或者政府授权的机构可以规定,除国家监狱与缓刑管理局之外的另一监狱与缓刑管理局有权决定假释的延缓或延期。

对有关第1款之事项所做的决定立即生效,另有规定除外。(1998

---

① 英文版是"第6条",根据该条文的表述以及含义,译者认为是"第2条"。——中文译者注

年604号法)

第10条 假释之后的缓刑期相当于判决的剩余刑期,但至少1年。(1998年604号法)

第11条 在决定假释的同时或之后,如果认为有必要,可以决定监督被假释者。由地方监狱与缓刑管理局①作出有关监督的决定。命令监督但是发现不再需要时,监督委员会可以决定不再继续监督。1年缓刑期后没有作出任何特别决定的,除出现第18条规定的事由外,应当停止监督。(1998年604号法)

第12条 一般在地方监狱与缓刑管理局的管理下执行监督和缓刑。管理局也可以委派一个监督员,必要时可以委派一人或多人协助监督。(1998年604号法)

第13条 被监督的被假释者,应当保持向监督员报告住处、就业情况和其他对监督有意义的状况,在监督员要求时向其汇报情况,一般应当依照监督员的指示与其保持联系。地方监狱与缓刑管理局如此决定监督的,前述有关监督员的规定也应当适用于地方监狱与缓刑管理局的官员以及其他人。(1998年604号法)

第14条 在缓刑期间,被假释者应当生活守秩序,努力要求自己发挥最大才能,以及遵守本法或者依据本法所制定的条件或给予的指示的要求。一经传唤,就应当向地方监狱与缓刑管理局报到。被命令赔偿犯罪造成的损失的,被假释者应当竭尽所能履行该义务。

地方监狱与缓刑管理局应当对被监督的被假释者实行监督和提供支持与帮助,以确保被假释者不重新犯罪,并帮助其适应社会。最后,地方监狱和缓刑当局应当保持自己被告知有关被假释者的生活举止和总体状况。(1998年604号法)

第15条 如果有理由认为,为了帮助被假释者适应社会,被假释者需要在缓刑期间必须遵守的特殊条件的支持,可以在规定的时期或者直到另行通知时制定该条件。条件可以涉及:

1. 住所地或者一次至多1年的规定时期的居住地;
2. 职业、其他有报酬的工作、教育或培训;

---

① 瑞典监狱与缓刑机构由国家监狱与缓刑管理局、地区监狱与缓刑管理局以及地方监狱和缓刑管理局组成。每个地方监狱与缓刑管理局都有自己的局长,其任务就是统一管理监狱和缓刑活动。单独的监狱或缓刑办事处则没有长官。——英文译者注

3. 医疗服务、酒精中毒治疗、在医院或其他类似机构内外进行的其他服务或治疗。

被假释者必须接受第 1 款第 3 项规定的服务或治疗的,可以规定其提供血液、尿和气味样本以监控其是否受依赖性物质的影响。

被假释者被命令赔偿犯罪损失的,可以制定关于履行该义务的时间和方式的条件,如果考虑被假释者的经济状况和其他情况,该条件被认为与其适应社会相抵触的除外。

被假释者被监督的,可以给予关于监督条件的特殊指示。指示可以明确被假释者应当与监督员或地方监狱与缓刑管理局保持联系的方式和程度;也可以在条件中规定,被假释者在离开工作、学习的地方或其他职业、机构时,有义务通知监督员或地方监狱与缓刑管理局。(1998 年 604 号法)

第 16 条 监督委员会应当依照第 15 条的规定给予指示。地方监狱与缓刑管理局可以临时给予该指示,直至监督委员会就该事务作出决定。

监督委员会可以根据被假释者的进步和其他个人情况,更改、撤销既定的条件或者制定新的条件。(1998 年 604 号法)

第 17 条 监督员可以就执行第 15 条所涉及的条件给予指示,也可以准许暂缓指示,并进行任何紧急必要的调整。

第 18 条 被假释者不遵守本法或依据本法所制定的条件或给予的指示的要求,监督委员会除依照第 15 条制定条件或者决定第三十七章第 7 条第 1 款规定的事务外,还可以:

1. 决定警告被假释者;

2. 决定在 1 年缓刑期之后的规定期间内监督被假释者,最长可延至缓刑期届满。(1983 年 240 号法)

第 19 条 被假释者严重怠于履行义务,可以认为其不会因为监督委员会可能采取的任何措施而改正自己的,监督委员会可以宣布取消附条件许可的自由,每次最长 15 天。(1998 年 604 号法)

第 20 条 缓刑期届满后,不能决定采取第 18 条规定的措施。即使缓刑期届满,只要监督委员会此前已经开始过问该问题,可以决定采取第 19 条规定的措施。(1973 年 918 号法)

第 21 条 被判处监禁的人被发现犯有他罪的,依照第三十四章的规定取消附条件许可的自由和施加其他一些措施。

第 22 条 宣布取消附条件许可的自由,采取第 18 条规定的措施或采取要求被假释者接受服务或治疗的措施出现问题,或者被假释者逃避监督的,如果情况许可,监督委员会可以命令适当控制被假释者,直至另外作出决定。只要有理由,应当时常考虑该决定。

因此被拘留的,不能超过 1 周。如果存在充分的理由,可以作出新命令,最长再拘留 1 周,但是不能在缓刑期届满后继续拘留。(1983 年 240 号法)

第 23 条 宣布全部或部分取消附条件许可的自由的,为了可以考虑假释,被取消的期间应当被认为是判处的新刑罚。(1983 年 240 号法)

第 24 条 不能再宣布取消附条件许可的自由的,缓刑期届满时刑罚应当视为全部执行完毕。

第二十七章 附条件之刑

第 1 条 法院认为适用罚金的制裁不适当的,可以对犯罪判处附条件之刑。(1988 年 942 号法)

第 2 条 附条件之刑可以与罚金并处,最多 200 日罚金,无论是否对犯罪规定了罚金。(1991 年 240 号法)

第 2a 条 被告人同意的,附条件之刑可以适用社区服务的条件。该条件应当规定一项义务,即从事 40 小时以上 240 小时以下的无偿劳动。

法院决定适用社区服务的条件时,应当在判决中说明选择监禁作为制裁时可能判处的监禁期。

如果存在理由,应检察官的要求可以修改或终止社区服务的条件。(1998 年 604 号法)

第 3 条 被判处附条件之刑的人应当经过 2 年的缓刑期。

缓刑期自法院对已决犯的犯罪的制裁获得终局法律效力之日起计算,无论是否因为声明服从判决致使判决获得终局效力。

第 4 条 缓刑期间,罪犯应当生活守秩序,并努力要求自己发挥最大才能。

附条件之刑与社区服务并处的,已决犯应当按照地方监狱与缓刑管理局拟订的劳动计划从事社区服务。(1998 年 604 号法)

第 5 条 罪犯被责令赔偿犯罪造成的损害的,应当尽其所能履行义务。法院可以指示,在缓刑期间,罪犯应当按照判决规定的次数和方式力图履行自己的义务,全额或部分赔偿损害。

如果犯罪导致财产损害并且帮助罪犯适应社会是适当的,法院可以指示罪犯按照判决规定的次数和方式帮助受害方修复或弥补损害,或者考虑犯罪的性质及导致的损害,可以制定其他适当的条件。但是只有经受害方同意,才能制定条件。

根据检察官、罪犯的申请,可以修改、取消根据第 1 款、第 2 款的规定制定的条件。(1987 年 761 号法)

第 6 条 罪犯不能遵守附条件之刑的要求,如果检察官在缓刑期届满之前继续予以追究的,法院考虑各种因素后可以采取下列措施:

1. 决定警告罪犯;
2. 根据第 5 条的规定制定条件或更改先前规定的条件;
3. 撤销附条件之刑,决定对犯罪判处其他制裁。

缓刑期届满之后,不能采取上述第 1 项、第 2 项规定的措施。

如果撤销附条件之刑,在决定制裁时,应当平衡考虑依照第 2 条和第三十四章第 5 条之规定判处的罚金以及已决犯在社区服务的条件的经历,可以判处比该罪法定刑较短的监禁。判决声明具有第 2a 条涉及的情况并且判处监禁的,决定刑期时应当予以考虑。

第 7 条 罪犯被发现犯他罪的,适用第三十四章的规定撤销附条件之刑和采取其他一些措施。

第二十八章 缓 刑

第 1 条 认为适用罚金的制裁不适当的,可以判处缓刑。(1988 年 42 号法)

第 2 条 缓刑可以与日罚金并处,最多 200 日,无论是否规定了罚金。(1991 年 240 号法)

第 2a 条 经被告人同意,缓刑可以适用社区服务的条件。该条件应当规定一项义务,即从事 40 小时以上 240 小时以下的无偿劳动。

法院决定适用社区服务的条件的,应当在判决中说明选择监禁作为制裁时可能判处的监禁期。

如果存在理由,监督委员会可以修改或终止社区服务的条件。

(1998 年 604 号法)

第 3 条 缓刑可以与 14 天以上 3 个月以下的监禁并处。

法院判处监禁和缓刑的,不应当根据第 2 条的规定判处罚金或社区服务的条件。

如果情况要求,尽管判决还没有获得终局法律效力,法院可以命令开始执行监禁。(1998 年 604 号法)

第 4 条 缓刑应当自开始执行制裁之日起持续 3 年的缓刑期。(1983 年 240 号法)

第 5 条 缓刑应当自判决之日起执行监督。但是,法院可以指示暂缓执行监督,直至对已决犯的判决获得终局法律效力。对判决提起上诉的,上级法院可以指示不再执行。

1 年缓刑期之后,没有任何特别命令的,不应当继续监督,依照第 4 款或第 5a 条、第 7 条、第 9 条之规定承担结果的除外。

上级法院已决定中断执行,此后被告人仍然被判处缓刑的,没有执行的期间不应当被计入缓刑期或第 2 款规定的期间。

缓刑适用一项罪犯保证完成的计划治疗的,法院可以在判决中命令监督期长于第 2 款规定的时间。但是,不应当长于完成治疗所需要的时间,也不应当超过缓刑期。(1987 年 761 号法)

第 5a 条 附条件之刑适用社区服务的,已决犯应当根据地方监狱与缓刑管理局拟订的劳动计划进行社区服务。

有必要监督已决犯直至完成社区服务的,监督委员会可以决定在 1 年缓刑期之后监督一定时期,但不能超过剩余的缓刑期。(1998 年 604 号法)

第 6 条 有关与缓刑犯的联系方式,应当适用第二十六章第 12 条至第 17 条的规定。然而,法院应当在判决中指定一名监督员,有特别反对理由的除外。此外,法院也可以根据第二十六章第 15 条第 2 款的规定附加条件。如果有理由,监督委员会可以修改或终止该条件。(1993 年 209 号法)

第 6a 条 在适用第三十章第 9 条第 2 款第 3 项的案件中,如果计划治疗对决定判处缓刑具有决定性作用的,法院应当在判决中说明选择监禁作为制裁时可能判处的监禁期。

此外,在该案件中,判决应当说明缓刑犯保证完成的治疗计划的适用条件。

对该治疗计划可以规定一项条件,即负责治疗的人必须向地方监狱与缓刑管理局和检察官报告缓刑犯是否严重怠于履行规定的义务。(1998 年 604 号法)

第 6b 条 在适用第 6a 条的案件中,如果已决犯被还押候审的,法院可以命令适当拘留已决犯,直至移交给治疗机构或治疗计划中规定的提供治疗的人。拘留持续时间不得超过 1 周。(1992 年 373 号法)

第 7 条 缓刑犯不履行缓刑判决规定的义务的,除依照第二十六章第 15 条的规定附加条件或依照第三十七章第 7 条第 1 款的规定决定事项之外,监督委员会还可以:

1. 决定警告缓刑犯;
2. 决定在 1 年缓刑期后应当继续监督缓刑犯一定时期,最长不能超过缓刑期届满之时。

根据第 1 款第 2 项的规定命令监督,但又认为不再需要的,监督委员会可以指示不再继续监督。法院根据第三十四章第 6 条的规定命令监督并且已经监督 1 年的,同样适用本规定。

在缓刑期届满之后,监督委员会不能命令采取本条第 1 款规定的措施。(1988 年 942 号法)

第 8 条 已决犯严重怠于履行义务,并且可以推定监督委员会可能采取的措施不会有效的,监督委员会应当申请检察官向法院提交该事项,要求撤销缓刑命令。对适用第 6a 条第 1 款的案件,缓刑犯严重怠于履行根据治疗计划应当承担的义务的,监督委员会无需申请,可直接向法院提交该事项。

应当在缓刑期届满之前提起本条规定的法院诉讼程序。(1988 年 942 号法)

第 9 条 缓刑命令被撤销的,法院应当适当考虑缓刑犯已经受过缓刑以及根据第 2 条、第 3 条或第三十四章第 6 条的规定判处的罚金、监禁之刑,对犯罪决定另一制裁。在该案件中,法院可以判处短于规定的监禁期限的监禁。判决已经说明具有第 2a 条第 2 款、第 6a 条第 1 款涉及的信息并且将处监禁的,决定刑期时应当适当考虑该信息。

目前没有撤销缓刑的充足理由的,法院可决定处第 7 条规定的一项措施,但不能在缓刑期届满之后决定。(1998 年 604 号法)

第 10 条 缓刑犯被发现犯他罪的,应当适用第三十四章的规定撤销缓刑和采取其他措施。

第11条 需要撤销缓刑,或需要采取第7条规定的措施,或需要采取一项措施可以照管或治疗缓刑犯,或缓刑犯逃避监督的,如果情况允许,监督委员会或法院可以在根据第8条的规定提起诉讼前,命令适当拘留等待另行决定的缓刑犯。

因此被拘留的,不得超过1周。然而,存在例外根据的,新的决定可以继续拘留最长1周。

法院决定撤销缓刑判决时缓刑犯被拘留的,法院可以命令继续拘留直至决定获得终局法律效力。

缓刑期届满之后不得羁押缓刑犯。(1987年761号法)

第二十九章 刑罚的确定及制裁的免除

第1条 适当考虑判决一致性的需要,根据对犯罪判处刑罚的价值,在刑罚的范围内确定刑罚。

判断刑罚的价值,应当特别考虑犯罪造成的损害、错误或危险,被告人认识到或者应当认识到上述后果,以及被告人可能具有的意图或动机。(1988年942号法)

第2条 判断刑罚的价值,除适用于每个及每类犯罪的情节外,应当特别考虑下列加重情节:

1. 被告人是否意图造成比犯罪的实际后果明显更严重的后果;
2. 被告人是否特别残忍;
3. 被告人是否利用他人易受攻击的地位或他人保护自己的特别困难;
4. 被告人是否严重利用自己的职位或滥用特别的信任、信赖;
5. 被告人是否以胁迫、欺诈或利用他人年幼、缺乏理解力或从属状态诱使他人参加犯罪;
6. 犯罪是否是被特别详细计划或大规模实施的犯罪活动的组成部分,并且被告人在其中是否具有重要作用;
7. 犯罪的动机是否基于种族、肤色、民族或种族起源、宗教信仰或其他类似情况而侵害他人、种族或其他类似群体。(1994年306号法)

第3条 判断刑罚的价值,除其他规定外,在特殊案件中还应当特别考虑下列减轻情节:

1. 由他人的严重攻击性行为引起犯罪;

2. 由于精神紊乱、情绪激动或其他原因，被告人控制行为的能力明显减弱；

3. 被告人的行为与发育、经历或判断能力明显不足有关；

4. 由强烈的同情引起犯罪；

5. 实施第二十四章规定的行为，没有免除刑事责任的。

如果需要考虑犯罪的刑罚价值，对犯罪判处刑罚时可以比照规定减轻处罚。（1994 年 458 号法）

第 4 条 法院在确定适当的刑罚时，如果在选择制裁或取消附条件许可的自由时没有充分考虑各种情节，那么除犯罪的刑罚价值外，还应当合理考虑被告人先前是否犯罪。在这点上，应当特别考虑先前犯罪的程度，两次犯罪之间的时间间隔，以及先前犯罪和新的犯罪是否具有类似性质或是否都特别严重。

第 5 条 在确定适当的刑罚时，除犯罪的刑罚价值外，法院还应当合理考虑下列情形：

1. 作为犯罪的结果，被告人是否遭受严重的身体损害；

2. 被告人是否已经竭尽所能努力去阻止、补救或者限制犯罪的损害后果；

3. 被告人是否自首；

4. 被告人是否会由于犯罪被驱逐出瑞典王国而遭受损失；

5. 作为犯罪的结果，被告人是否被免职或解雇或者有合理理由推定其会被免职或解雇，或者在求职时会遭遇任何其他的障碍或特别的困难；

6. 根据犯罪的刑罚价值对被告人处刑罚时，被告人是否会因为年老或身体不佳而遭受不合理的困难；

7. 考虑犯罪的性质，犯罪自实施以来是否持续异常长的时间；

8. 是否存在任何其他情形，可以减轻依犯罪的刑罚价值所确定的刑罚。

具有第 1 款规定的任何情形，并且有特别根据的，法院可以比照犯罪的法定刑减轻处罚。

第 6 条 具有第 5 条规定的情形之一，科处制裁明显不合理的，法院应当免除制裁。

第 7 条 不满 21 岁的人犯罪，确定刑罚时应当特别考虑其年轻。比照犯罪的法定刑，可以处较轻的刑罚。不满 21 岁的人犯罪，不得处终身监禁。

第三十章 制裁的选择

第 1 条 选择制裁时,监禁是比附条件之刑、缓刑更严厉的制裁。关于特别照管的制裁的规定见第三十一章。

第 2 条 任何人不得因同一犯罪而被判处超过一种制裁,另有规定除外。(1988 年 942 号法)

第 3 条 因数罪被判决,法院应当对正在审理中的数罪合并制裁,另有规定除外。

存在特别理由的,法院可以对一罪或数罪处罚金,对任何剩余一罪或数罪处其他制裁。此外,法院可以对一罪或数罪处监禁,对任何剩余一罪或数罪处附条件之刑或缓刑。(1988 年 942 号法)

第 4 条 选择制裁时,法院应当特别注意可处比监禁较轻的刑罚的任何情形。因此,法院应当考虑第二十九章第 5 条规定的情形。

作为处监禁的理由,除刑罚价值和犯罪性质之外,法院可以考虑被告人先前犯一罪或数罪的事实。(1988 年 942 号法)

第 5 条 不满 18 岁的人犯罪,仅在有多项特别理由时,法院才可以处监禁。依照第三十一章第 1a 条的规定,法院应当首先处封闭式青少年照管①。

已满 18 岁不满 21 岁的人犯罪,如果考虑犯罪的刑罚价值或其他特别理由,处监禁正当的,法院才可处监禁。(1998 年 604 号法)

第 6 条 在严重精神紊乱的影响下犯罪,不得处监禁。法院认为不应当判处其他制裁的,应当对被告人免除制裁。(1991 年 1138 号法)

第 7 条 选择制裁时,法院应当考虑因为担心被告人会继续犯罪所以科处附条件之刑是否欠缺理由。

如果被告人愿意接受社会服务的条件,并且考虑被告人的个人和总体情况,条件是适当的,法院可以考虑对附条件之刑适用社会服务的条件,作为科处附条件之刑替代监禁的特别理由。(1988 年 942 号法)

---

① 封闭式青少年照管在别的地方被翻译为"对青少年罪犯的慈善对待"。——英文译者注

第 8 条 附条件之刑应当和日罚金并处,如果考虑履行社会服务的义务或其他犯罪后果,罚金会造成被告人过度困难或有不处罚金的其他特别理由的除外。(1998 年 604 号法)

第 9 条 选择制裁时,法院应当考虑处缓刑是否能帮助被告人不再继续犯罪。

作为缓刑的特别根据,法院可以考虑下列因素:

1. 可认为与被告人犯罪有关的个人或社会处境是否出现明显改进;

2. 因为滥用依赖性物质或其他可认为与犯罪有关的疾病,被告人是否正接受治疗;

3. 滥用依赖性物质或其他必须进行必要照管和其他治疗的特别情形是否帮助犯罪,以及被告人是否宣称自己愿意接受依照能与执行制裁合并实施的个人计划进行的治疗;

4. 被告人是否愿意缓刑适用社会服务的条件,并且考虑被告人的个人和总体情况,条件是适当的。(1998 年 604 号法)

第 10 条 考虑犯罪的刑罚价值、犯罪的性质或被告人先前的犯罪,法院应当判断是否需要将缓刑与日罚金并处。(1988 年 942 号法)

第 11 条 考虑犯罪的刑罚价值或被告人先前的犯罪,只有不可避免时才将缓刑与监禁并处。(1988 年 942 号法)

第三十一章 交付特别照管

第 1 条 不满 21 岁犯罪的人,依照《社会服务法》(1980 年 620 号法)或《青少年照管特别规定法》(1990 年 52 号法)接受治疗或其他措施,法院可以将案件提交给社会福利委员会,由社会福利部门根据委员会为被告人准备的治疗计划安排必要的治疗。考虑犯罪的刑罚价值、犯罪性质以及被告人先前的犯罪,如果认为社会福利部门的计划措施具有充分干预性的,才能提交案件。必要时可以根据下述第 3 款的规定与罚金或青少年服务同时适用的。

根据治疗计划,显然被告人应当接受本法有关社会福利部门的规定的治疗或其他措施的,法院应当签署命令,要求被告人接受治疗或措施。

根据犯罪的刑罚价值、犯罪的性质或被告人先前的犯罪,法院可以将交付社会福利部门治疗与下列措施合并适用：

1. 最高数额为 200 日的日罚金,无论有待判决之罪是否规定了罚金;

2. 特殊条件,即如果被告人同意,被告人应当从事 24 小时以上 100 小时以下的无偿工作或参加其他特别安排的活动(青少年服务)。

如果有理由,应检察官的要求可以修改或取消青少年服务的条件。

犯罪造成财产损害,如果根据第 1 款规定交付治疗适合帮助已决犯适应社会的,法院可以命令已决犯以判决规定的次数和方式帮助受害方,进行可以帮助恢复或限制损害的工作,或者考虑犯罪的性质及造成的损害,进行其他适当的工作。只有受害方同意,才能签署该命令。(1998 年 604 号法)

第 1a 条 不满 18 岁的人犯罪,法院在适用第三十章的规定时发现应当判处的制裁是监禁的,应当决定替代判处一定期限的封闭式青少年照管之制裁。如果考虑被告人被起诉时的年龄或其他情况,存在特殊的反对理由的,不适用本规定。

法院可以处 14 天以上 5 年以下封闭式青少年照管。

关于封闭式青少年照管的执行,见《封闭式青少年照管执行(1998 年 604 号)法》的规定。(1998 年 603 号法)。

第 2 条 依照《毒品滥用者治疗法》(1988 年 870 号法)的规定,罪犯被要求接受治疗的,法院可以将案件移交给社会福利委员会;待决犯已经被送入提供该治疗的机构的,移交给该机构的委员会安排必要的治疗。法院决定移交前应当征询社会福利委员会或治疗机构的委员会的意见。

如果犯罪的法定刑重于 1 年监禁的,有特别根据时,才能根据第 1 款的规定命令移交给治疗机构。(1994 年 97 号法)

第 3 条 犯不限处罚金之罪的人严重精神紊乱,考虑其精神状况和个人情况,认为需要送入精神照管机构、剥夺自由和采取其他强制措施的,法院可以将其提交司法精神病照管。

在严重精神紊乱的影响下犯罪,由于精神紊乱有再犯严重类型之重罪的危险的,法院可以决定在照管期间实行《司法精神病照管法》(1991 年 1129 号)规定的特别释放调查。

如果考虑被告人先前的犯罪或有其他特别理由,法院认为有必要的,可以将交付司法精神病照管与除监禁或交付其他特别照管之外的

其他制裁并处。(1991年1138号法)

第4条 废除。(1991年1138号法)

第三十二章 废除(1986年645号法)

第三十三章 逮捕和还押候审期间的扣除

第1条 废除。(1988年42号法)
第2条 废除。(1988年942号法)
第3条 废除。(1973年43号法)
第4条 废除。(1988年942号法)

第5条 判处固定期限的监禁或封闭式青少年照管,或者法庭根据第三十四章第1条的规定命令该制裁应当涵括其他犯罪,如果因为怀疑已决犯涉嫌犯已经被审理和判决之罪,通过逮捕、还押候审或者《司法精神病调查法》(1991年1137号法)第10条规定的送入司法精神病部门对已决犯剥夺自由至少24小时的,剥夺自由并且没有同时执行其他判决的期间应当视为在监狱或特殊青少年机构的服刑期间。法院应当在判决中声明该期间视为服刑期间。判处的监禁期超出被剥夺自由的期间很短的,法庭可以指明,被剥夺自由应当视为服完监禁。

撤销附条件之刑或缓刑,替代判处固定期限的监禁,如果没有根据第1款、第3款的规定进行扣除的,第1款的规定也应当适用于下列情形:

1. 在附条件之刑或缓刑之前剥夺自由的;
2. 在判决指出附条件之刑或监禁应当涵括其他犯罪之前剥夺自由的;
3. 第二十八章第6条、第11条第3款规定的任何拘留。

被处罚金并且由于涉嫌犯已受刑罚之罪被以第1款规定的方式剥夺自由的,法庭可以指明,作为剥夺自由的结果,刑罚已全部或部分执行完毕。(1998年604号法)

第6条 对瑞典王国外发生的被剥夺自由的情形,可合理适用第5条关于把剥夺自由的期间计入执行刑罚时间的规定。

第 7 条 废除。(1987 年 761 号法)

第 8 条 上级法院审理有关科处制裁的上诉,可以修正对第 5 条和第 6 条中涉及的问题的决定,即使没有对该决定提起上诉。(1988 年 942 号法)

第 9 条 废除。(1988 年 942 号法)

第三十四章 数罪并发和变更制裁的一般规定

第 1 条 被判处监禁、附条件之刑、缓刑或者封闭式青少年照管的人,被发现在判决前曾犯他罪,或者在判决后制裁被执行完毕或终止前又犯新罪的,适当考虑第 2 条至第 7 条有关特定案件的规定以及特别情况后,法院可以:

1. 命令先前判处的制裁适用于新罪;
2. 对新罪单独判处制裁;
3. 先前的判决已经获得终局法律效力的,撤销先前判决的制裁,对所有犯罪判处一种不同类型的制裁。

根据第二十八章第 3 条的规定并处缓刑与监禁的,适用本章规定时,科处的监禁应当视为缓刑的一部分。(1998 年 604 号法)

第 2 条 对正在服终身监禁之刑的罪犯,仅可以根据第 1 条第 1 项发布命令。

第 3 条 先前的判决判处固定期限的监禁,只有新罪的制裁与前罪的制裁相比明显不重要,或者有其他特别的理由时,才可以根据第 1 条第 1 项的规定发布命令。

适用第 1 条第 2 项对开始执行先前判决之前的犯罪科处刑罚,确定刑罚时应当尽可能注意,合并的刑罚不能超过依照第二十六章第 2 条的规定为两罪科处的刑罚,但可以处比该罪法定刑较轻的刑罚。

只有在刑罚执行完毕前宣告判决,才可以根据第 1 条第 3 项的规定撤销监禁。

第 4 条 对从监禁被假释的人适用第 1 条第 1 项、第 2 项的规定,如果在缓刑期间犯罪并且没有特别的反对理由,应当宣告全部或部分取消附条件许可的自由。

法院可以考虑下列特别理由,不宣告取消或者宣告部分取消附条件许可的自由：

1. 新罪是否比前罪具有较轻的性质；
2. 两次犯罪是否间隔很长时间；
3. 取消是否不合理。

根据第 1 款不应当宣告取消的，法院可以依照第二十六章第 18 条的规定决定一项措施，或者在第二十六章第 10 条规定的时间之外延长缓刑期间至多 1 年。

只能在缓刑期届满之前根据第 3 款决定一项措施。只有被假释的人被还押候审或者在缓刑期届满 1 年内收到起诉通知的，才可以决定取消。（1998 年 604 号法）

第 5 条 先前判处的制裁是附条件之刑，只有在缓刑期开始之前犯罪的，才可以根据第 1 条第 1 项的规定发布命令。

根据第 1 条第 1 项的规定发布命令，考虑新罪的刑罚价值或性质，法院可以判处 200 日以下的日罚金，无论该罪是否规定了罚金。

如果法院必须适用第 1 条第 1 项的规定判处监禁，而不是根据第 1 条第 3 项的规定撤销附条件之刑，并且存在第三十章第 7 条规定的特定理由的，法院可以决定附条件之刑适用社区服务的条件。如果命令适用社区服务的条件，法院应当适用第二十七章第 2a 条第 2 款的规定。

如果适用第 1 条第 1 项、第 2 项的规定，只有已决犯已经被还押候审或在缓刑期届满前收到起诉通知的，法院才可以根据第二十七章第 6 条第 1 项、第 2 项的规定决定一项措施，或者延长缓刑期至 3 年。

根据第 1 条第 3 项的规定撤销附条件之刑的，法院确定新的制裁时应当合理考虑根据第 2 款、第二十七章第 2 条的规定科处的任何罚金，以及命令适用社区服务条件对已决犯造成的后果。因此，法院可以比照该罪的法定刑，判处较短的监禁。具有第二十七章第 2a 条第 2 款规定的情况的，法院在确定刑期时应当予以考虑。

只有已决犯已经被还押候审或在缓刑期届满 1 年内收到起诉通知的，才能根据第 1 条第 3 项的规定撤销附条件之刑。（1998 年 604 号法）

第 6 条 先前判处的制裁是缓刑，考虑新罪的刑罚价值、性质或先前的犯罪，法院在适用第 1 条第 1 项时可以判处日罚金至多 200 日，无论有待判决之罪是否规定了罚金。

如果法院必须适用第 1 条第 1 项的规定判处监禁，而不是根据第 1 条第 3 项撤销缓刑，存在第三十章第 9 条第 2 款第 4 项规定的特定理由的，法院可以判处缓刑适用社区服务条件。如果命令适用社区服务条件的，法院应当适用第二十八章第 2a 条第 2 款的规定。

如果新罪规定了监禁，并且如果考虑第三十章第 11 条的规定，除依照第 1 条第 1 项之命令同时剥夺自由之外，不能适用第 1 条第 1 项的规定，法院可以根据第二十八章第 3 条的规定判处监禁而不是罚金。

如果适用第 1 条第 1 项、第 2 项的规定，法院可以决定第二十八章第 9 条规定的一项措施，或者延长缓刑期至多五年。已决犯承诺遵守第三十章第 9 条第 2 款第 3 项规定的治疗计划的，应当适用第二十八章第 6a 条的规定。

如果根据第 1 条第 3 项的规定对被告人判处监禁的，法院在确定刑期时应当合理考虑：被告人已经被判处缓刑，或根据本条第 1 款、第二十八章第 3 条的规定被告人已经服监禁刑的时间，或根据本条第 1 款、第二十八章第 2 条的规定被告人已经被判处的任何罚金。因此，可以比照犯罪的法定刑，处较短的监禁。判决声明具有第二十八章第 6a 条第 1 款规定的情况，如果判处监禁的，确定刑期时应当予以适当考虑。

只有已决犯已经被还押候审或在缓刑期届满前收到起诉通知的，才能根据第 3 款的规定判处罚金，根据第 2 款的规定作决定，根据第 4 款的规定作决定或者决定撤销缓刑。(1998 年 604 号法)

第 7 条 先前判处的制裁是封闭式青少年照管，只有与前罪的制裁相比，新罪的制裁明显没有任何特殊意义，或有其他特殊理由时，法院才能根据第 1 条第 1 项的规定发布命令。

如果根据第 1 条第 2 项的规定对开始执行先前制裁之前的犯罪判处制裁，法院在决定制裁时应当确保合并的制裁不超过本可以对两罪判处的制裁。因此，法院可以判处比该罪法定刑较轻的刑罚。

如果根据第 1 条第 3 项的规定对被告人判处监禁，法院在确定刑期时应当合理考虑被告人已受封闭式青少年照管之制裁。只有在固定的执行期届满之前判处监禁的，才可以撤销封闭式青少年照管。(1998 年 604 号法)

第 8 条 废除。(1979 年 680 号法)

第 9 条 废除。(1981 年 211 号法)

第 10 条 如果适用第 1 条第 1 项的规定的判决已经获得终局法律效力,先前判决所判处的监禁、附条件之刑、缓刑或封闭式青少年照管已经视为涵括新罪,但是如果上级法院获得终局法律效力的判决变更先前判决的,根据检察官的通知,法院应当重新考虑所谓新罪的制裁问题。根据第 3 条第 2 款、第 7 条第 2 款的规定决定制裁,如果先前制裁已经被变更的,同样适用本规定。

将要执行处固定期限的监禁或封闭式青少年照管的判决时,发现已决犯在开始执行另一犯罪的制裁之前犯该罪,如果判决没有显示已经考虑该制裁,一旦该判决获得终局法律效力,根据检察官的通知,法院在适用第 3 条第 2 款、第 7 条第 2 款的规定时,应当确定已决犯应当受的刑罚作为最后被执行的判决。(1998 年 604 号法)

第 11 条 终身监禁将与罚金、替代罚金的监禁、固定期限的监禁、附条件之刑、缓刑或封闭式青少年照管同时执行的,终身监禁应当取代其他制裁。

2 年以上固定期限的监禁、2 年以上的封闭式青少年照管将与开始执行前述制裁之前判处的罚金、替代罚金的监禁同时执行的,前述监禁、封闭式青少年照管应当取代其他制裁。(1998 年 604 号法)

第 12 条 废除。(1979 年 680 号法)

第 13 条 废除。(1981 年 211 号法)

第 14 条至第 17 条 废除。(1975 年 667 号法)

第 18 条 为执行对 2 个或多个犯罪判处监禁作为合并制裁的判决,引渡至瑞典时出现问题,并且根据外国政府的立法,不能对所有犯罪都引渡的,法院应当根据检察官的通知,撤销先前判处的合并制裁,对可以引渡的犯罪判处制裁。

根据《刑事案件判决执行国际协作法》(1972 年 260 号)、《关于监督被处附条件之刑或假释的罪犯的国际协作法》(1978 年 801 号)的规定,将在国外执行涉及 2 罪或更多犯罪的瑞典刑事案件的判决,但是根据外国政府有关一罪或数罪的法律,存在执行障碍的,同样适用第 1 款的规定。

第三十五章 制裁的限制

第 1 条 除犯罪嫌疑人在下列期限内被还押候审或收到犯罪起诉

书外，不能判处任何制裁：

1. 对犯罪可以判处至多 1 年监禁的，在 2 年内；
2. 最高刑是 1 年以上 2 年以下监禁的，在 5 年内；
3. 最高刑是两年以上 8 年以下监禁的，在 10 年内；
4. 最高刑是 8 年以上固定期限的监禁的，在 15 年内；
5. 对犯罪可以判处终身监禁的，在 25 年内。

一行为构成数罪的，如果可以对其中任一犯罪判处制裁，就可以对所有犯罪判处制裁，无需考虑上述规定。

第 2 条 废除。（1975 年 667 号法）

第 3 条 被还押候审的人没有收到犯罪起诉书就被释放或者收到后对其提起的诉讼被否决或驳回，出现判处制裁的可能性的，还押候审或通知应当视为从未发生。

第 4 条 第 1 条规定的期限应当自犯罪实行之日起开始计算。特定的犯罪结果是判处制裁的必要条件的，应当自结果发生之日起开始计算。

对 15 岁以下的儿童犯第六章第 1 条至第 4 条和第 6 条之罪，或者犯该罪未遂的，第 1 条规定的期限应当自被害人已满或应满 15 岁之日起开始计算。

在并不轻微的簿记罪中，负责簿记的人在犯罪的 5 年之内被宣告破产或被准许和解，或者提出和解或中止偿债的，应当自前述情形发生之日起开始计算期限。负责簿记的人在犯罪的 5 年之内成为税务审计或税务评估审计的对象的，应当自决定审计之日起开始计算期限。（1996 年 659 号法）

第 5 条 废除。（1971 年 964 号法）

第 6 条 自第 4 条规定之日起经过下列期限，不能判处制裁：

1. 犯罪不应当受重于罚金的刑罚，并且根据第 1 条第 1 项对犯罪确定判处制裁的时间的，经过 5 年；
2. 除第 1 项之规定外，犯罪不应当受 2 年以上监禁的，经过 15 年；
3. 其他案件，经过 30 年。（1971 年 964 号法）

第 7 条 自判决获得终局法律效力之日起，处罚金的判决经过 5 年失效。在规定的期限届满时已决犯被通知申请变更罚金，且申请尚未被最终确定的，不适用本规定。经申请但未获准变更罚金的，法院就该案件的最终决定获得终局法律效力时,处罚金的判决失效。变更罚金的判决的失效,适用特别规定。

已决犯死亡的,判处的罚金失效。但是,在已决犯生存期间判决获得终局法律效力,并且为支付罚金,动产已被扣押或处于政府监管之下的,可以以该财产支付罚金。

依附于支付令的附条件的罚金,同样适用前述有关罚金的条款。(1983 年 351 号法)

第 8 条 自判决获得终局法律效力之时起,经过下列期限没有开始执行监禁的,处监禁的判决失效:

1．处 1 年以下监禁的,经过 5 年;
2．处 1 年以上 4 年以下监禁的,经过 10 年;
3．处 4 年以上 8 年以下监禁的,经过 15 年;
4．处 8 年以上固定期限监禁的,经过 20 年;
5．处终身监禁的,经过 30 年。(1971 年 964 号法)

第 9 条 执行固定期限的监禁中断的,其继续执行应当适用第 8 条的规定。期限计算应当考虑剩余的刑期。应当自执行中断之日起开始计算期限。批准假释但宣告撤销的,应当自撤销决定获得终局法律效力之日起开始计算期限。

第 10 条 自判决获得终局法律效力之日起,经过 5 年没有开始执行的,处封闭式青少年照管的判决失效。

执行封闭式青少年照管中断的,应当适用第 1 款的规定继续执行。应当自中断之日起开始计算期限。(1998 年 604 号法)

第 11 条 废除。(1986 年 645 号法)

第三十六章 没收财产、法人罚金以及犯罪的其他法律后果

第 1 条 本法规定的犯罪的收益应当宣告没收,宣告没收明显不合理的除外。收受作为有关犯罪的成本的报酬之物,根据本法构成犯罪的,同样适用本规定。收受之物的价值可以代替收受之物本身被宣告没收。

判断根据第 1 款的规定宣告没收犯罪收益是否明显不合理,应当特别考虑是否有理由相信会施加或解除赔偿犯罪损失的义务。(1986

年1007号法）

第2条 财产被用作犯本法规定之罪的辅助手段，或属于犯罪的产出，为预防犯罪或有其他特别理由的，可以宣告没收财产。使用财产构成本法规定之罪或以构成该罪的方式使用财产的，同样适用本规定。

财产的价值可以代替财产本身被宣告没收。（1968年165号法）

第3条 除第2条之规定外，对下列物也可以宣告没收：

1. 由于其特殊性质和其他情况，可能用作犯罪之物；

2. 计划用作侵害人的生命、健康的犯罪武器，并且有会被如此使用的可能之物；

3. 计划用作损害财产的犯罪的辅助手段，并且有明显会被用作该用途的可能之物。（1989年136号法）

第4条 企业家在商业活动中犯罪获得经济利益的，应当宣告没收其中的价值，即使第1条、第2条另有规定或有其他特殊规定。

没收不合理的，不适用第1款的规定。判断是否合理，应当特别注意是否有理由相信会对企业家施加支付相当于犯罪经济所得的金额的义务或该义务会被他解除。

不能或很难对将被宣告没收之物提供证据的，可以根据各种情形把该物的价值评估为一个合理的数额。（1986年1007号法）

第5条 如无其他规定，可以对下列人没收财产或犯罪收益：

a) 罪犯或犯罪的共犯；

b) 曾经的罪犯或共犯；

c) 从犯罪受益的人或第4条规定的企业家；

d) 在犯罪后通过分割婚姻共有财产、继承、遗嘱、赠予或以其他方式获得财产，明知或有合理根据怀疑该财产与犯罪有关的任何人。

财产不属于第1款第(a)—(c)项的任何人的，不能宣告没收。

被宣告没收的财产的特定权利没有被宣告没收的，仍然保留。

宣告没收财产的，为偿付而扣押或担保所获的权利终止，为特殊理由命令保留的除外。（1987年791号法）

第6条 法院可以规定一项防止滥用财产的措施替代没收。（1986年118号法）

法 人 罚 金

第7条 在商业活动中犯罪，有下列情形的，依检察官的请求，应当命令企业家支付法人罚金：

1. 严重怠于履行与商业活动有关的特定义务,或具有其他严重性质,且

2. 企业家没有为防止犯罪采取可以合理要求他采取的措施。

针对企业家犯罪或处法人罚金明显不合理的,不适用第1款的规定。(1986年1007号法)

第8条 法人罚金为1万以上300万以下瑞典克朗。(1986年118号法)

第9条 确定法人罚金的数额时,应当特别考虑犯罪的性质和程度以及犯罪与商业活动的关系。(1986年118号法)

第10条 有下列情形之一的,比照第9条规定的数额,可以免除或减少法人罚金:

1. 对企业家或其代表科处犯罪制裁的;
2. 犯罪导致企业家承担某种其他支付义务或特定法律后果的;
3. 有其他特别根据的。(1986年118号法)

一般规定

第11条 判处第一章第3条规定的其他制裁时,应当同样适用有关判处刑罚所引起的特定法律后果的法令或行政立法性文件的规定。

适用第1款规定时,除判决另有说明外,附条件之刑、缓刑和交付特别照管应当视为和监禁等同。依此指示,缓刑和交付特别照管应当视为与6个月以上的监禁等同。(1986年118号法)

第12条 只有对犯罪判处制裁,才能命令没收财产或承担其他特定法律后果的,即使免除犯罪制裁,法院也可以依各种情形命令判处该法律后果。(1986年118号法)

第13条 不满15岁的人犯罪,或者在严重精神紊乱的影响下犯罪,只有考虑罪犯的精神状态、犯罪性质和其他情形,认为合理的,法院才能命令没收财产或承担其他特定法律后果。(1986年118号法)

第14条 罪犯死亡或有其他原因不判处制裁的,只有在相关的诉讼程序中自犯罪实施之时起5年内签发传票,才可以宣告没收财产、科处法人罚金或为避免滥用而规定措施。对该类案件,公诉人为公共利益才提起诉讼。

对本条规定的案件,同样适用第三十五章第3条的规定。(1986

年 118 号法)

第 15 条 涉及没收、避免滥用的措施或者法人罚金的判决,自获得终局法律效力之日起 10 年内未执行的,失效。(1986 年 118 号法)

第 16 条 法令或行政立法性文件规定应当宣告没收或承担其他特定法律后果,如果这么做明显不合理的,可以免除。(1986 年 1007 号法)

第 17 条 没收的财产和法人罚金应当上缴国家,另有规定的除外。

向某人宣告没收相当于造成的损失的第 1 条规定的犯罪收益后,国家应当代替该人向受害方赔偿,数额相当于上缴国家的价值。在执行判决的过程中,被没收的一方证明自己已经向受害方赔偿一定数额的,有权要求扣除。(1986 年 1007 号法)

第三十七章 监督委员会

第 1 条 政府决定将全国划分为若干个监督委员会辖区。

监督委员会由主席、副主席和 3 名委员组成,政府规定某特定的委员会应当拥有更多委员的除外。主席和 2 名委员组成一个法定人数的小组。主席可以代表委员会独自决定紧急事务和不重要的事项,但应当在下次委员会会议上进行汇报。

政府可以命令一个监督委员会应当分区工作。管理该委员会的法律的可适用部分应当适用于该区。(1983 年 240 号法)

第 2 条 政府或政府指定的行政部门任命各监督委员会的主席和副主席。没有主席时,由副主席担任主席。没有主席和副主席时,由国家监狱与缓刑管理局任命一名临时代理人。主席、副主席和代理人应当拥有和担任法官一样的法律资格和职业经历。

通过选举任命其他委员。通过选举产生同等数量的委员的代理人。一个监督委员会辖区由单个市组成的,由市议会主持选举,否则由郡议会主持。一个监督委员会辖区内的某个市不属于郡议会辖区的,由郡议会和地区议会根据两者之间的比例进行选举,该比例由郡行政委员会根据人口数量决定。一个监督委员会辖区包括了数个郡或各郡的数个部分的,政府按照相同的原则决定各郡或某郡某部分的委员和代理人的人数。

以应当获选的人数加上 1 再除以现有委员数,至少有和所取得的商一样多的郡议会或地区议会议员提出请求的,委员或代理人的代表比例应当在郡议会或市选举过程中获得通过。商是分数的,必须把其上舍入,调高为整数。规范这种代表比例计算程序的规定见诸关于按比例选举之程序的 1992 年 339 号法令。不是按比例选举代理人的,他们被召唤去就职的顺序也必须在选举过程中决定。

监督委员会委员和非临时代理人任期 4 年。在按比例选举中被任命的委员在任期届满之前辞职的,根据选举时决定的代理人之间的顺序来任命一名代理人。一名并非在按照比例选举代表过程中获得任命的委员或代理人辞职的,为剩余的任期任命一名新的委员或者代理人。临时代理人的任期至多为 6 个月。

要任命委员或代理人时,监督委员会必须向任命机关通报详情。(1998 年 598 号法)

第 3 条 在市选举中享有投票权,在监督委员会管辖权范围内的行政区进行了正式登记,年龄不超过 70 岁,并且在将来在位期间也不会达到这一年龄的,就符合作为一名监督委员会委员或代理人的参选资格。任何处于《父母与儿童法》第十一章第 7 条规定的监护人监护之下的人都不能被选举为监督委员会的委员或代理人。符合法定资格的法官、公诉人、警官、监狱与缓刑机构官员、律师或者其职业就是在法庭上为他人之案件提供辩护的人,也不应当被选举为监督委员会的委员或代理人。监督委员会应当根据自己的意向来决定当选委员或代理人是否合格。

委员不再适合任职的,他在该身份方面的义务应当被视为已经终止。(1991 年 510 号法)

第 4 条 国家假释委员会由 5 人组成,其中 1 名具有或已经具有一个司法职位且应当是该委员会的主席。根据政府确定的数量任命代理人。政府任命主席、其他委员和代理人。没有主席时,主席的职责应当由政府指定的具有被任命为主席资格的一名委员或代理人行使。

在紧急情况下和对于不太重要的问题,主席可以代表委员会独自作出决定。这样的决定应当在下次委员会会议上进行汇报。

主席、其他委员和代理人任期 5 年。委员或代理人在任期届满之前离职的,应当为剩余的任期任命一名新的委员或代理人。(1983 年 240 号法)

第5条 监督委员会和国家假释委员会的委员或代理人必须像法官一样宣誓。适用于法官的剥夺资格的理由同样应当适用于委员或代理人,但《司法程序法》第四章第13条第7项的规定不应当适用于监督委员会的委员或代理人。

至于第1款提到的委员会所作出的决定,必须遵守关于高级法院刑事案件投票表决规定的可适用部分。(1981年211号法)

第6条 已决犯就监督委员会处理的事项请求口头听审的,应当准许。

对于国家假释委员会处理的事项,应当准许已决犯获得当面听审的机会,只要这样做被认为是有用而且是可以便利地安排的。(1981年211号法)

第7条 被判处监禁的人可以请求监督委员会审查辖区内的地方监狱与缓刑管理局根据第二十六章第11条、第12条第2句或第13条第2句的规定所作的决定。委员会也可以主动决定审查该决定,还可以决定地方监狱与缓刑管理局根据前述任一规定负责解决的事项。地方监狱与缓刑管理局可以将该事项提交委员会决定。

被判处监禁的人不服监督委员会根据第二十六章第11条、第15条、第18条、第19条或第22条的规定所作决定的,应当被准许请求国家假释委员会复查该决定。(1998年604号法)

第8条 第7条第1款的规定应当适用于被判处缓刑的人。

被判处缓刑的人可以对监督委员会就第二十六章第15条或第二十八章第7条、第11条规定的事项所作的决定向上诉法院提起上诉。允许提出上诉的时间自他收到该决定通知之日起计算。上诉法院应当适用《司法程序法》关于针对地区法院判决提起上诉的规定。(1994年1037号法)

第9条 根据第二十六章的规定撤销从监狱假释的案件,应当指派公设辩护人帮助受该措施影响的人,不需要帮助的除外。(1996年1604号法)

第10条 地方监狱与缓刑管理局和监督委员会根据第7条和第8条之规定所作的决定立即生效,另有规定的除外。

第11条 只能针对监督委员会根据本法就第7条和第8条规定之外的事项所作的决定提起上诉。可以根据第8条的规定向上诉法院或国家假释委员会提起上诉。(1981年211号法)

第三十八章 程序性规定及其他

第1条 被判处附条件之刑的人可以在上诉期届满之前声明满意判决的制裁。声明也可以涉及根据第二十七章第2条判处的罚金。必须以政府规定的方式作出声明。

一旦以规定的方式作出声明即不可撤回。罪犯对判决提起上诉,又对犯罪的制裁作出声明的,应当视为撤销上诉。

声明满意监禁及封闭式青少年照管之刑的,适用特殊规定。(1998年604号法)

第2条 法院根据第三十一章第1条交付某人给社会福利机构照管之后,已决犯严重违反根据第三十一章第1条第1款、第3款的规定发布的命令的,依检察官的申请,法院可以取消交付照管的命令,判处另一制裁。应当合理考虑根据第三十一章第1条第3款第1项的规定判处的罚金,根据第三十一章第1条第3款第2项发布的有关青少年服务的命令所经历的制裁。

警告已足够的,法院可以决定发布警告,而非根据第1款取消命令。

对于不适用第一款规定的案件,有计划的照管和社会福利委员会根据有关青少年罪犯的特殊规定之法(1964年167号)第11条在报告中提出的措施不会发生,或者有计划的照管与报告中提出的计划有实质性差别的,应当比照适用第1款的规定。法院根据第三十一章第2条的规定将某人交付照管,社会福利委员会在提交法院的报告中宣称意图提供该照管,但证明不可能提供的,同样适用第1款的规定。(1998年604号法)

第2a条 在确定刑罚或选择制裁时,判决表明特别考虑了被告人是否因为犯罪可能被解雇或停职,且作为判决根据的假定是错误的,案件的一审判决法院可以根据检察官或已决犯的申请,撤销制裁并为犯罪判处一项新的制裁,先前制裁被执行完毕的除外。一旦提出申请,法院可以裁定中止执行先前制裁直到另行通知。

先前制裁是附条件之刑或缓刑,新的制裁是监禁的,法院在确定监禁的刑期时,应当适当考虑罪犯因附条件之刑或缓刑所经历的制裁。因此,法院可以判处比犯罪的法定刑较短的监禁。废除处监禁或封闭式青少年照管的判决,并且法院科处相同性质的判决的,服先前制裁的期间应当视为执行新制裁。法院在判决中必须说明已执行的期间。(1998 年 604 号法)

第 3 条 首次判处附条件之刑的法院必须考虑与根据第二十七章第 2a 条第 3 款、第 5 条第 3 款或第 6 条采取措施有关的事项。首次判处交付社会福利机构照管的制裁的法院必须考虑与根据第三十一章第 1 条第 4 款采取措施有关的事项。

第二十八章第 8 条规定的事项应当向质询该事项的监督委员会所属辖区的地区法院或首次对该案件判处缓刑的法院呈递。

考虑到将进行的调查、成本和其他情况,法院认为合适的,可以向审理指控已决犯犯罪的法院或向已决犯主要居住地的法院,呈递涉及本条规定的案件。(1998 年 604 号法)

第 4 条 第三十四章第 10 条规定的通告应当向每一案件的一审法院发布。

第三十四章第 18 条规定的申请应当向案件的一审法院提出。(1981 年 211 号法)

第 5 条 受理案件的申请已告知罪犯的,应当视为就第二十七章第 6 条、第二十八章第 8 条提及之事项提起诉讼。(1981 年 211 号法)

第 6 条 业余法庭顾问应当参与一审法院对第二十七章第 2 条、第 2a 条、第二十八章第 9 条或第三十四章第 10 条第 2 款、第 18 条规定之事项的判决。本规定同样适用于根据第三十四章第 1 条第 3 项的规定撤销制裁,根据第三十四章第 4 条的规定取消附条件许可的自由或者根据第三十四章第 5 条第 3 款、第 6 条第 2 款的规定采取措施。

一名合格法官参与审理的一审法庭,应当有能力判决第二十七章第 2a 条第 3 款、第 5 条第 3 款、第二十八章第 11 条第 1、2 款或第三十一章第 1 条第 4 款规定之事项。(1998 年 604 号法)

第 7 条 废除。(1981 年 211 号法)

第 8 条 对根据第 2 条或第 2a 条、第二十七章第 2a 条第 3 款、第 5 条第 3 款、第 6 条、第二十八章第 9 条、第三十一章第 1 条第 4 款或第三十四章第 10 条第 2 款的规定采取措施的案件,一审法院应当为已决犯提供充分表达意见的机会。已决犯请求口头诉答的,应当提供适当的机会。对根据第三十四章第 18 条的规定采取措施的案件,应当尽可能为已决犯提供充分表达意见的机会。法院应当以判决处理该事项。

在没有给罪犯提供充分表达意见机会的情况下,可以决定根据第二十八章第11条第1款、第2款的规定采取措施。(1998年604号法)

第9条 法院决定根据第二十七章第2a条第3款、第5条第3款、第二十八章第11条第1款、第2款、第三十一章第1条第4款、三十四章第10条第2款或第18条采取措施的,除另有命令外,立即生效。根据第二十七章第6条、第二十八章第9条、第三十四章第4条、第5条或第6条的规定确定条件以及监督或缓刑期间的,同样适用本规定。(1998年604号法)

第10条 法院的判决或监督委员会的通知应当迅速送达罪犯本人。不能送达的,可以请求其他法院或监督委员会送达。

第11条 废除。(1973年918号法)

第12条 警察当局应当协助法院、监督委员会、国家假释委员会和地方监狱与缓刑管理局,确保罪犯参与诉讼或与本法有关之事务,或确保根据第二十六章第22条或第二十八章第6b条、第11条的规定拘留罪犯。

第13条 国家监狱与缓刑管理局或经该局授权的地方监狱与缓刑管理局局长可以变更本地监狱与缓刑管理局根据本法所作的决定。国家监狱与缓刑管理局对该事项的决定不能上诉。地方监狱与缓刑管理局局长的决定,同样不能上诉,但国家监狱与缓刑管理局可以修改。

与第二十六章第6条第3款、第7条、第11条、第12条第2句,第13条第2句,或第16条第1款第2句有关的决定,不适用第1款的规定。(1998年604号法)

第14条 国家监狱与缓刑管理局可以变更另一监狱与缓刑管理局根据第二十六章第9条第2款的授权规定所作的推迟或延期假释的决定。如果决定对其不利,与决定有关的人可以请求国家监狱与缓刑管理局复查该决定。

对国家监狱与缓刑管理局根据第二十六章第6条第3款和第7条的规定所作的决定,可以上诉至行政法院。

向行政上诉法院提出上诉需要有上诉许可。(1998年604号法)

第15条 国家监狱与缓刑管理局可以根据1971年291号法第7条关于行政诉讼程序的规定向郡行政法院和上诉行政法院提交正式案件。(1998年604号法)

国家监狱与缓刑管理局向最高行政法院提交正式案件。

第 16 条 政府或政府指定的部门可以决定为已决犯根据第二十七章第 2a 条第 1 款、第二十八章第 2a 条第 1 款和第三十一章第 1 条第 3 款第 2 项的规定从事无偿劳动所造成的损害支付国家赔偿。(1998 年 604 号法)

PART ONE GENERAL PROVISIONS

Chapter 1
On Crimes and Sanctions for Crime

Section 1

A crime is an act defined in this Code or in another law or statutory instrument for which a punishment as stated below is provided. (Law 1994:458)

Section 2

Unless otherwise stated, an act shall be regarded as a crime only if it is committed intentionally.

If the act has been committed during self-induced intoxication or if the perpetrator has in some other way himself brought about the temporary loss of the use of his senses, this shall not cause the act to be considered non-criminal. (Law 1994:458)

Section 3

In this Code a sanction for a crime means the punishments of fines and imprisonment, and conditional sentence, probation and committal for special care. (Law 1988:942)

Section 4

The use of punishments is regulated by the provisions on the particular crimes and any further special provisions. Other sanctions may be im-

PART ONE GENERAL PROVISIONS

posed in accordance with the provisions.

concerning their use, even if they are not mentioned in the provisions concerning particular crimes. (Law 1988:942)

Section 5

Imprisonment is to be considered a more severe punishment than a fine.

Provisions on imprisonment in relation to conditional sentence and probation are to be found in Chapter 30, Section 1. (Law 1988:942)

Section 6

No sanction shall be imposed upon a person for a crime committed before attaining the age of fifteen. (Law 1988:942)

Section 7

Repealed (Law 1988:942)

Section 8

Apart from a sanction, a crime may, in accordance with what is provided, result in forfeiture of property, corporate fines or some other special consequence defined by law and may also entail liability for the payment of damages. (Law 1986:118)

Chapter 2

On the Applicability of Swedish Law

Section 1

Crimes committed in this Realm shall be adjudged in accordance with Swedish law and by a Swedish court. The same applies when it is uncertain where the crime was committed but grounds exist for assuming that it was committed within the Realm. (Law 1972:812)

Section 2

Crimes committed outside the Realm shall be adjudged according to Swedish law and by a Swedish court where the crime has been committed:

1. by a Swedish citizen or an alien domiciled in Sweden,

2. by an alien not domiciled in Sweden who, after having committed the crime, has become a Swedish citizen or has acquired domicile in the Realm or who is a Danish, Finnish, Icelandic, or Norwegian citizen and is present in the Realm, or

3. by any other alien, who is present in the Realm, and the crime under Swedish Law can result in imprisonment for more than six months.

The first, paragraph shall not apply if the act is not subject to criminal responsibility under the law of the place where it was committed or if it was committed within an area not belonging to any state and, under Swedish law, the punishment for the act cannot be more severe than a fine.

In cases mentioned in this Section, a sanction may not be imposed which is more severe than the severest punishment provided for the crime under the law in the place where it was committed. (Law 1972:812)

Section 3

Even in cases other than those listed in Section 2, crimes committed outside the Realm shall be adjudged according to Swedish law and by a Swedish court:

1. if the crime was committed on board a Swedish vessel or aircraft or was committed in the course of duty by the officer in charge or a member of its crew,

2. if the crime was committed by a member of the armed forces in an area in which a detachment of the armed forces was present, or if it was committed by some other person in such an area and the detachment was present for a purpose other than an exercise,

3. if the crime was committed in the course of duty outside the Realm by a person employed in a foreign contingent of the Swedish armed forces,

4. if the crime committed was a crime against the Swedish nation, a Swedish municipal authority or other assembly, or against a Swedish public institution,

5. if the crime was committed in an area not belonging to any state

and was directed against a Swedish citizen, a Swedish association or private institution, or against an alien domiciled in Sweden,

6. if the crime is hijacking, maritime or aircraft sabotage, airport sabotage, an attempt to commit such crimes, a crime against international law, unlawful dealings with chemical weapons, unlawful dealings with mines or false or careless statement before an international court, or

7. if the least severe punishment prescribed for the crime in Swedish law is imprisonment for four years or more. (Law 1998:1703)

Section 3a

Besides the cases described in Sections 1—3, crimes shall be adjudged according to Swedish law and by a Swedish court in accordance with the provisions of the Act on International Collaboration concerning Proceedings in Criminal Matters (1975:19). (Law 1976:20)

Section 4

A crime is deemed to have been committed where the criminal act was perpetrated and also where the crime was completed or, in the case of an attempt, where the intended crime would have been completed.

Section 5

Prosecution for a crime committed within the Realm on a foreign vessel or aircraft by an alien, who was the officer in charge or member of its crew or otherwise travelled in it, against another alien or a foreign interest shall not be instituted without the authority of the Government or a person designated by the Government.

Prosecution for a crime committed outside the Realm may be instituted only following the authorisation referred to in the first paragraph. However, prosecution may be instituted without such an order if the crime consists of a false or careless statement before an international court or if the crime was committed:

1. on a Swedish vessel or aircraft or by the officer in charge or some member of its crew in the course of duty,

2. by a member of the armed forces in an area in which a detachment of the armed forces was present,

3. in the course of duty outside the Realm by a person employed by

a foreign contingent of the Swedish armed forces,

4. in Denmark, Finland, Iceland or Norway or on a vessel or aircraft in regular commerce between places situated in Sweden or one of the said states, or

5. by a Swedish, Danish, Finnish, Icelandic or Norwegian citizen against a Swedish interest. (Law 1993:350)

Section 5a

If the question of responsibility for an act has been determined by a judgement which has entered into legal force pronounced in a foreign state where the act was committed, or by a foreign state in which the European Convention of 28 May 1970 on the International Validity of Criminal Judgements or the European Convention of 15 May 1972 on the Transfer of Proceedings in Criminal Matters was in force, the accused may not be prosecuted for the same act in this Realm:

1. if he has been acquitted,

2. if he has been declared guilty of the crime without a sanction being imposed,

3. if the sanction imposed has been enforced in its entirety or enforcement is in process,

4. if the sanction imposed has lapsed under the law of the foreign state.

The first paragraph shall not apply to a crime under Section 1 or Section 3, points 4, 6 and 7, unless legal proceedings in the foreign state were instituted at the request of a Swedish authority.

If the question of responsibility for an act has been determined by a judgement pronounced by a foreign state and no impediment to legal proceedings exists by reason of what has been previously stated in this Section, the act may be prosecuted in the Realm only by order of the Government or a person authorised by the Government. (Law 1987:761)

Section 6

If a person is sentenced in the Realm for an act for which he has been subjected to a sanction outside the Realm, the sanction shall be determined with due consideration for what he has undergone outside the

Realm. If he should be sentenced to a fine or imprisonment and he has been sentenced to a sanction of deprivation of liberty outside the Realm, what he has undergone therewith shall be taken fully into consideration when determining the sanction.

In cases referred to in the first, paragraph a less severe punishment than that provided for the act may be imposed or a sanction completely waived. (Law 1972:812)

Section 7

In addition to the provisions of this Chapter on the applicability of Swedish law and the jurisdiction of Swedish courts, limitations resulting from generally recognised fundamental principles of public international law or from special provisions in agreements with foreign powers, shall be observed.

Section 7a

If an alien has committed a crime in the exercise of an office or duty comprising a general position held on behalf of another state or international organisation, a prosecution for the crime may only be instituted on order of the Government. The foregoing does not apply if, by means of misleading information, disguise or other means, the perpetrator has attempted to conceal the capacity in which he acted. (Law 1985:518)

Section 7b

If, on the occasion of a visit to Sweden of a foreign power's military forces within the framework of international co-operation, a crime is committed by personnel of the foreign power belonging to its forces, a prosecution for the crime may only be instituted on order of the Government. (Law 1996:401)

Section 8

Special provisions apply to extradition for crimes.

Conditions stipulated in connection with extradition from a foreign state to Sweden shall be complied with in the Realm.

PART TWO ON CRIMES

Chapter 3
On Crimes against Life and Health

Section 1

A person who takes the life of another shall be sentenced for *murder* to imprisonment for ten years or for life.

Section 2

If, in view of the circumstances that led to the act or for other reasons, the crime referred to in Section 1 is considered to be less serious, imprisonment for *manslaughter* shall be imposed for at least six and at most ten years.

Section 3

A woman who kills her child at birth or at a time, when, owing to her confinement, she is in a disturbed mental state or in grave distress, shall be sentenced for *infanticide* to imprisonment for at most six years.

Section 4

Repealed (Law 1974:596)

Section 5

A person who inflicts bodily injury, illness or pain upon another or renders him or her powerless or in a similar helpless state, shall be sentenced for *assault* to imprisonment for at most two years or, if the crime is petty, to a fine or imprisonment for at most six months. (Law 1998: 393)

PART TWO ON CRIMES

Section 6

If the crime referred to in Section 5 is considered gross, the sentence for *gross assault* shall be imprisonment for at least one and at most ten years.

In assessing if the crime is gross special consideration shall be given to whether the act constituted a mortal danger or whether the offender inflicted grievous bodily harm or severe illness or otherwise displayed particular ruthlessness or brutality. (Law 1988:2)

Section 7

A person who through carelessness causes the death of another shall be sentenced for *causing another's death* to imprisonment for at most two years or, if the crime is petty, to a fine.

If the crime is gross, imprisonment shall be imposed for at least six months and at most six years. If the act was committed by driving a motor vehicle, special consideration shall be given, in assessing whether the crime is gross, to whether the sentenced person was under the influence of alcohol or other substance. (Law 1993:1462)

Section 8

A person who through carelessness causes another to suffer bodily injury or illness not of a petty nature, shall be sentenced for *causing bodily injury or illness* to a fine or imprisonment for at most six months.

If the crime is gross, imprisonment for at most four years shall be imposed. If the act was committed by driving a motor vehicle, special consideration shall be given, in assessing whether the crime is gross, to whether the sentenced person was under the influence of alcohol or other substance. (Law 1993:1462)

Section 9

A person who through gross carelessness exposes another to mortal danger or danger of severe bodily injury or serious illness, shall be sentenced for *creating danger to another* to a fine or imprisonment for at most two years.

Section 10

Where a crime referred to in Sections 7—9 has been committed by a person with intent or by carelessly neglecting his duty under the Work Environment Act (1977:1160) to prevent sickness or accidents, the punishment shall be for an *environmental offence* and as provided for in the said provisions. (Law 1991:679)

Section 11

Sentences concerning liability for attempt or preparation to commit murder, manslaughter, infanticide or an assault not of a petty nature, as well as conspiracy to commit murder, manslaughter or gross assault or failure to reveal such a crime, shall be imposed in accordance with the provisions of Chapter 23. (Law 1991:679)

Section 12

Causing bodily injury or illness shall, if the crime is not of serious nature, only be prosecuted by a prosecutor if the injured party reports the crime for prosecution and prosecution is called for in the public interest. (Law 1991:679)

Chapter 4
On Crimes against Liberty and Peace

Section 1

A person who seizes and carries off or confines a child or some other person with intent to injure him or her in body or health or to force him or her into service, or to practise extortion, shall be sentenced for *kidnapping* to imprisonment for a fixed period of at least four and at most ten years, or for life.

If the crime is of a less serious nature, imprisonment for at most six years shall be imposed. (Law 1998:393)

Section 2

A person who, in cases other than those stated in Section 1, kidnaps or confines someone or in some other way deprives him or her of liberty, shall be sentenced for *unlawful deprivation of liberty* to imprisonment for at least one and at most ten years.

PART TWO ON CRIMES

If the crime is of a less serious nature, a fine or imprisonment for at most two years shall be imposed. (Law 1998:393)

Section 3

A person who otherwise than as stated in Section 1 or 2, by unlawful coercion or deceit, causes the entry of someone into military or work service or other similar condition of restraint or induces someone to go or remain in a place abroad where he or she may be in danger of being exposed to persecution or exploited for casual sexual relations or otherwise fall into distress, shall be sentenced for *placing a person in a distressful situation* to imprisonment for at least one and at most ten years.

If the crime is of a less serious nature, a fine or imprisonment for at most two years shall be imposed. (Law 1998:393)

Section 4

A person who, by assault or otherwise by force or by threat of a criminal act, compels another to do, submit to or omit to do something, shall be sentenced for *unlawful coercion* to a fine or imprisonment for at most two years. Anyone who to such effect exercises coercion by threatening to prosecute or report another for a crime or give detrimental information about another, shall also be sentenced for unlawful coercion, provided that the coercion is wrongful.

If the crime referred to in the first paragraph is gross, imprisonment for at least six months and at most six years shall be imposed. In assessing whether the crime is gross special consideration shall be given to whether the act included the infliction of pain to force a confession, or other torture.

Section 4a

A person who commits criminal acts as defined in Chapters 3, 4 or 6 against another person having, or have had, a close relationship to the perpetrator shall, if the acts form a part of an element in a repeated violation of that person's integrity and suited to severely damage that person's self-confidence, be sentenced for *gross violation of integrity* to imprisonment for at least six months and at most six years.

If the acts described in the first paragraph were committed by a man against a woman to whom he is, or has been, married or with whom he is, or has been cohabiting under circumstances comparable to marriage, he shall be sentenced for *gross violation of a woman's integrity* to the same punishment. (Law 1998:393)

Section 5

A person who raises a weapon against another or otherwise threatens to commit a criminal act, in such a manner that the nature thereof evokes in the threatened person a serious fear for the safety of his own or someone else's person or property, shall be sentenced for *unlawful threat* to a fine or imprisonment for at most one year.

If the crime is gross, imprisonment for at least six months and at most four years shall be imposed. (Law 1993:207)

Section 6

A person who unlawfully intrudes or remains where another has his living quarters, whether it is a room, a house, a yard or a vessel, shall be sentenced to a fine for *breach of domiciliary peace*.

A person, who, without authorisation, intrudes or remains in an office, factory, other building or vessel or at a storage area or other similar place, shall be sentenced for *unlawful intrusion* to a fine.

If the crime mentioned in the first or second paragraph is gross, imprisonment for at most two years shall be imposed.

Section 7

A person who physically molests or by discharging a firearm, throwing stones, making loud noise or other reckless conduct molests another, shall be sentenced for *molestation* to a fine or imprisonment for at most one year. (Law 1993:207)

Section 8

A person who unlawfully obtains access to a communication which a postal or telecommunications firm delivers or transmits in the form of mail or as a telecommunication, shall be sentenced for *breach of postal or telecommunication secrecy* to a fine or imprisonment for at most two years. (Law 1993:601)

Section 9

A person who, in a case not covered by Section 8, unlawfully opens a letter or a telegram or otherwise obtains access to something kept under seal or lock or otherwise enclosed, shall be sentenced for *intrusion into a safe depository* to a fine or imprisonment for at most two years.

Section 9a

A person who, in a case other than as stated in Section 8, unlawfully and secretly listens to or records by technical means for sound reproduction, speech in a room, a conversation between others or discussions at a conference or other meeting to which the public is not admitted and in which he himself does not participate, or to which he has improperly obtained access, shall be sentenced for *eavesdropping* to a fine or imprisonment for at most two years. (Law 975:239)

Section 9b

A person who employs technical means with the intention of committing a breach of telecommunication secrecy in the manner stated in Section 8 or to commit a crime as defined in Section 9a, shall be sentenced for preparation of such a crime to a fine or imprisonment for at most two years if he is not responsible for a completed crime. (Law 1975:239)

Section 9c

A person who, in cases other than those defined in Sections 8 and 9, unlawfully obtains access to a recording for automatic data processing or unlawfully alters or erases or inserts such a recording in a register, shall be sentenced for *breach of data secrecy* to a fine or imprisonment for at most two years. A recording in this context includes even information that is being processed by electronic or similar means for use with automatic data processing. (Law 1998:206)

Section 10

Attempt, preparation or conspiracy to commit kidnapping, unlawful deprivation of liberty or placing a person in a distressful situation, and any failure to reveal such crimes, shall be adjudged in accordance with the provisions of Chapter 23. The same shall apply to an attempt or preparation to commit unlawful coercion of a serious nature or breach of data secrecy, which if it had been completed, could not be considered petty. (Law 1998:206)

Section 11

Breach of domiciliary peace or unlawful intrusion not of a serious nature, unlawful eavesdropping not committed in a public place or preparation for such a crime, molestation which did not occur in a public place, or intrusion into a safe depository, may be prosecuted by a prosecutor only if the injured party reports the crime for prosecution or if prosecution is called for in the public interest. This also applies to unlawful coercion by threatening to prosecute or to inform on another for a crime or to give detrimental information about another, as well as an attempt to commit or prepare such a crime. (Law 1975:239)

Chapter 5
On Defamation

Section 1

A person who points out someone as being a criminal or as having a reprehensible way of living or otherwise furnishes information intended to cause exposure to the disrespect of others, shall be sentenced for *defamation* to a fine.

If he was duty-bound to express himself or if, considering the circumstances, the furnishing of information on the matter was defensible, or if he can show that the information was true or that he had reasonable grounds for it, no punishment shall be imposed.

Section 2

If the crime defined in Section 1 is regarded as gross, a fine or imprisonment for at most two years shall be imposed for *gross defamation*.

In assessing whether the crime is gross, special consideration shall be given to whether the information, because of its content or the scope of its dissemination or otherwise, was calculated to bring about serious damage.

Section 3

A person who vilifies another by an insulting epithet or accusation or by other infamous conduct towards him, shall be sentenced, if the act is not punishable under Section 1 or 2, for *insulting behaviour* to a fine.

If the crime is gross, a fine or imprisonment for at most six months shall be imposed.

Section 4

Defamation of a deceased person shall result in liability under Section 1 or 2 if the act is offensive to the survivors or if, having regard to the time that has passed since the deceased was alive and other circumstances, the act can be regarded as disturbing the peace to which the deceased should be entitled.

Section 5

Crimes mentioned in Sections 1—3 may not be prosecuted by other than the injured party. If, however, the injured party notifies the crime for prosecution, and if for special reasons prosecution is considered necessary in the public interest, a prosecutor may prosecute for:

1. defamation and gross defamation,
2. insulting behaviour towards a person exercising, or for the exercise of, his or her duties in office,
3. insulting behaviour towards a person with allusion to his or her race, colour, national or ethnic origin or religious belief, or
4. insulting behaviour towards a person with allusion to his or her homosexual inclination.

If defamation is directed against a deceased person, prosecution may be instituted by the surviving spouse, direct heir or heirs, father, mother or siblings and by a prosecutor if prosecution for special reasons is considered to be called for in the public interest.

If a crime mentioned in Sections 1—3 entails an outrage against the head of state of a foreign power who is at that time in Sweden, or against the representative of a foreign power in Sweden, and has thereby insulted the foreign power, the crime may be prosecuted by a public prosecutor notwithstanding the provisions of the first paragraph. However, such prosecution may not be instituted without an order of the Government or a person authorised by the Government. (Law 1998:393)

Chapter 6
On Sexual Crimes

Section 1

A person who by violence or threat which involves, or appears to the threatened person to involve an imminent danger, forces another person to have sexual intercourse or to engage in a comparable sexual act, that having regard to the nature of the violation and the ircumstances in general, is comparable to enforced sexual intercourse, shall be sentenced for *rape* to imprisonment for at least two and at most six years. Causing helplessness or a similar state of incapacitation shall be regarded as equivalent to violence.

If having regard to the nature of the violence or the threat and the circumstances in general, the crime is considered less serious, a sentence to imprisonment for at most four years shall be imposed.

If the crime is gross, a sentence to imprisonment for at least four and at most ten years shall be imposed for *gross rape*. In assessing whether the crime is gross, special consideration shall be given to whether the violence involved a danger to life or whether the perpetrator caused serious injury or serious illness or, having regard to the method used or the victim's youth or other circumstances, exhibited particular ruthlessness or brutality. (Law 1998:393)

Section 2

A person who, under circumstances other than those defined in Section 1, makes someone engage in a sexual act by unlawful coercion shall be sentenced for *sexual coercion* to imprisonment for at most two years.

If the person who committed the act exhibited particular ruthlessness or if the crime is otherwise considered gross, a sentence of at least six months and at most four years shall be imposed for *gross sexual coer-*

cion. (Law 1992:147)

Section 3

A person who induces another person to engage in a sexual act by gross abuse of his or her dependent state shall be sentenced for *sexual exploitation* to imprisonment for at most two years. The same shall apply to a person who engages in a sexual act with another person by improperly taking advantage of the fact that the latter is helpless or in some other state of incapacitation or is suffering from a mental disturbance.

If the accused has exhibited particular ruthlessness or if the crime is otherwise to be considered gross, imprisonment for at least six months and at most six years shall be imposed for *gross sexual exploitation*. (Law 1998:393)

Section 4

A person who engages in a sexual act with someone under eighteen years of age and who is that person's offspring or for whose upbringing he or she is responsible, or for whose care or supervision he or she is responsible by decision of a public authority, shall be sentenced for *sexual exploitation of a minor* to imprisonment for at most four years. This also applies to a person who, in circumstances other those mentioned previously in this Chapter, engages in a sexual act with a child under fifteen years.

If the person who committed the act exhibited particular lack of regard for the minor or if the crime by reason of the minor's young age or otherwise is regarded as gross, imprisonment for at least two and at most eight years shall be imposed for *gross sexual exploitation of a minor*. (Law 1998:393)

Section 5

Repealed (Law 1994:1499)

Section 6

If a person has sexual intercourse otherwise than as previously provided in this Chapter with his or her own child or its offspring imprisonment for at most two years shall be imposed for *sexual intercourse with an offspring*.

A person who has sexual intercourse with a blood sibling shall be sentenced to imprisonment for at most one year for *sexual intercourse with a sibling*.

The provisions of this Section do not apply to a person who has been made to commit the act by unlawful coercion or other improper means. (Law 1992:147)

Section 7

If a person sexually touches a child under fifteen years of age otherwise than as previously provided in this Chapter, or induces the child to undertake or participate in an act with sexual implication a fine or imprisonment for at most two years shall be imposed for *sexual molestation*.

A sentence for sexual molestation shall also be imposed on a person who by coercion, seduction or other improper influence induces a person who has attained the age of fifteen but not eighteen to undertake or participate in an act with sexual implication if the act is an element in the production of pornographic pictures or constitutes pornographic posing in circumstances other than those relating to the production of a picture.

This shall also apply if a person exposes himself or herself in such a manner that the nature thereof gives offence or otherwise manifestly behaves indecently by word or deed towards the latter in a way that flagrantly violates a sense of propriety. (Law 1994:1499)

Section 8

A person who promotes or improperly financially exploits the casual sexual relations for payment of another person shall be sentenced for *procuring* to imprisonment for at most four years.

A person who, holding the right to the use of premises, grants the right to use them to another in the knowledge that the premises are wholly or to a substantial extent used for casual sexual relations for payment and omits to do what can reasonably be expected to terminate the granted right, he or she shall, if the activity continues or is resumed at the premises, be considered to have promoted the activity and shall be sentenced in accordance with the first paragraph. (Law 1998:393)

PART TWO ON CRIMES

Section 9

If the crime provided for in Section 8 is gross, imprisonment for at least two and at most six years shall be imposed for *gross procuring*.

In assessing whether the crime is gross, special consideration shall be given to whether the accused promoted casual sexual relations for payment on a large scale or ruthlessly exploited another. (Law 1984:399)

Section 10

A person who, by promising or giving recompense, obtains or tries to obtain casual sexual relations with someone under eighteen years of age, shall be sentenced for *seduction of youth* to a fine or imprisonment for at most six months. (Law 1984:399)

Section 11

Criminal responsibility as provided for in this Chapter for an act committed against someone under a given age shall be required of a perpetrator who did not realise, but had reasonable grounds for assuming, that the other person had not attained such age. (Law 1998:393)

Section 12

An attempt to commit rape, gross rape, sexual coercion, gross sexual coercion, sexual exploitation, gross sexual exploitation, sexual exploitation of a minor, gross sexual exploitation of a minor, procuring and gross procuring shall be dealt with in accordance with the provisions of Chapter 23. This also applies to preparation for and conspiracy to commit rape, gross rape, gross sexual exploitation of a minor and gross procuring, together with failure to reveal such crime. (Law 1998:393)

Section 13

If, in a case of sexual exploitation of a minor under Section 4, first paragraph, second sentence or an attempt to commit such a crime, or in a case of sexual molestation under Section 7, first paragraph, there is little difference in age and development between the person who committed the act and the child, public prosecution shall not occur unless it is called for in the public interest. (Law 1994:1499)

Chapter 7
On Crimes against the Family

Section 1

A married person who enters into a new marriage or a single person who marries someone who is already married, shall be sentenced for *bigamy* to a fine or imprisonment for at most two years.

A person who is a partner in a registered partnership and enters into a marriage, shall be sentenced for *unlawfully entering a marriage* to a fine or imprisonment for at most two years. (Law 1994:1119)

Section 1a

A married person who permits a partnership to be registered or being already in a registered partnership permits a partnership to be registered, shall be sentenced for *unlawful partnership* to a fine or imprisonment for at most two years. The same shall apply if some other person permits the registration of a partnership although his or her partner is already married or is a partner in a registered partnership. (Law 1994:1119)

Section 2

Repealed (Law 1973:648).

Section 3

A person who conceals or exchanges a child or otherwise, by giving incorrect notice to the authorities or by failing to give notice, appropriates for himself or another a false family status or deprives another of his rightful family status, shall be sentenced for *tampering with family status* to a fine or imprisonment for at most two years.

Section 4

A person who without authorisation separates a child under fifteen years of age from the person who has the custody of the child, shall, unless the crime is one against personal liberty, be sentenced for *arbitrary conduct concerning a child* to a fine or imprisonment for at most one year. The same applies if a person having joint custody with another of a

PART TWO ON CRIMES

child under fifteen years of age without good reason arbitrarily carries off the child or if the person who is to have the custody of the child without authorisation takes possession of the child and thereby takes the Law into his or her own hands.

A person is also criminally responsible under the first paragraph who without authorisation separates a child under fifteen years of age from the person who has the custody of the child by virtue of the Care of Young Persons Special Provisions Act (Law 1990:52), unless the crime is one against personal liberty or of furtherance of flight.

If the crime against the provisions of the first or second paragraph is gross, the accused shall be sentenced to imprisonment for at least six months and at most two years. (Law 1993:207)

Section 5

An attempt to tamper with family status or a gross crime of arbitrary conduct concerning a child shall be sentenced in accordance with the provisions of Chapter 23. (Law 1993:207)

Section 6

Arbitrary conduct concerning a child may not be prosecuted by a public prosecutor unless prosecution is called for in the public interest. (Law 1973:648)

Chapter 8

On Theft, Robbery and Other Crimes of Stealing

Section 1

A person who unlawfully takes what belongs to another with intent to acquire it, shall, if the appropriation involves loss, be sentenced for *theft* to imprisonment for at most two years.

Section 2

If the crime under Section 1, having regard to the value of the stolen goods and other circumstances of the crime, is regarded as petty, a fine or imprisonment for at most six months shall be imposed for *petty theft*.

Section 3

Repealed (Law 1987:791)

Section 4

If the crime under Section 1 is considered to be gross, imprisonment for at least six months and at most six years shall be imposed for *gross theft*.

In assessing whether the crime is gross, special consideration shall be given to whether the unlawful appropriation took place after intrusion into a dwelling, whether it concerned the appropriation of property borne by a person, whether the accused was equipped with a weapon, explosive or similar aid, or whether the act was otherwise of an especially dangerous or ruthless nature, concerned property of considerable value or entailed a keenly felt loss. (Law 1988:2)

Section 5

If a person steals from another by means of violence or by a threat implying or appearing to the threatened person to imply an imminent danger, or who, after committing a theft and being caught in the act, resists by such violence or threat a person who attempts to recover the stolen property, imprisonment for at least one and at most six years shall be imposed for *robbery*. The same shall apply to a person who by such violence or threat forces another to commit or omit to commit some act so that gain results to the accused and loss to the person so forced or to someone he represents. Causing helplessness or a similar state of incapacitation shall be regarded as equivalent to violence.

If the conduct under the first paragraph, having regard to the violence, threat or other circumstances, is of a less serious nature the sentence shall not be for robbery but for such other crime as the conduct entails. (Law 1975:1395)

Section 6

If the crime under Section 5 is regarded as gross, imprisonment for at least four and at most ten years shall be imposed for *gross robbery*.

In assessing whether the crime is gross, special consideration shall be given to whether the violence was dangerous to life or whether the accused caused serious bodily injury or a severe illness or otherwise exhibited considerable brutality or ruthlessly took advantage of the victim's defenceless or exposed situation.

Section 7

A person who unlawfully takes or uses a motor vehicle or other motor-driven conveyance belonging to another, shall, unless the crime is punishable under the previous provisions of this Chapter, be sentenced for *vehicle theft* to imprisonment for at most two years or, if the crime is of a petty nature, to a fine.

If the crime is gross, imprisonment for at least six months and at most four years shall be imposed.

Section 8

If a person, in a case other than those specially provided for in this Chapter, unlawfully takes and uses or otherwise appropriates something, a fine or imprisonment for at most six months shall be imposed for *unlawful dispossession*. The same shall apply to a person who, without any appropriation, by fitting or breaking a lock or by other means unlawfully disturbs another's possession or by violence or threat of violence prevents another from exercising his right to retain or take something.

If the crime is gross, imprisonment for at most two years shall be imposed.

Section 9

A person who, in order to restore a personal right, unlawfully interferes with another's possession shall be sentenced for *selfrepossession* to a fine or imprisonment for at most six months.

Section 10

A person who unlawfully diverts electric energy, shall be sentenced for *unlawful diversion of energy* to a fine or imprisonment for at most one year.

If the crime is gross a sentence to imprisonment for at least six months and at most four years shall be imposed. (Law 1993:207)

Section 11

If a person unlawfully takes such objects as are mentioned in Chapter 12, Section 2, second, paragraph from a forest or field, and if the crime is not to be considered as trespassing as there defined, the provisions of the present Chapter on misappropriation of property shall apply.

If a person disturbs another's possession of real property, by, for instance unlawfully raising or breaking down a fence, or by building, digging, ploughing, making a road or letting animals graze, or without authorisation deprives another of possession of real property or a part thereof, the provisions of Sections 8 and 9 on unlawful dispossession and unlawful repossession shall apply.

Section 12

An attempt or preparation to commit theft, gross theft, robbery, gross robbery, vehicle theft or unlawful diversion of energy, and also conspiracy to commit or failure to reveal robbery or gross robbery shall be punished in accordance with the provisions of Chapter 23. If, however, a completed vehicle theft would have been regarded as petty such punishment shall not be imposed.

Section 13

If a crime as defined in this Chapter other than gross theft, robbery or gross robbery has been committed against:

1. a person living with the accused other than on a temporary basis,

2. a spouse or a blood relation in a direct ascending or descending line or a relative by marriage, sibling, brother-in-law or sister-in-law, or

3. any other person similarly closely related to the accused, a public prosecutor may institute a prosecution only if the injured party has reported the crime for prosecution or if prosecution is called for in the public interest.

In application of the present provisions, any person accessory to the crime and any person guilty of receiving stolen goods or petty receiving of stolen goods shall be deemed equivalent to an accused. (Law 1987:791)

PART TWO ON CRIMES

Chapter 9
On Fraud and Other Dishonesty

Section 1

If a person by deception induces someone to commit or omit to commit some act which involves gain for the accused and loss for the deceived or someone represented by the latter imprisonment for at most two years shall be imposed for *fraud*.

A sentenced for fraud shall also be imposed on a person who, by delivering incorrect or incomplete information, or by making alterations to a programme or recording or by other means, unlawfully affects the result of automatic data processing or any other similar automatic process so that gain accrues to the offender and loss is entailed by any other person. (Law 1986:123)

Section 2

If, having regard to the extent of the loss and other circumstances of the crime mentioned in Section 1, the crime is regarded as petty, a fine or imprisonment for at most six months shall be imposed for *fraudulent conduct*.

A person who avails himself of accommodation, meals, transportation or admission to a performance or anything similar offered on condition of cash payment, and fails to meet his obligation, shall, whether anyone was deceived or not, be sentenced for fraudulent conduct. However, this shall not apply if the act concerns a value that is inconsiderable and is in other respects as defined in Section 1. (Law 1976:1139)

Section 3

If a crime as defined in Section 1 is regarded as gross, imprisonment for at least six months and at most six years shall be imposed for *gross fraud*.

In assessing whether the crime is gross, special consideration shall be given to whether the offender abused public trust or employed a false document or misleading bookkeeping, or whether the crime otherwise had been of a particularly dangerous nature, involved a substantial value or resulted in a keenly felt loss. (Law 1976:1139)

Section 4

A person who by unlawful coercion induces someone to do or not do something which involves gain for the offender and loss for the coerced person or someone represented by the latter, shall, unless the crime is regarded as robbery or gross robbery, be sentenced for *extortion* to imprisonment for at most two years or, if the crime is petty, to a fine.

If the crime is gross, imprisonment for at least six months and at most six years shall be imposed.

Section 5

A person who in connection with a contract or other legal transaction takes advantage of someone's distress, innocence or thoughtlessness or dependent relationship to him in order to obtain a benefit which is clearly disproportionate to the consideration afforded or for which no consideration will be provided, shall be sentenced for *usury* to a fine or imprisonment for at most two years.

A person shall also be sentenced for usury who, in connection with the granting of credit in a business activity or other activity that is conducted habitually or otherwise on a large scale, procures interest or other financial benefit which is manifestly disproportionate to the counter-obligation.

If the crime is gross, imprisonment for at least six months and at most four years shall be imposed. (Law 1986:123)

Section 6

A person who

1. takes possession of something of which another has been dispossessed by a crime, and does so in such a manner that the nature thereof renders its restitution difficult,

2. procures an improper gain from another's proceeds of crime,

3. improperly promotes the opportunity for another to take advantage of property emanating from the proceeds of crime, or the value of

such property,

4. assists in the removal, transfer, or sale of property which is derived from the proceeds of crime, or takes some similar measure, with the intent of concealing the origin of property, or

5. by a demand, transfer or other similar means asserts a claim arising from a crime, shall be sentenced for *receiving* to imprisonment for at most two years.

A person who, in business activities or as a part of business activities which are conducted habitually or otherwise on a large scale, acquires or receives something which may reasonably be assumed to have been misappropriated from another person by a crime, and does so in such a manner that the nature thereof renders its restitution difficult, shall be similarly sentenced for receiving.

If the crime referred to in the first or second paragraph is gross, imprisonment for at least six months and at most six years shall be imposed. (Law 1993:207)

Section 7

If a crime under Section 6 is considered to be petty, imprisonment for at most six months or a fine shall be imposed for *petty receiving*.

A sentence for petty receiving shall also be imposed on a person who

1. in a case other than that provided for in Section 6, second paragraph, acquires or receives something in such a manner that the nature thereof renders restitution difficult which may reasonably be assumed to have been misappropriated from another person by a crime,

2. in a case as provided for in Section 6, first paragraph, did not realise, but had reasonable cause to assume that a crime was involved, or

3. in a manner as provided for in Section 6, first paragraph, point 1, participated in the crime whereby property was misappropriated from another and did not realise, but had reasonable cause to assume, that a crime had been committed. (Law 1991:451)

Section 8

A person who in a case other than those referred to earlier in this Chapter, acts dishonestly by misleading someone and inducing him to do or omit to do something, thereby harming him or someone he represents, shall be sentenced to a fine or imprisonment for at most two years shall be imposed for *dishonest conduct*. (Law 1970:414)

Section 9

A person who publishes or otherwise disseminates misleading information among the public in order to influence the price of an article, a security or other property, shall be sentenced for *swindling* to imprisonment for at most two years or, if the crime is petty, to a fine or imprisonment for at most six months.

A person who assists in organising a share company or other firm or who, because of his position ought to possess special knowledge about a firm, intentionally or through gross carelessness publishes or otherwise disseminates misleading information among the public or among those holding an interest in the firm of a nature to influence the assessment of the firm from a financial point of view, and thereby causes damage, shall be sentenced in accordance with the first paragraph.

If a crime as defined in this Section is gross, imprisonment for at least six months and at most six years shall be imposed. (Law 1993:207)

Section 10

A person who accepts for use as a means of exerting pressure in connection with a claim, a document that is false, drawn up for the sake of appearance or otherwise incorrect, or a cheque drawn on insufficient funds, shall be sentenced for *usurious acquisition* to a fine or imprisonment for at most two years.

Section 11

An attempt or preparation to commit fraud, gross fraud, extortion or usury shall be punished in accordance with the provisions of Chapter 23. The provisions of Chapter 23, Section 3, however, shall not apply to attempt at extortion.

A person who, in order to defraud an insurer, or otherwise with fraudulent intent, inflicts bodily harm on himself or on another or harm to property of his own or of another, shall be sentenced for preparation to commit fraud or gross fraud. The same shall apply if a person with the

PART TWO ON CRIMES

intent previously mentioned endeavours to bring about such harm. If, before the harm has been inflicted, he has voluntarily refrained from carrying out the act, he shall be free from criminal responsibility.

Section 12

The provisions of Chapter 8, Section 13, concerning limitation of a public prosecutor's right to prosecute shall also apply to the crimes defined in this Chapter with the exception of gross fraud.

A prosecution for fraud or fraudulent conduct which consists of making a withdrawal from a personal credit or deposit account in breach of agreement, and fraudulent conduct under Section 2, second paragraph, may only be initiated by the public prosecutor if this is in the public interest. (Law 1994:141)

Chapter 10

On Embezzlement and Other Breaches of Trust

Section 1

A person who, through a contract or public or private service or a similar situation, has gained possession of property on behalf of another with the obligation to deliver it or account for it, and appropriates the property or otherwise disregards what he has to comply with in order to be able to fulfil his obligation, shall, if the act results in gain for him and loss to the owner, be sentenced for *embezzlement* to imprisonment for at most two years.

Section 2

If, having regard to the value of the property and other circumstances, the crime defined in Section 1 is regarded as petty, a fine or imprisonment for at most six months shall be imposed for *withholding property*.

Section 3

If the crime defined in Section 1 is regarded as gross, imprisonment for at least six months and at most six years shall be imposed for *gross embezzlement*.

In assessing whether the crime is gross, special attention shall be given to whether the offender abused a responsible position or used a false document or misleading bookkeeping or whether the act was otherwise of a specially dangerous nature, involved a substantial amount or resulted in a particularly keenly felt loss.

Section 4

A person who, in a case other than one provided for earlier in this Chapter, takes any step concerning property in his possession to which the right of ownership or legal security is reserved for, guaranteed to or otherwise belongs to another and by such step the latter is dispossessed of his property or otherwise deprived of his right, shall be sentenced for *unlawful disposal* to a fine or imprisonment for at most two years.

Section 5

A person who, by reason of a position of trust has been given the task of managing another's financial affairs or independently handling an assignment requiring qualified technical knowledge, or exercising supervision over the management of such affairs or assignment, abuses his position of trust and thereby injures his principal, shall be sentenced for *breach of faith committed by an agent against his principal* to a fine or imprisonment for at most two years. The foregoing does not apply if the crime is punishable under Sections 1—3.

If the crime is gross, imprisonment for at least six months and at most six years shall be imposed. In assessing whether the crime is gross, special attention shall be given to whether the offender used a false document or misleading bookkeeping or caused his principal a substantial or particularly keenly felt loss.

A person who has been given the task of managing another's legal affairs and abuses his position of trust to the detriment of his principal, shall be sentenced in accordance with the first paragraph even if the affairs are not of a financial or technical nature. (Law 1986:123)

PART TWO   ON CRIMES

Section 6

A person who, in a case not previously provided for in this Chapter, by misusing his authority to take legal action on behalf of another, harms that person, or, by misuse of his authority to call in a promissory note or like instrument, lays claim to something that belongs to another, shall be sentenced for *misuse of authority* to a fine or imprisonment for at most two years. The same shall apply if a person demands payment in conformity with a document that has not been issued or payment of a debt already settled or demands the delivery of goods he has already received or, when presented with a demand, adduces a receipt which has not been given.

Section 7

A person who unlawfully uses something belonging to another and thereby causes damage or inconvenience, shall be sentenced for *unlawful use* to a fine or imprisonment for at most six months.

The same shall apply if the owner of a property uses it to the prejudice of another's right to it by unlawfully building, digging, ploughing, making a road, letting animals graze or taking some other similar action.

If the crime as defined in the first paragraph is gross, imprisonment for at least six months and at most four years shall be imposed. (Law 1993:207)

Section 8

A person who does not comply with the law's provisions concerning the obligation to give notice of property found or belonging to another, of which possession was gained by error or by chance, shall be sentenced for *failure to return lost property* to a fine. If such obligation was disregarded with intent to appropriate the property or if otherwise the property was dealt with in a manner defined in Section 4, the provisions of that Section shall apply.

Section 9

Attempted embezzlement, gross embezzlement or disloyalty to principal shall be punished in accordance with the provisions of Chapter 23.

Section 10

The provisions of Chapter 8, Section 13, concerning restriction of a public prosecutor's right to prosecute shall also apply to crimes as defined in this Chapter with the exception of gross embezzlement and such disloyalty to a principal which is considered gross.

Unlawful conversion of property, which has come into the possession of the accused through an agreement on the hire of the property or an agreement according to which the right of ownership shall be transferred only after payment has been made, or which the accused otherwise possesses by virtue of a credit purchase subject to a right of recovery, may only be prosecuted by a public prosecutor if such prosecution is, for a special reason, called for in the public interest. (Law 1994:1411)

Chapter 11
On Crimes against Creditors

Section 1

A person who, being insolvent or in manifest danger of becoming insolvent, destroys, or by gift or other like action disposes of property of substantial value, shall be sentenced for *dishonesty to creditors* to imprisonment for at most two years. This also applies to any person who by means of a like act or acts renders himself insolvent or brings about a manifest danger of becoming insolvent.

A debtor who, in connection with the rescheduling of debts under the Debt Rescheduling Act (Law 1994:334), bankruptcy or negotiation of a public accord with creditors, conceals an asset, reports a non-existent debt, or gives other erroneous information of like nature, shall also, unless the statement is corrected before it is attested on oath or otherwise made the basis of the proceeding, be sentenced for dishonesty to creditors. The same shall apply if a debtor, in connection with some other executive proceeding, invokes an erroneous document or a fictitious contract and thereby hinders the seizure, in conformity with the proceeding, of

PART TWO ON CRIMES

property necessary to provide a creditor with payment or security.

Any debor who, with impending bankruptcy, removes from the Realm an asset of substantial value with the intention of withholding such asset from the bankruptcy estate, or any debtor who, being bankrupt, withholds an asset from the bankruptcy administration shall likewise be sentenced for dishonesty to creditors. (Law 1994:335)

Section 2

If a crime under Section 1 is considered to be gross, imprisonment shall be imposed for not less than six months and not more than six years for *gross dishonesty to creditors*.

In assessing whether a crime is gross, special attention shall be given to whether the offender attested a false statement, or made use of a false document or misleading bookkeeping, or if the crime was on a considerable scale. (Law 1986:43)

Section 3

Any person who, being insolvent or in manifest danger of becoming insolvent, continues to run an enterprise, utilising thereby considerable means without corresponding benefit to the enterprise, or who lives in a wasteful or extravagant manner, or who enters into a hazardous undertaking or thoughtlessly assumes onerous commitments, or who embarks upon a similar course of action and thereby intentionally or through gross carelessness substantially worsens his economic status, shall be sentenced for *careless disregard of creditors* to imprisonment for at most two years. The same shall apply even though the perpetrator did not realise, but had good reason to assume, that he was insolvent or in manifest danger of becoming insolvent.

A debtor who in connection with the rescheduling of debts under the Debt Rescheduling Act (Law 1994:334), bankruptcy or negotiation of a public accord with creditors, through gross carelessness conceals an asset, reports a non-existent debt or provides some other erroneous information of like nature, shall also, unless the statement is corrected before it is attested on oath or otherwise made the basis of the proceeding, be sentenced for careless disregard of creditors. (Law 1994:335)

Section 4

A person who, being insolvent or in manifest danger of becoming insolvent, favours a particular creditor by paying a debt which has not fallen due, making payment by means other than is customary, or furnishing security not agreed upon when the debt was incurred, or by taking some other such action, shall, if the measure entails a manifest lessening of the rights of other creditors, be sentenced for *favouritism to a creditor* to imprisonment for at most two years.

The same shall apply to a person who, being insolvent, shows favouritism to a creditor for an improper purpose by means other than those defined here and thereby occasions a manifest danger that the rights of other creditors will thereby be substantially diminished.

A debtor who, for the purpose of promoting an accord, secretly makes or promises payment or other advantage, shall also be sentenced for favouritism to creditors. (Law 1986:43)

Section 5

A person who intentionally or through carelessness neglects the obligation to maintain accounts in accordance with the Bookkeeping Act (1976:125), The Act on Foundations (Law 1994:1220) or the Pension Obligations Protection Act (1967:531) by failing to enter business transactions into the accounts or to preserve accounting material, or by entering false information into the accounts or in some other way, shall, if in consequence the course of the business or its financial results or status cannot in the main be assessed from the accounts, be sentenced for *bookkeeping crime* to imprisonment for at most two years, or, if the crime is petty, to a fine. If the crime is gross imprisonment for not less than six months and not more than four years shall be imposed. (Law 1994:1220)

Section 6

Attempted dishonesty to creditors under Section 1, first paragraph or attempted dishonesty to creditors under Section 1, third paragraph, which means that an asset is removed from the Realm, shall be punished in accordance with the provisions of Chapter 23. (Law 1986:43)

PART TWO   ON CRIMES

Section 7

A person who, whilst acting for or on behalf of a debtor, commits an act for which a debtor is criminally responsible under the provisions of this Chapter, shall be sentenced as if he himself were a debtor.

A creditor who, in a case defined in Section 4, accepts or permits himself to be promised a payment, security or other benefit shall only be sentenced for complicity if he used an improper threat or improper promise of a benefit or acted in collusion with the perpetrator. (Law 1986:43)

Section 8

Careless disregard of creditors under Section 3, first paragraph, may be prosecuted by a public prosecutor only if prosecution is called for in the public interest. (Law 1982:150)

Chapter 12

On Crimes Inflicting Damage

Section 1

A person who destroys or damages property, real or moveable, to the detriment of another's right thereto, shall be sentenced for *inflicting damage* to a fine or imprisonment for at most six months.

Section 2

If, having regard to the insignificance of the damage to property and other circumstances, the crime mentioned in Section 1 is considered to be petty, a fine shall be imposed for *trespass*.

A person who in a forest or field unlawfully takes growing trees or grass or from growing trees takes twigs, branches, bark, leaves, bast, acorns, nuts or resin, or takes windfall trees, stone, gravel, sod or similar things not prepared for use, shall be sentenced for trespass if the crime is considered to be petty having regard to the value of what is taken and other circumstances.

Section 3

If the crime defined in Section 1 is regarded as gross, imprisonment for at most four years shall be imposed for *gross infliction of damage*.

In assessing whether the crime is gross, special attention shall be paid to whether the act gave rise to an extreme risk to anyone's life or health or the damage was to something of great cultural or financial importance or was otherwise a particularly keenly felt loss.

Section 4

A person who unlawfully makes his way across a building lot, a plantation or other land that can be damaged thereby, he shall be sentenced for *taking an unlawful path* to a fine.

Section 5

Attempt or preparation to commit the crime of gross infliction of damage and failure to reveal such a crime is punishable in accordance with the provisions of Chapter 23.

Section 6

Trespass or taking an unlawful path may, if the crime only infringes the right of a private person, be prosecuted by a prosecutor only if prosecution is called for in the public interest.

Chapter 13
On Crimes Involving Public Danger

Section 1

A person who starts a fire which entails danger to another's life or health or extensive destruction of another's property shall be sentenced for *arson* to imprisonment for at least two and at most eight years.

If the crime is less serious, imprisonment of at least one and at most three years shall be imposed. (Law 1993:207).

Section 2

If the crime defined in Section 1 is considered gross, imprisonment for a fixed term of at least six and at most ten years, or for life, shall be

PART TWO ON CRIMES

imposed for *gross arson*.

In assessing whether the crime is gross, special attention shall be paid to whether the fire was started in a densely populated area, where it could easily spread, or otherwise constituted a danger to a number of persons or to property of special importance.

Section 3

A person who causes an explosion, flooding, landslide, shipwreck, an aircraft or train accident or other like calamity and thereby gives rise to a danger to another's life or health or to extensive destruction of another's property, shall be sentenced for *devastation endangering the public* to imprisonment for at least two and at most eight years.

If the crime is less serious, imprisonment for at least one and at most three years shall be imposed.

If the crime is gross, imprisonment for a fixed term of at least six and at most ten years, or for life, shall be imposed. (Law 1993:207)

Section 4

A person who destroys or damages property of considerable importance for the defence of the Realm, public subsistence, the administration of justice or public administration, or the maintenance of public order and security in the Realm, or by some other action, not limited to the withholding of labour or encouraging such action, seriously disturbs or obstructs the use of such property, shall be sentenced for *sabotage* to imprisonment for at most four years. This shall also apply if a person otherwise, by inflicting damage or by other action of the kind just described, seriously disturbs or obstructs public traffic or the use of telegraph, telephone, radio or other similar public service or use of an installation for the supply of water, light, heat or power to the public.

Section 5

If a crime as defined in Section 4 is considered gross, imprisonment for at least two and at most ten years, or for life, shall be imposed for *gross sabotage*.

In assessing whether the crime is gross, special attention shall be paid to whether it caused danger to the security of the Realm, to the lives of a number of persons, or to property of special importance.

Section 5a

A person who, by means of unlawful coercion, seizes or interferes with the operation of an aircraft or a vessel used in civil commercial maritime traffic for the transport of goods or passengers, towing, salvaging, fish or other catch, shall be sentenced for *hijacking* to imprisonment for at most four years. The same shall apply to a person who by unlawful coercion seizes a platform in the sea which is intended for activities in connection with the exploration or exploitation of natural resources or for some other financial purpose.

A person who in other cases:

1. destroys or seriously damages such a vessel or such a platform as is mentioned in the first paragraph or an aircraft in traffic, or

2. undertakes an action of a nature to present a danger to the safety of such vessel or such platform as is mentioned in the first paragraph or to the safety of such an aircraft during flight, shall be sentenced for *maritime or air traffic sabotage* to imprisonment for at most four years.

If the crime described in the first or second paragraph is considered to be gross, a sentence for a fixed term, of at least two and most ten years, or for life shall be imposed. In assessing

whether the crime is gross, special attention shall be given to whether danger was thereby caused to a number of persons or whether the act was otherwise of a particularly dangerous nature. (Law 1990: 416).

Section 5b

A person who:

1. uses serious violence or threatens such violence against a person who is at an airport open to international traffic,

2. destroys or seriously damages an installation belonging to such an airport or which is used for its traffic, or an aircraft which is not in traffic but is parked at the airport, or

3. by the use of violence or threat of violence thwarts the operations conducted at such an airport,

shall be sentenced, if the act is of a nature to endanger the operations at or safety of the airport, for *airport sabotage*, to imprisonment for at most four years.

If the crime is considered to be gross, a sentence to imprisonment for a fixed term of at least two and at most ten years, or for life shall be imposed. In assessing whether the crime is gross, special attention shall be paid to whether it presented danger to the lives of a number of persons or if the act was otherwise of a particularly dangerous nature. (Law 1990:416)

Section 6

A person who carelessly, by the careless handling of fire or explosives or in some other way causes

1. a fire or some calamity mentioned in Sections 1, 2 or 3 or a danger of its occurring, or

2. causes the damage or obstruction described in Section 4, or

3. the damage described in Section 5a, second paragraph, or Section 5b, first paragraph, second point,

shall be sentenced for *carelessness endangering the public* to a fine or imprisonment for at most six months.

If the crime is gross, imprisonment for at most two years shall be imposed. (Law 1990:416)

Section 7

A person who creates a general danger to human life or health by poisoning or infecting food, water, or the like, or in other ways by spreading poison or the like, or by transmitting or spreading serious disease, shall be sentenced for *spreading poison or a contagious substance* to imprisonment for at most six years.

If the crime is gross, imprisonment for at least four and at most ten years, or for life, shall be imposed. In assessing whether the crime is gross, special attention shall be paid to whether it was committed with intent to harm another's life or health or exposed a number of persons to danger.

Section 8

A person who creates a general danger to animals or plants by means of poison or by transmitting or spreading malignant disease or by spreading noxious animals or weeds or by other like means, shall be sentenced for *causing destruction* to a fine or imprisonment for at most two years.

If the crime is gross, imprisonment for at least six months and at most six years shall be imposed. In assessing whether the crime is gross, special attention shall be paid to whether it was committed with intent to cause damage or whether property of substantial value was exposed to danger.

Section 8a

Repealed (Law 1998:809)

Section 9

A person who through carelessness commits an act defined in Section 7 or 8, shall be sentenced for *careless handling of poison or contagious substance* to a fine or imprisonment for at most of two years. (Law 1998: 809)

Section 10

A person who, without being criminally responsible under the preceding provisions of this Chapter, while handling fire, explosives or poison or in some other way creates a danger of fire or calamity as described in Sections 1, 2, or 3 or general danger as described in Sections 7 or 8, and neglects, after becoming aware of the danger, to do what can be reasonably expected to avert it, he shall be sentenced for *neglect to avert public danger* to a fine or imprisonment for at most one year.

Section 11

A person who has incurred criminal responsibility under Sections 1, 2, 3, 6, 7, 8, 9 or 10, or under Section 5a, second paragraph, point 2, or Section 5b, first paragraph, points 2 or 3, but has voluntarily averted the danger or effect therein mentioned before considerable inconvenience or nuisance has arisen, may be sentenced to a less severe punishment than is provided for the act. No punishment shall be imposed if the danger occasioned by the act was slight and the punishment provided for the act does not exceed imprisonment for one year. (Law 1998:809)

Section 12

Attempt, preparation or conspiracy to commit arson, gross arson, devastation endangering the public, sabotage, gross sabotage, hijacking, maritime or aircraft sabotage, airport sabotage, spreading poison or a contagious substance, or causing destruction, and also for failure to reveal such a crime, shall be punished in accordance with the provisions of Chapter 23. (Law 1990:416)

Chapter 14
On Crimes of Falsification

Section 1

A person who, by writing the name of another person, real or fictitious, or by deceit obtains another's signature or in other ways produces a false document or deceitfully alters or adds to a genuine document, shall, if the act jeopardises proof, be sentenced for *falsification of a document* to imprisonment for at most two years.

A document is to be considered as including a protocol, contract, promissory note, certificate or other record established as evidence or otherwise important as evidence and also an identification card, ticket or similar evidential token.

Section 2

If the crime defined in Section 1 is regarded as petty, a fine or imprisonment for at most six months shall be imposed for *falsifying a document*.

In assessing whether a crime is petty, special attention shall be paid to whether the document was of little importance, such as a cash register receipt, counter token or like proof of receipt, or the act was committed to aid a person to gain his right.

Section 3

If the crime defined in Section 1 is considered gross, imprisonment for at least six months and at most six years shall be imposed for *gross falsification of a document*.

In assessing whether the crime is gross, special attention shall be paid to whether the falsification involved a public authority's important archival document or a document of special importance in general commerce such as a bond, a share certificate or a mortgage or whether the act was in other ways of an especially harmful nature.

Section 4

A person who destroys, renders unserviceable or removes a document which he has no right at the time to dispose of in such manner, shall, if the act jeopardises proof and is not to be regarded as a bookkeeping crime, be sentenced for *suppression of a document* to imprisonment for at most two years or, if the crime is petty, to a fine or imprisonment for at most six months.

If the crime is gross, imprisonment for at least six months and at most four years shall be imposed. (Law 1982:150)

Section 5

A person who without permission affixes to or otherwise forges another person's name or signature on a work of art or applied art or on some similar such product and thereby makes it appear that the latter has confirmed himself to be the originator of the product, shall be sentenced for *forgery of signature* to imprisonment for at most two years or, if the crime is petty, to a fine or imprisonment for at most six months.

If the crime is gross, imprisonment for at least six months and at most four years shall be imposed. (Law 1970:489)

Section 6

A person who counterfeits a banknote or coin valid within or outside the Realm or otherwise forges a banknote or coin, shall be sentenced for *counterfeiting currency* to imprisonment for at most four years or, if the crime is petty, to a fine or imprisonment for at most six months.

If the crime is gross, imprisonment for at least two and at most eight years shall be imposed.

Section 7

A person who counterfeits a valid postage stamp, cover stamp or other domestic or foreign stamp indicating value, whether official or meant for general use, or an official domestic or foreign control stamp on a measure, weight, merchandise, document or other thing, or affixes such false stamp or falsely affixes a genuine stamp, or otherwise forges such a stamp or the object stamped, shall, if the act jeopardises proof, be sentenced for *stamp forgery* to imprisonment for at most two years or, if the crime is petty, to a fine or imprisonment for at most six months.

If the crime is gross, imprisonment for at least six months and at most four years shall be imposed.

Section 8

A person who falsely affixes a mark or other object which can be taken to be a valid boundary mark, water mark, fixed point or other mark for the measure of surface or height, or moves, takes away, damages or destroys such a mark, shall, if the act jeopardises proof, be sentenced for *falsification of fixed mark* to imprisonment for at most four years or, if the crime is petty, to a fine or imprisonment for at most six months.

Section 9

A person who invokes a false document, offers or holds for sale a work with a false signature, passes a counterfeit banknote or coin, uses a false mark indicating value or a false control stamp, invokes a false fixed mark or otherwise makes use of anything that has been falsified in a manner described above, shall, if the act jeopardizes proof, be sentenced for the use of that which was falsified as if he himself had made the falsification.

Section 10

A person who, in a case other than as described in Section 9, distributes generally something that can easily be mistaken for a valid banknote, coin or other official token of value, shall be sentenced for *illegal distribution of imitations* to a fine.

Section 11

A person, who has incurred criminal responsibility under the above provisions of this Chapter, but voluntarily and before any considerable inconvenience has arisen has averted in the matter of proof the jeopardy presented by the act, may be sentenced to a lesser punishment than that provided for the crime. No punishment shall be imposed if the danger occasioned by the act was slight and the punishment provided for the act does not exceed imprisonment for one year.

Section 12

An attempt or preparation to commit document forgery, gross document forgery, suppression of document, forgery of signature, counterfeiting of currency, stamp forgery, falsification of fixed mark, or to use something which is falsified, and also for failure to disclose the counterfeiting of currency, shall be punishable under the provisions of Chapter 23. However, no punishment shall be imposed if the crime, had it been completed, would have been regarded as petty.

Chapter 15
On Perjury, False Prosecution and Other Untrue Statements

Section 1

A person who, under legal oath, gives untrue information or withholds the truth, shall be sentenced for *perjury* to imprisonment for at most four years or, if the crime is petty, to a fine or imprisonment for at most six months.

If the crime is gross, imprisonment for at least two and at most eight years shall be imposed. In assessing whether the crime is gross, special attention shall be paid to whether it was done with the intent that an innocent person be convicted of a serious crime or that very considerable harm was done to someone. (Law 1975:1292)

PART TWO ON CRIMES

Section 2

A person who, during a hearing in court proceedings, after declaring that he will tell the truth gives untrue information or withholds the truth, shall be sentenced for *untrue statement by a party* to imprisonment for at most two years or, if the crime is petty, to a fine or imprisonment for at most six months.

Section 3

A person who commits an act, as described in Section 1 or 2, through gross carelessness, shall be sentenced for *careless statement* to a fine or imprisonment for at most six months.

Section 4

No punishment shall be imposed if a statement described in Sections 1—3 is proved to be without significance for the issue.

The foregoing shall also apply if a person has given untrue information or has withheld the truth with regard to something about which he would have had the right to refuse to express himself and the circumstances furnish him with a reasonable excuse.

Section 4a

A person who under liability to punishment gives untrue information or withholds the truth from a court in Denmark, Finland, Iceland or Norway, shall be sentenced for *false statement before a Nordic court* to a sanction as provided in Section 1, if the testimony would have been given under legal oath in this Realm, and in accordance with Section 2 in the case of testimony by a party to a civil case. If the act is committed through gross carelessness, the person shall be sentenced for *careless statement before a Nordic* court to a sanction as provided in Section 3.

The provisions of Sections 4, 14 and 15 shall be applied correspondingly to an act referred to in the first paragraph. (Law 1975:1292)

Section 4b

If a witness or expert under oath before the Court of Justice of the European Communities, before the Court of First Instance of that Court or before the European Free Trade Area Court (the EFTA Court), gives untrue information or withholds the truth, a sentence for *untrue state-*

ment *before an international court* shall be imposed in accordance with Section 1, provided the statement would have been given under legal oath in this Realm. If the act is committed through gross carelessness, a sentence for *careless statement before an international court* shall be imposed in accordance with Section 3.

The applicable parts of the provisions of Sections 4, 14 and 15 shall also apply to an act described in the first paragraph. (Law 1995:316)

Section 5

If a person institutes the prosecution of an innocent person with the intent that the latter be convicted, a sentence shall be imposed for *false prosecution* to imprisonment for at most two years or, if the crime was petty, to a fine or imprisonment for at most six months.

If the crime is gross, imprisonment for at least six months and at most four years shall be imposed. In assessing whether the crime is gross, special attention shall be paid to whether the prosecution related to a serious crime or involved misuse of an official position.

A person who institutes prosecution without probable cause for so doing shall be sentenced for *unjustified prosecution* to a fine or imprisonment for at most six months.

Section 6

If someone denounces an innocent person for prosecution with the intent that such person be convicted, a sentence shall be imposed for *false accusation* to imprisonment for at most two years or, if the crime is petty, to a fine or imprisonment for at most six months.

If the accused did not realise, but had reasonable grounds for assuming, that the person denounced was innocent, a sentence shall be imposed for *unjustified accusation* to a fine or imprisonment for at most six months.

Section 7

A person who, in a case other than as provided for in Section 6, untruthfully charges another before a public prosecutor, police authority or other authority, with a criminal act, alleges some compromising circumstance, or denies an exonerating or extenuating circumstance, shall, if the authority is bound to receive reports of this kind, be sentenced for *false incrimination* to imprisonment for at most two years or, if the crime is petty, to a fine or imprisonment for at most six months.

If the accused did not realise but had reasonable grounds for assuming that the information was untrue, he shall be sentenced for *careless incrimination* to a fine or imprisonment for at most six months.

Section 8

A person who tampers with or removes evidence with the intent that an innocent person be convicted, or with such intent invokes false evidence, shall be sentenced for *tampering with evidence* to imprisonment for at most two years or, if the crime is petty, to a fine or imprisonment for at most six months.

If the crime is gross, imprisonment for at least six months and at most four years shall be imposed.

Section 9

If person not being liable to punishment under previous provisions in this Chapter has by any act there described given rise to a danger that someone, without legal cause, be sentenced or otherwise suffer considerable harm, and if once having realised this, neglects to do what can be reasonably required to avert the harm, he shall be sentenced for *neglect to avert judicial error* to a fine or imprisonment for at most six months.

Section 10

A person who in a written deposition which according to law or statute is made under oath or on one's faith and honour or like affirmation, gives untrue information or withholds the truth, shall, if the act jeopardises proof, be sentenced for *untrue affirmation* to a fine or imprisonment for at most six months or, if the crime is gross, imprisonment for at most two years.

If such action is due to gross carelessness, a sentence to a fine or imprisonment for at most six months shall be imposed for *careless affirmation*.

Section 11

A person who gives untrue information about his identity or about other than his own affairs in a certificate or other document, or for the sake of appearances prepares a document concerning a legal document shall, if the act jeopardises proof, be sentenced for *false certification* to a fine or imprisonment for at most six months. If the crime is considered gross because it involves misuse of official position or for other reasons, imprisonment for at most two years shall be imposed.

A person who invokes or otherwise uses a false document referred to in the first paragraph, shall, if the act jeopardises proof, be sentenced, as there provided, for *using a false document*.

Section 12

A person who misuses a passport, certificate or similar document issued in the name of a given individual, by representing himself or another as being that individual or imparts the document to be thus misused, or if he imparts a false document, which has come into being as a carbon copy or photographic reproduction or otherwise, as being a correct copy of a certain document, shall, if the act jeopardises proof, be sentenced for *misuse of document* to a fine or imprisonment for at most six months or, if the crime is gross, to imprisonment for at most two years.

Section 13

A person who denies his signature on a document, shall, if the act jeopardises proof, be sentenced for *denial of signature* to a fine or imprisonment for at most six months or, if the crime is gross, imprisonment for at most two years.

Section 14

A person who, having incurred criminal responsibility under the previous provisions of this Chapter, has voluntarily and before considerable inconvenience has arisen, corrected the mistake or by other means averted the risk of further inconvenience may be sentenced to a less severe punishment than is provided for the act. If the risk was slight and a punishment not exceeding six months imprisonment is provided for the act, no punishment shall be imposed.

Section 15

Punishment shall be imposed in accordance with the provisions of

PART TWO   ON CRIMES

Chapter 23 for preparation to commit perjury or conspiracy to commit perjury involving efforts to instigate such act, as well as attempt to tamper with evidence. If the crime, had it been completed, would have been regarded as petty, no punishment as here provided shall be imposed.

Chapter 16
On Crimes against Public Order

Section 1

If a crowd of people disturbs public order by demonstrating an intention to use group violence in opposition to a public authority or otherwise to compel or obstruct a certain measure and does not disperse when ordered to do so by the authority, the instigators and leaders shall be sentenced for *riot* to imprisonment for at most four years and other participants in the crowd's proceedings to a fine or imprisonment for at most two years.

If the crowd disperses on order of the authority, the instigators and leaders shall be sentenced for riot to a fine or imprisonment for at most two years.

Section 2

If a crowd, with intent referred to in Section 1, has proceeded to use group violence on a person or property, whether a public authority was present or not, sentences to imprisonment for *violent riot* shall be imposed on instigators and leaders for at most ten years whilst participants in the crowd's proceedings shall be sentenced to a fine or imprisonment for at most four years.

Section 3

A member of a crowd that disturbs the public order who neglects to obey a command aimed at maintaining order, or intrudes into an area that, for such purpose, is enclosed or has been fenced off, shall, if no riot occurs, be sentenced for *disobeying police orders* to a fine or imprisonment for at most six months.

Section 4

A person who by act of violence, loud noise or other like means disturbs or tries to interfere with a public religious service, other public devotional exercise, wedding, funeral or like ceremony, a court session or other state or municipal official function, or a public gathering for deliberation, instruction or to hear a lecture, shall be sentenced for *disturbing a function or public meeting* to a fine or imprisonment for at most six months.

Section 5

A person who orally, before a crowd or congregation of people, or in a publication distributed or issued for distribution, or in other message to the public, urges or otherwise attempts to entice people to commit a criminal act, evade a civic duty or disobey public authority, shall be sentenced for *inciting rebellion* to a fine or imprisonment for at most six months.

A sentence for inciting rebellion shall also be imposed upon any person who orally before a gathering of members of the armed forces or by other communication with members of the armed forces urges or otherwise attempts to entice them to an act or omission in dereliction of their service duty.

Punishment shall not be imposed in petty cases. In assessing whether the crime is petty, special consideration shall be given to whether there was only an insignificant risk that the enticement or attempted enticement would in fact have effect.

If the crime, in view of the fact that the offender attempted to instigate the commission of a serious crime or in view of other circumstances, must be regarded as gross, imprisonment for at most four years shall be imposed. (Law 1986:645)

Section 6

If a gathering of members of the armed forces collectively threaten to overthrow or resist a lawful authority of those forces, they shall be sentenced for *mutiny* to a fine or imprisonment for at most four years. Instigators and leaders of the mutiny, however, shall be sentenced to impris-

PART TWO ON CRIMES

onment for at most six years.

If the participants in a mutiny have used collective force or violence against a person or property, they shall be sentenced to imprisonment for at most of six years. The instigators and leaders, however, shall be sentenced to imprisonment for at most ten years, or for life.

If the crime is otherwise considered to be gross, the accused shall be sentenced to imprisonment for at most ten years, or for life.

In assessing whether the crime is gross, special consideration shall be given to whether the act or actions were committed during battle or at a time when a breach of military discipline would otherwise result in special danger. (Law 1986:645)

Section 7

Repealed (Law 1970:225)

Section 8

A person who, in a disseminated statement or communication, threatens or expresses contempt for a national, ethnic or other such group of persons with allusion to race, colour, national or ethnic origin or religious belief shall, be sentenced for *agitation against a national or ethnic group* to imprisonment for at most two years or, if the crime is petty, to a fine. (Law 1988:835)

Section 9

A businessman who in the conduct of his business discriminates against a person on grounds of that person's race, colour, national or ethnic origin or religious belief by not dealing with that person under the terms and conditions normally applied by the businessman in the course of his business with other persons, shall be sentenced for *unlawful discrimination* to a fine or imprisonment for at most one year.

The provisions of the foregoing paragraph relating to discrimination by a businessman shall also apply to a person employed in a business or otherwise acting on behalf of a businessman and to a person employed in public service or having a public duty.

A sentence for unlawful discrimination shall also be imposed on any organiser of a public assembly or gathering, and on any collaborator of such organiser, who discriminates against a person on grounds of his race, colour, national or ethnic origin or religious belief by refusing him access to the public assembly or gathering under the terms and conditions normally applied to other persons.

A sentence for unlawful discrimination shall also be imposed on any person designated in the first to third paragraphs above who, in the manner there indicated, discriminates against another on the ground that the latter has a homosexual disposition. (Law 1987:610)

Section 10

A person who, without authorisation, moves, injures or outrageously treats the corpse or ashes of the dead, opens a grave or otherwise inflicts damage on or abuses a coffin, urn, grave or other resting place of the dead or a tombstone, shall be sentenced for *crime against the peace of the tomb* to a fine or imprisonment for at most six months. (Law 1993:207)

Section 10a

A person who

1. portrays a child in a pornographic picture;

2. disseminates, transfers, grants use, exhibits or in any other way makes such a picture of a child available to some other person;

3. acquires or offers such a picture of a child;

4. brings about contact between a buyer and a seller of such pictures of children or takes any other similar step to facilitate dealing in such pictures; or

5. possess such a picture of a child shall be sentenced for *child pornography crime* to imprisonment for at most two years, or, if the crime is petty, to a fine or imprisonment for at most six months.

By child is meant a person whose pubertal development is not complete or, if it is apparent from the picture and its attendant circumstances, who is less than 18 years of age.

A person who in the course of business or otherwise for the purpose of making money disseminates a picture of the kind described in the first paragraph through negligence shall be sentenced as there stated.

PART TWO ON CRIMES

If the crime described in the first paragraph is considered to be gross a sentence of at least six months and at most four years shall be imposed for *gross child pornography crime*. In assessing whether the crime is gross special consideration shall be given to whether it was committed in the course of business or otherwise for profit, was a part of criminal activity that was systematically practised or practised on a larger scale, or concerned a particularly large number of pictures or pictures in which children are exposed to especially ruthless treatment.

The prohibitions against depiction and possession do not apply to a person who draws, paints or in some other similar hand-crafted fashion produces a picture of the kind described in the first paragraph as long as it is not intended for dissemination, transfer, granted use, exhibition or in any other way be made available to others. Even in other cases the act shall not constitute a crime if, having regard to the circumstances, it is justifiable. (Law 1998:1444)

Section 10b

Any person who in a picture depicts sexual violence or coercion with intent to disseminate the picture or pictures or disseminates such depiction, shall, unless the act in view of the circumstances is justifiable, be sentenced for *unlawful depiction of violence* to a fine or imprisonment for at most two years. This also applies to any person who in moving pictures intrusively or extensively depicts extreme violence towards humans or animals with intent to disseminate such pictures, or disseminates such a depiction.

A person who through negligence disseminates a depiction mentioned in the first paragraph in the course of business or otherwise for the purpose of making money, shall be punished in accordance with the provisions of the first paragraph.

The provisions of the first and second paragraphs shall not apply to films or video recordings approved for public showing by the National Board of Film Censors. Nor shall they apply to a technical recording of moving pictures the contents of which are identical with those of a film or video recording approved by the Board. In addition, the first and second paragraphs do not apply to public showings of films or video recordings.

If a technical recording of moving pictures is furnished with a certificate confirming that a film or video recording with an identical content has been approved by the National Board of Film Censors, no criminal responsibility exists under the provisions of the first or second paragraph for the dissemination of the recording.

This shall however not apply if the certificate was false and the person who disseminated the recording realised or should have realised that this was so. (Law 1998:1444)

Section 10c

Any person who, intentionally or through gross negligence in the course of business or otherwise for the purpose of making money purveys to a person under the age of fifteen a film, video recording or other technical recording with moving pictures explicitly and realistically depicting violence or the threat of violence towards humans or animals shall be convicted of *illicit purveyance of a technical recording* and sentenced to a fine or imprisonment for at most six months.

The provisions of the first paragraph do not apply to films or video recordings approved by the National Board of Film Censors for showing to children under the age of fifteen. Nor shall they apply to a technical recording of moving pictures with an identical content to a film or video recording approved by the Board of Film Censors. In addition, the first paragraph does not apply to public showings of films or video recordings.

If a technical recording of moving pictures is furnished with a certificate confirming that a film or video recording with an identical content has been approved by the National Board of Film Censors for showing to children under the age of fifteen, no criminal responsibility exists under the provisions of the first paragraph.

This shall not, however, apply if the certificate was false and the person who purveyed the recording realised or should have realized that this was so. (Law 1998:1444)

Section 11

A person who, on or at a public place, exhibits pornographic pic-

PART TWO ON CRIMES

tures by means of displays or other similar procedure in a manner which is apt to result in public annoyance, shall be sentenced for *unlawful exhibition of pornographic pictures* to a fine or imprisonment for at most six months. This also applies to a person who sends through the mail to or otherwise furnishes another with unsolicited pornographic pictures. (Law 1970:225)

Section 12

A person who distributes among children or young persons a writing, picture or technical recording which owing to its content may brutalise or otherwise involve serious danger to the moral nurture of the young, shall be sentenced for *leading youth astray* to a fine or imprisonment for at most six months. (Law 1998:1444)

Section 13

A person who, with intent or through gross carelessness, by maltreating, overworking, neglecting or in some other way unjustifiably exposes an animal to suffering, shall be sentenced for *cruelty to animals* to a fine or imprisonment for at most two years. (Law 1972:629)

Section 14

If a person unlawfully organises for the public a game or other similar activity the outcome of which is entirely or essentially dependent on chance and, if in view of the nature of the activity, the financial value of the stakes and other circumstances it appears hazardous or of a nature to bring a considerable financial gain for the organiser, he shall be sentenced for *illicit gambling* to a fine or imprisonment for at most two years. The same applies to a person who permits such activity in an apartment or other premises which he has opened to the public. (Law 1986:1007)

Section 14a

If the crime referred to in Section 14, first paragraph, is regarded as gross, the offender shall be sentenced for *gross illicit gambling* to imprisonment for at least six months and at most four years.

In assessing whether the crime is gross, special attention shall be paid to whether the activity was conducted professionally, comprised considerable amounts or otherwise had been of a specially hazardous nature.

(Law 1982:1061)

Section 15

A person who, by furnishing a false statement that danger exists for the life or health of one or more people or for extensive destruction of property, occasions unnecessary safety measures, shall be sentenced for *false alarm* to a fine or imprisonment for at most one year.

If the crime referred to in the first paragraph is regarded as gross, imprisonment for at least six and at most four years shall be imposed.

A person who, by improper use of an alarm, emergency signal or other similar device, causes an unnecessary turn out of the police, rescue service, fire brigade, ambulance service, the military, searescue service or other public security service shall be sentenced for *improper use of an alarm* to a fine or imprisonment for not more than six months. (Law 1993:207)

Section 16

A person who is noisy in a public place or who otherwise publicly behaves in a manner apt to arouse public indignation, shall be sentenced for *disorderly conduct* to pay a fixed fine. (Law 1991:240)

Section 17

A person preparing or conspiring to mutiny, or who fails to disclose a mutiny, shall be sentenced in accordance with the provisions of Chapter 23. The same shall also apply to the crime of attempt or preparation of gross illicit gambling, to the crime of attempt of child pornography crime described in Section 10a, first paragraph if it is not petty, and attempt or preparation to gross child pornography crime. (Law 1998:1444)

Section 18

A person who, having granted the usufructuary right to a dwelling, acquires knowledge that the property is wholly or to a substantial extent used for illicit gambling or gross illicit gambling or for an attempt to, or preparation for, gross gambling and fails to do what can reasonably be required to bring the grant to an end, shall be considered, if the criminal activity continues or is resumed at the property, to have promoted it and be sentenced under the provisions governing complicity in Chapter 23.

(Law 1980:892)

Section 19

Public prosecution of a crime defined in Section 10 c may only be instituted with the prior consent of the National Board of Film Censors. For crimes defined in Section 10 b, the National Board of Film Censors shall express their opinion before a public prosecution is instituted concerning films and video recordings. (Law 1991:1560)

Chapter 17
On Crimes against Public Activity

Section 1

A person who, by violence or threat of violence, attacks anyone in his exercise of public authority or compels him to perform or to prevent him from performing an official act or for the purpose of taking revenge for such act, shall be sentenced for *violence or threat to public servant* to imprisonment for at most four years or, if the crime is petty, to a fine or imprisonment for at most six months. This also applies if a person assaults someone who has previously exercised public authority for something the latter did or failed to do while in office. (Law 1975:667)

Section 2

A person who, otherwise than as stated in Section 1, in order to compel or prevent someone in his exercise of public authority or in order to take revenge for an official action, wrongfully engages in an act which causes such person suffering, injury or inconvenience, or threatens to have such consequence, shall be sentenced for *outrageous conduct toward a public servant* to a fine or imprisonment for at most six months.

If the crime is gross, imprisonment for at most four years shall be imposed. (Law 1975:667)

Section 3

Repealed (Law 1975:667)

Section 4

Even in cases not previously provided for in this Chapter, a person who resists or otherwise seeks to prevent anyone in his exercise of public authority shall be sentenced for *violent resistance* to a fine or imprisonment for at most six months. (Law 1975:667)

Section 5

The provisions of Sections 1, 2 and 4 shall also apply if a person, as stated in those Sections, commits an outrage against or hinders anyone who, by special order, shall enjoy the same protection as is associated with the exercise of public authority or who is or has been summoned to assist a public servant with a measure for which such protection is provided. (Law 1975:667)

Section 6

Repealed (Law 1976:509)

Section 7

A person who gives, promises or offers a bribe or other improper reward to an employee or other person defined in Chapter 20, Section 2, for the exercise of official duties, shall be sentenced for *bribery* to a fine or imprisonment for at most two years. (Law 1977:103)

Section 8

A person who, in an election to public office or in connection with some other exercise of suffrage in public matters, attempts to prevent voting or to tamper with its outcome or otherwise improperly influence the vote, shall be sentenced for *improper activity at election* to a fine or imprisonment for at most six months.

If the crime is gross, imprisonment for at most four years shall be imposed. In assessing whether the crime is gross, special attention shall be paid to whether it had been committed by use of violence or the threat of violence or had involved misuse of an official position.

A person who receives, accepts a promise of or demands an improper favour for voting in a certain manner or for abstaining from voting on a public matter, shall be sentenced, unless it is a crime of taking a bribe, for *accepting an improper reward for voting* to a fine or imprisonment for at most six months. (Law 1977:103)

Section 9

A person who without authorisation seeks to secure information about matters which, with respect to the exercise of suffrage on public questions shall be kept secret, shall be sentenced for *violating the privacy of suffrage* to a fine or imprisonment for at most six months.

Section 10

A person who, by violence or threat of violence, assaults someone because he has, in court or before another authority, filed a complaint, pleaded a cause, testified, or else made a statement at a hearing, or to prevent him from so doing, shall be sentenced for *interference in a judicial matter* to a fine or imprisonment for at most two years. The same shall apply to a person who by some other act causes suffering, injury or inconvenience, or by threat of such act, assaults someone because the latter testified or made some other statement at an official hearing, or does so to prevent the making of such a statement.

If the crime is gross, imprisonment for at least six months and at most six years shall be imposed (Law 1997:389)

Section 11

A person who hides someone who has committed a crime, helps him to escape, destroys evidence concerning the crime, or in other like ways thwarts its discovery or prosecution, shall be sentenced for *protecting a criminal* to a fine or imprisonment for at most one year.

If the crime is gross, imprisonment for at least six months and at most four years shall be imposed.

A person who did not realise but had reasonable grounds to assume that the other was a criminal, shall be sentenced to pay a fine.

No sentence shall be imposed if having regard to the relationship of the accused to the criminal and other circumstances the crime is to be considered petty. (Law 1993:207)

Section 12

A person who assists someone who is an inmate of a prison, or who is remanded in custody or arrested, or otherwise lawfully deprived of his liberty, to gain his freedom or, after such escape, aids him by hiding him or by other like action, shall be sentenced for *aiding escape* to a fine or imprisonment for at most one year.

If the crime is gross, imprisonment for at least six months and at most four years shall be imposed.

Punishment shall not be imposed if the act is considered petty having regard to the nature and purpose of the deprivation of liberty, the means employed by the perpetrator and his relationship to the person whose escape he has aided. (Law 1993:207)

Section 13

A person who unlawfully moves, damages or otherwise disposes of property that is subject to distraint, provisional attachment, security of payment, confiscation or other similar measure, damages or removes an official notice or seal or otherwise unlawfully opens something officially closed or breaches some similar officially proclaimed order, shall be sentenced for *violation of official order* to a fine or imprisonment for at most one year.

A person who refuses admittance which a functionary has the right to demand, shall be sentenced for *obstructing a functionary* to a fine. (Law 1981:827)

Section 14

Repealed (Law 1975:667)

Section 15

An unauthorised person who claims to be exercising public authority, shall be sentenced for *pretence of public office* to a fine or imprisonment for at most six months. This also applies to a person who without authority wears a uniform, symbol or other service token which makes him appear to belong to the armed services or some other branch of public service or to a service dealing with public communications or the public supply of water, light, heat or power.

If the crime has caused considerable harm to the public or to any individual or is otherwise to be regarded as gross, the offender shall be sentenced to imprisonment for at most two years.

PART TWO ON CRIMES

An unauthorised person who claims to be an advocate, shall be sentenced for *pretending to be an advocate* to a fine. (Law 1975:667)

Section 16

Attempt or preparation to commit violence or threat against a public servant shall be punishable under the provisions of Chapter 23 unless the crime would have been considered petty had it been completed. Attempt or preparation to aid escape shall also be punishable under the provisions of Chapter 23. (Law 1981:463)

Section 17

If a bribe has been given to a person who is neither an employee of the State or a local authority nor defined by Chapter 20, Section 2, second paragraph, points 1—4, a public prosecutor may only prosecute if the crime is reported for prosecution by the employer or principal of the person exposed to bribery or if prosecution is called for in the public interest. (Law 1977:103)

Chapter 18
On Crimes of Lese-majesty

Section 1

A person who, with intent that the form of government be overthrown by force of arms or other violent means or that a measure or decision of the Head of State, the Government, Parliament or the supreme judicial bodies be thus forced or obstructed, takes action which involves a danger of the realisation of such intent, shall, if it is not high treason, be sentenced for *sedition* to imprisonment for ten years, or for life or, if the danger was slight, to at least four and at most ten years. (Law 1974:565)

Section 2

If the act referred to in Chapters 3—5 involves an assault against the King or other member of the Royal Family or against a Regent acting in place of the King, imprisonment for at most four years shall be imposed if otherwise at most six months imprisonment can be imposed for the crime, and for at most six years if the crime otherwise would be subject to imprisonment for more than six months but at most four years. (Law 1974:565)

Section 3

A person who, with the intent that the crime be committed against public security or the liberty of citizens, gathers or leads an armed force or keeps it assembled or furnishes a force with arms, ammunition or other like equipment or trains it in the use of arms, shall be sentenced for *armed threat against the legal order* to imprisonment for at least six and at most ten years.

Section 4

A person who founds or participates in an association which must be considered to constitute or, in view of its character and the purpose for which it has been organised, is easily capable of developing into, an instrument of force such as a military troop or a police force, and which does not with due authority reinforce the national defence or the police, or who on behalf of such association deals in arms, ammunition or other like equipment, makes available a building or land for its activity or supports it with money or in other ways, shall be sentenced for *unlawful military activity* to a fine or imprisonment for at most two years.

Section 5

A person who exerts illegal coercion or illegal threat with the intent of influencing the shaping of public opinion or of encroaching on freedom of action within a political organisation or a trade or industrial association and thereby endangers freedom of speech, assembly or association, shall be sentenced for *crime against civil liberty* to imprisonment for at most six years.

Section 6

A person who, by mutilation or otherwise, for a short or long period incapacitates himself for military service which it was his duty to perform in the armed forces or otherwise for the defence of the Realm, or by feigning illness or by means of other deception evades such service, shall

PART TWO ON CRIMES

be sentenced for *evading defence duty* to a fine or imprisonment for at most two years or, if the Realm was at war, to a fine or imprisonment for at most four years.

Section 7

Attempt, preparation or conspiracy to commit sedition or armed threat against the legal order, failure to reveal such crime, as well as attempt to commit crime against civil liberty, or evading defence duty shall be punished under the provisions of Chapter 23.

Section 8

An act referred to in Chapters 3—5 which involves an outrage against the King or any other person defined in Section 2 may not be prosecuted by a prosecutor without an order from the Government, unless someone's death occurred as a result of the act. The same applies to attempt, preparation or conspiracy to commit an act here mentioned or failure to reveal such act. (Law 1974:565)

Chapter 19
On Crimes against the Security of the Realm

Section 1

A person who with the intent that the Realm or a part thereof, by violent or otherwise illegal means or with foreign aid, be placed under foreign domination or made dependent on a foreign power, or that a part of the Realm be thus torn loose, takes action which involves danger that such intent be realised, shall be sentenced for *high treason* to imprisonment for ten years or for life or, if the danger was slight, for at least four and at most ten years.

A person who, with the intent that a measure or decision of the Head of State, the Government, Parliament or the supreme judicial bodies be coerced or obstructed with foreign aid, engages in an act involving a danger of this occurring, shall also be sentenced for high treason. (Law

1974:565)

Section 2

A person who by violent means or foreign aid causes a danger of the Realm being involved in war or other hostilities, shall, unless it is high treason, be sentenced for *instigating war* to imprisonment for at least two and at most eight years.

Section 3

A person who has been commissioned to negotiate with a foreign power on behalf of the Realm or otherwise to protect the concerns of the Realm in dealings with someone who represents the interests of a foreign power and misuses his authority to represent the Realm or otherwise his position of trust and thereby causes the Realm considerable harm, shall be sentenced for *disloyalty in negotiation with a foreign power* to imprisonment for a fixed term of at least two and at most ten years, or for life.

Section 4

A Swedish citizen who, without permission from the Government or a person designated by the Government, allows himself to be used as an agent of a foreign power in a diplomatic matter which concerns the Realm, and also anyone who in the alleged capacity of an authorised agent enters into negotiation about such a matter with someone who represents the interests of a foreign power, shall be sentenced for *arbitrary conduct in negotiation with a foreign power* to imprisonment for at most two years, or if the Realm was at war, for at most four years.

If the crime jeopardised the Realm's right of self-determination or its peaceful relations with a foreign power, imprisonment for at least one and at most six years shall be imposed or, if the Realm was at war, for a fixed term of at least four and at most ten years, or for life. (Law 1976: 509)

Section 5

A person who, in order to aid a foreign power, without authorisation obtains, transmits, gives or otherwise reveals information concerning a defence facility, arms, supplies, imports, exports, means of produc-

PART TWO ON CRIMES

tion, negotiations, decisions or other conditions, the disclosure of which to a foreign power can cause harm to the total defence of the Realm, or otherwise to the security of the Realm, shall be sentenced, whether the information is correct or not, for *espionage* to imprisonment for at most six years. This also applies if person with the intent here described, produces or takes possession of a writing, drawing or other object containing such information without authority. (Law 1981:1165)

Section 6

If a crime referred to in Section 5 is regarded as gross, imprisonment for a fixed term of at least four and at most ten years, or for life, shall be imposed for *gross espionage*.

In assessing whether the crime is gross, special attention shall be paid to whether the act was of an especially dangerous nature in view of an ongoing war or concerned matters of great importance or whether the perpetrator disclosed something entrusted to him by reason of his position in public or private service.

Section 7

A person who, without intent to aid a foreign power, without authority obtains, transmits, gives or reveals information concerning matters of a secret nature, the disclosure of which to a foreign power can cause harm to the defence of the Realm or to the maintenance of necessary supplies to the people during war or during extraordinary conditions caused by war, or otherwise to the security of the Realm, shall be sentenced, whether the information is correct or not, to *unauthorised dealing with secret information* to a fine or imprisonment for at most two years. (Law 1981:1165)

Section 8

If a crime under the provisions of Section 7 is regarded as gross, imprisonment for at most four years shall be imposed for *gross unauthorised dealing with secret information*.

In assessing whether the crime is gross special attention shall be paid to whether the act involved assistance of a foreign power or was of an especially dangerous nature having regard to an ongoing war, or related to a matter of great significance, or whether the accused disclosed what had been confided to him by reason of public or private service. (Law 1976: 509)

Section 9

A person who through gross carelessness transmits, gives or reveals information described in Section 7 shall be sentenced to a fine or imprisonment for at most six months or, if the Realm was at war, to a fine or imprisonment for at most two years. (Law 1981:1165)

Section 10

A person who, with the intent of aiding a foreign power, conducts activities designed to acquire information relating to military or other matters, the revelation of which to that foreign power could cause harm to the security of another foreign power, or lends assistance not solely of an incidental nature to such activities in the Realm, shall be sentenced for *unlawful intelligence activities* to a fine or imprisonment for at most one year.

A person who, with the intent of aiding a foreign power, secretly or by fraudulent means conducts in the Realm activities designed to acquire information concerning the personal circumstances of another individual or lends assistance not solely of an incidental nature to such activities, shall likewise be sentenced for unlawful intelligence activities.

If a crime under this Section is gross, imprisonment for at least six months and at most four years shall be imposed. (Law 1993:207)

Section 11

If an act referred to in Chapter 3 or 4 involves an affront to a foreign power by an outrage against the foreign power's Head of State or its representative in this Realm, imprisonment for at most two years shall be imposed, if the crime otherwise is subject to imprisonment for at most six months, and for at most four years if the crime is otherwise subject to imprisonment for more than six months and at most two years. These provisions shall have corresponding application if a foreign power is affronted because someone intrudes into premises occupied by its representatives or causes damage to such premises or to property therein contained. (Law 1970:225)

Section 12

A person who within this Realm and without the authority of the Government recruits people for foreign military service or comparable service, or induces people to leave the country unlawfully in order to enter such service, shall be sentenced for *unlawful recruiting* to a fine or imprisonment for at most six months or, if the Realm was at war, to imprisonment for at most two years. (Law 1974:565)

Section 13

A person who accepts money or other property from a foreign power or from any person abroad who is acting in the interest of a foreign power in order, through the publication or dissemination of writings or otherwise, to influence public opinion in a matter affecting any of the foundations of the Realm's form of government or in any question of significance for the security of the Realm and which it lies in the power of Parliament or the Government to decide on, shall be sentenced for *acceptance of foreign assistance* to imprisonment for at most two years. (Law 1981:1165)

Section 14

Attempt, preparation or conspiracy to commit high treason, disloyalty in negotiation with foreign power, espionage, gross espionage, gross unauthorised dealing with secret information, or unlawful intelligence activity, as well as attempt or preparation to engage in unauthorised dealing with secret information, shall be in accordance with the provisions of Chapter 23. Entering into contact with a foreign power for the purpose of preparing, making possible or facilitating high treason shall also be regarded as conspiracy to commit such crime.

A person who fails to reveal high treason, disloyalty in negotiation with a foreign power, espionage, gross espionage or gross unauthorised dealing with secret information, shall also be punished in accordance with the provisions of Chapter 23 and shall be so liable even though he did not realise but should have realised that a crime was being committed. (Law 1976:509)

Section 15

A person who, in view of what is known to him by reason of warnings given or otherwise, should have realised that high treason, disloyalty in negotiation with a foreign power, espionage, gross espionage or gross unauthorised dealing with secret information is taking place, and contributes to the act, shall be punishable as an accessory. However, no more severe punishment than imprisonment for two years may be imposed. (Law 1976:509)

Section 16

Unlawful intelligence activity, acceptance of foreign assistance or unlawful recruiting, or attempt, preparation or conspiracy to undertake unlawful intelligence activity, may not be prosecuted by a public prosecutor without authorisation by the Government.

An act referred to in Chapters 3 or 4 and involving such an affront to a foreign power as is referred to in Section 11, as well as attempt, preparation or conspiracy to commit or failure to reveal such act, may not be prosecuted by a public prosecutor without authorisation by the Government or a person designated by the Government. (Law 1981:1165)

Chapter 20
On Misuse of Office, etc.

Section 1

A person who in the exercise of public authority by act or by omission, intentionally or through carelessness, disregards the duties of his office, shall be sentenced for *misuse of office* to a fine or imprisonment for at most two years. If, having regard to the perpetrator's official powers or the nature of his office considered in relation to his exercise of public power in other respects or having regard to other circumstances, the act may be regarded as petty, punishment shall not be imposed.

If a crime mentioned in the first paragraph has been committed intentionally and is regarded as gross, a sentence for *gross misuse of office* to imprisonment for at least six months and at most six years shall be imposed. In assessing whether the crime is gross, special attention shall be given to whether the offender seriously abused his position or whether the crime occasioned serious harm to an individual or the public sector or a substantial improper benefit.

A member of a decision-making national or municipal assembly shall not be held responsible under the provisions of the first or second paragraphs of this Section for any action taken in that capacity.

Nor shall the provisions of the first and second paragraphs of this Section apply if the crime is subject to a punishment under this or some other Law. (Law 1989:608)

Section 2

An employee who receives, accepts a promise of or demands a bribe or other improper reward for the performance of his duties, shall be sentenced for *taking a bribe* to a fine or imprisonment for at most two years. The same shall apply if the employee committed the act before obtaining the post or after leaving it. If the crime is gross, imprisonment for at most six years shall be imposed.

The provisions of the first paragraph in respect of an employee shall also apply to:

1. a member of a directorate, administration, board, committee or other such agency belonging to the State, a municipality, county council, association of local authorities, parish, religious society, or social insurance office,

2. a person who exercises a assignment regulated by statute,

3. a member of the armed forces under the Act on Disciplinary Offences by Members of the Armed Forces, etc. (Law 1986:644), or other person performing an official duty prescribed by Law,

4. a person who, without holding an appointment or assignment as aforesaid, exercises public authority, and

5. a person who, in a case other than stated in points 1—4, by reason of a position of trust has been given the task of managing another's legal or financial affairs or independently handling an assignment requir-

ing qualified technical knowledge or exercising supervision over the management of such affairs or assignment. (Law 1993:207)

Section 3

A person who discloses information which he is duty-bound by Law or other statutory instrument or by order or provision issued under a Law or statutory instrument to keep secret, or if he unlawfully makes use of such secret, he shall, if the act is not otherwise specially subject to punishment, be sentenced for *breach of professional confidentiality* to a fine or imprisonment for at most one year.

A person who through carelessness commits an act described in the first paragraph shall be sentenced to a fine. In petty cases, however, punishment shall not be imposed. (Law 1980:102)

Section 4

A person elected to a national or local government assignment involving the exercise of public authority may be removed therefrom by a court if he has committed a crime for which the punishment is imprisonment for two years or more and, through the crime, has proved manifestly unsuited for the assignment.

An assignment with such other employers as are referred to in Section 2, second paragraph, point 1, shall be considered equivalent to a national or local government assignment. (Law 1988:942)

Section 5

A prosecutor may, without hindrance of other provisions which may exist, prosecute crimes through which a national or local government employee or other person referred to in Section 2, second paragraph, points 1—4, has neglected his obligations in the exercise of his appointment or assignment.

However, notwithstanding what is said in the first paragraph, the following shall apply:

1. the provisions of this Code specifying that prosecution may not take place without the authority of the Government or by a person empowered by the Government, and

2. the provisions of any other statute or statutory instrument con-

PART TWO ON CRIMES

cerning prosecution of an act for which a punishment may be imposed only if the act is committed by a holder of an appointment or assignment as defined in the first paragraph.

If a crime of taking a bribe has been committed by a person not covered by the first paragraph, a prosecutor may bring an action only if the crime is reported for prosecution by the employer or principal or if prosecution is called for in the public interest.

Unless otherwise prescribed for a given case, a prosecutor may prosecute a breach of professional confidentiality existing for the benefit of an aggrieved person only if the latter reports the crime for prosecution or if prosecution is called for in the public interest.

Prosecution for crimes committed in the exercise of the appointment or assignment by a Member of Parliament, Minister, Justice of the Supreme Court, Justice of the Supreme Administrative Court or holder of an appointment or assignment with the Parliament or its organs is subject to separate provisions. (Law 1977:103)

Sections 6—15

Repealed (Law 1975:667)

Chapter 21
On Crimes by Members of the Armed Forces

Section 1

The provisions of this Chapter shall be applied when the Realm is in a state of war.

If the Realm is in danger of entering a state of war, or if there prevail such extraordinary conditions or circumstances as may have been provoked by a war or by the perils of a war in which the Realm may have found itself, the Government may order that the provisions of this Chapter shall be applied. (Law 1986:645)

Section 2

Upon cessation of the conditions and circumstances described in Section 1, the Government shall order that the provisions of this Chapter shall no longer apply. (Law 1986:645)

Section 3

For the purposes of this Chapter, all those liable to serve in the armed forces shall be considered to be members of the armed forces.

The armed forces shall also be understood to comprise:

1. police officers who, without being liable to serve in the armed forces, are liable to take part in the defence of the Realm,

2. guards and protected area guards appointed under the Protection of Important Installations Act (Law 1990:217),

3. all other persons otherwise attached to detachments of the armed forces when such detachments are in the field or operating under similar circumstances, and

4. members of an organised resistance movement. (Law 1990:218)

Section 4

The provisions of this Chapter relating to members of the armed forces shall also apply to:

1. prisoners of war,

2. participants in a war interned during the course of a war in which the Realm is neutral, and

3. aliens residing or staying with prisoners of war or interned participants in a war for the purpose of administering medical or spiritual care. (Law 1986:645)

Section 5

A member of the armed forces who refuses or fails to obey an order given by a superior, or if unduly delays carrying out such order, shall be sentenced for *insubordination* to a fine or imprisonment for at most two years. However, he shall not be sentenced if it is clearly apparent that the order had no bearing on the duties of his office. (Law 1986:645)

Section 6

If a crime defined in the previous Section is considered to be gross, the offender shall be sentenced for *gross insubordination* to imprisonment for at most ten years, or for life. In assessing whether the crime is gross, special consideration shall be given to whether the criminal act or actions were committed during battle or at a time when a breach of military discipline would otherwise constitute a special danger. (Law 1986:645)

Section 7

A member of the armed forces who absconds or is unlawfully absent from duty, shall be sentenced for *desertion* to a fine or imprisonment for at most two years.

If the crime is considered gross, imprisonment for at most ten years, or for life shall be imposed. In assessing whether the crime is gross, special consideration shall be given to whether the offender absconded during battle or in conjunction with battle, or whether he went over to the enemy or otherwise voluntarily delivered himself into the hands of the enemy. (Law 1986:645)

Section 8

A member of the armed forces who by violence, or the threat of violence, assails a superior in the execution of his duty, whether to compel him to perform or prevent him from performing a duty of his office, or for reasons otherwise arising from the nature of his office, shall be convicted of *violence or threat against a superior* and sentenced to a fine or imprisonment for at most two years.

Sentries and other members of the armed forces serving as guards for the maintenance of order shall be accorded the status of a superior.

If the crime is considered gross, imprisonment for at most six years shall be imposed. In assessing whether the crime is gross, special consideration shall be given to whether the criminal act was committed during battle or at a time when a breach of military discipline would otherwise constitute a danger. (Law 1986:645)

Section 9

A member of the armed forces who unlawfully dispatches a message to or otherwise enters into contact with a member of the enemy's forces or someone residing in enemy territory, shall be sentenced for *consorting with the enemy* to a fine or imprisonment for at most two years. (Law 1986:645)

Section 10

A member of the armed forces who, during battle or at a time when a breach of military discipline otherwise constitutes a gross danger, counsels other members of the armed forces to deliver themselves up to the enemy, or if otherwise in the presence of other members of the armed forces without authorisation undertakes an action of a nature to foster disloyalty or despondency, shall be sentenced for *undermining the will to fight* to imprisonment for at most ten years, or for life. (Law 1986:645)

Section 11

A member of the armed forces who fails in the performance of his duty, to make defences ready for battle, to prepare a detachment for action, to procure property or material, or otherwise to prepare a military operation, shall be sentenced for *neglect of military preparation* to imprisonment for at most ten years, or for life. (Law 1986:645)

Section 12

A member of the armed forces who, whilst in command of a detachment of the armed forces without authorisation committals a combat position, materials of war or any object or objects of material significance for the conduct of war to the enemy, or committals himself and his detachment to the enemy, shall be sentenced for *unauthorised capitulation* to imprisonment for at most ten years, or for life. (Law 1986:645)

Section 13

A member of the armed forces who, during battle or in conjunction with battle, fails to carry out his duty to the utmost to further the waging of the war, shall be sentenced for *combat dereliction* to imprisonment for at most ten years, or for life. (Law 1986:645)

Section 14

A member of the armed forces who intentionally or through gross carelessness disregards the duties incumbent upon him and the fault is considered to be serious, shall be sentenced for *breach of duty* to imprisonment for at most two years.

PART TWO ON CRIMES

Punishment shall not be imposed under the provisions of the foregoing paragraph if a punishment for the act is prescribed in some other Section of this Chapter. (Law 1986:645)

Section 15

Attempt, preparation or conspiracy to desert or failure to reveal desertion as well as attempt, preparation or conspiracy to use violence or threat against a superior shall be punishable under the provisions of Chapter 23.

For aiding and abetting breach of duty, only the person who thereby disregarded his duty shall be punishable. (Law 1986:645)

Section 16

For the purposes of Sections 7, 9, 10 and 12, the enemy shall be considered to include a foreign power with which the Realm is not at war if there exists a danger that the Realm may come to be at war with that power. (Law 1986:645)

Chapter 22
On Treason, etc.

Section 1

A person who, when the Realm is at war:

1. obstructs, misleads or betrays those engaged in the defence of the Realm, or who inveigles into them mutiny, disloyalty or dispiritedness,

2. betrays, destroys or damages materials or property of importance for any aspect of its defence,

3. procures military manpower, materials, property or services for the enemy; or who

4. commits any another criminal act, shall, if the criminal act is of a nature to cause considerable harm to any aspect of defence of the Realm or furnish the enemy with considerable assistance, be sentenced for *treason* to imprisonment for a fixed term of not less than four years and at most ten years, or for life. (Law 1986:645)

Section 2

If an act described in Section 1 is such that it is likely only to a lesser extent to cause harm to any aspect of defence or consists of furnishing the enemy with assistance of less consequence than is described in that Section, the accused shall be sentenced for *treachery* to imprisonment for at most six years. (Law 1986:645)

Section 3

A person who through negligence commits an act described in Section 1 or 2 shall be sentenced for *negligence harmful to the country* to imprisonment for at most four years. (Law 1986:645)

Section 4

If an act described in Sections 1—3 consists of procuring materials, property or services for the enemy in an area occupied by the enemy, and if, having regard to the needs of the population or the sustenance of the perpetrator or other special circumstances, the act cannot be regarded as improper, punishment shall not be imposed. (Law 1986:645)

Section 5

A person who, when the Realm is at war, spreads or causes to spread false rumours or other untrue assertions of nature to imperil the security of the Realm among the public, or conveys or causes such false rumours or other untrue assertions to be conveyed to the enemy, shall be sentenced for *spreading rumours endangering the security of the Realm* to a fine or imprisonment for at most two years.

The above provision shall also apply if a person, when the Realm is at war, spreads false rumours or other untrue assertions of a nature to foster disloyalty or dispiritedness among members of the armed forces. (Law 1986:645)

Section 6

A person guilty of a serious violation of a treaty or agreement with a foreign power or an infraction of a generally recognised principle or tenet relating to international humanitarian Law concerning armed conflicts shall be sentenced for *crime against international Law* to imprisonment for at most four years. Serious violations shall be understood to include:

PART TWO ON CRIMES

1. use of any weapon prohibited by international law,

2. misuse of the insignia of the United Nations or of insignia referred to in the Act on the Protection of Certain International Medical Insignia (Law 1953:771), parliamentary flags or other internationally recognised insignia, or the killing or injuring of an opponent by means of some other form of treacherous behaviour,

3. attacks on civilians or on persons who are injured or disabled,

4. initiating an indiscriminate attack knowing that such attack will cause exceptionally heavy losses or damage to civilians or to civilian property,

5. initiating an attack against establishments or installations which enjoy special protection under international law,

6. occasioning severe suffering to persons enjoying special protection under international law; coercing prisoners of war or civilians to serve in the armed forces of their enemy or depriving civilians of their liberty in contravention of international law; and

7. arbitrarily and extensively damaging or appropriating property which enjoys special protection under international law in cases other than those described in points 1—6 above.

If the crime is gross, imprisonment for at most ten years, or for life shall be imposed. In assessing whether the crime is gross, special consideration shall be given to whether it comprised a large number of individual acts or whether a large number of persons were killed or injured, or whether the crime occasioned extensive loss of property.

If a crime against the international law has been committed by a member of the armed forces, his lawful superior shall also be sentenced in so far as he was able to foresee the crime but failed to perform his duty to prevent it. (Law 1994:1721)

Section 6a

A person who:

1. develops, produces or by other means acquires, stores or holds chemical weapons or directly or indirectly transfers chemical weapons to another person,

2. uses chemical weapons,

3. participates in military preparations for the use of chemical weapons, or

4. uses riot control materials as a means of warfare shall be sentenced, if the act is not regarded as a crime against international Law, for *unlawful handling of chemical weapons* to imprisonment for at most four years.

Chemical weapons in the first paragraph, points 1—3 means those weapons defined as such by the United Nations Convention on the Development, Production, Possession and Use of Chemical Weapons and their Destruction.

If the crime is gross, imprisonment for at most ten years, or for life, shall be imposed. In assessing whether the crime is gross special consideration shall be given to whether the act was likely essentially to contribute to the development, production or proliferation of chemical weapons or to their use against people. (Law 1994:119)

Section 6b

A person who uses, develops, manufactures, acquires, possesses or transfers anti-personnel mines shall be sentenced for *unlawful dealings with mines* to imprisonment for at most four years unless the act is to be considered as a crime against international law.

The first paragraph applies only to mines referred to in the Convention of 18 September 1997 on the Prohibition of the Use, Storage, Production and Transfer of Anti-Personnel Mines, and on their Destruction.

Such dealing with mines as is allowed by the Convention referred to in the second paragraph shall not constitute a crime.

If the crime is gross a sentence of imprisonment shall be imposed for at most ten years or for life. In assessing whether the crime is gross special consideration shall be given to whether the act contributed essentially to the mines being used in a way that constituted a danger to the life and health of many persons. (Law 1998:1703)

Section 6c

A person who, contrary to the United Nations treaty on a complete prohibition of nuclear explosions, takes part in or in any other way collaborates in carrying out a nuclear weapons test or other form of nuclear explosion shall be sentenced for *carrying out an unlawful nuclear explosion* to imprisonment for at most four years, unless the act is considered to be against international law.

If the crime is gross, imprisonment shall be imposed for at most ten years or for life. In assessing if the crime is gross special consideration shall be given to whether the act was of great importance for a nuclear explosion or constituted a danger to many persons or to property of special importance. (Law 1998:1703. To enter into force at a time to be decided by the Government)

Section 7

Attempt, preparation or conspiracy to commit treason or treachery shall be adjudged under the provisions of Chapter 23. Conspiracy to commit such crimes shall also be understood to include communicating with the enemy with a view to preparing, enabling or facilitating the commission of the foregoing crimes. Preparation and conspiracy to commit such crimes at a time when the Realm is imperilled by war, occupation or other hostilities shall be punishable even though hostilities have not actually broken out.

A person who fails to reveal treason or treachery shall be punished in accordance with the provisions of Chapter 23. He shall be punishable even though he did not realise, but should have realised, that the crime was in process of being committed. (Law 1986:645. To be repealed at a time to be decided by the Government)

Section 7

Attempt, preparation or conspiracy to commit treason or treachery shall be adjudged under the provisions of Chapter 23. Conspiracy to commit such crimes shall also be understood to include communicating with the enemy with a view to preparing, enabling or facilitating the commission of the foregoing crimes. Preparation and conspiracy to commit such crimes at a time when the Realm is imperilled by war, occupation or other hostilities shall be punishable even though hostilities have not actually broken out.

A person who fails to reveal treason or treachery shall be punished in accordance with the provisions of Chapter 23. He shall be punishable even though he did not realise, but should have realised, that the crime was in process of being committed. Attempt or preparation to carry out an unlawful nuclear explosion shall be sentenced in accordance with the provisions of Chapter 23. (Law 1998:1703. To enter into force at a time to be decided by the Government)

Section 8

If, during the course of a war, a crime is committed by a person who had reason to assume that the act was permitted under the usages of war, the sentence imposed may be less severe than that prescribed for the crime in question. If the circumstances were especially extenuating, no punishment shall be imposed. (Law 1986:645)

Section 9

If a crime described in Chapter 21 or in this Chapter is committed against a State allied with the Realm, or against the armed forces of such State or against a member of its armed forces, the provisions of law on such acts against the Realm, its armed forces or members of its armed forces, shall be applicable. (Law 1986:645)

Section 10

If the Realm is in danger of war, or if there prevail such extraordinary circumstances as may have been provoked by a war or by the danger of war involving the Realm, the Government may order that the provisions of Chapter 19 and this Chapter pertinent to the event of the Realm being at war shall be applicable. The Government shall revoke such an order when the aforesaid circumstances no longer obtain.

If the Realm is totally or partially occupied by a foreign power without there being military opposition, the provisions of the aforesaid Chapters and Chapter 21 on the defence of the Realm are applicable to resistance activities, and the provisions relating to the enemy are applicable to the occupying power. (Law 1986:645)

PART TWO ON CRIMES

Section 11
Enemy in this Chapter is also to be understood as including a foreign power with which the Realm is not at war if there is a risk that the Realm will enter into war with that power. (Law 1986:645)

Chapter 23
On Attempt, Preparation, Conspiracy and Complicity

Section 1
A person who has begun to commit a crime without bringing it to completion, shall, in cases where specific provisions exist for the purpose, be sentenced for attempt to commit crime if there was a danger that the act would lead to the completion of the crime or such danger had been precluded only because of fortuitous circumstances.

Punishment for attempt shall be at most what is applicable to a completed crime and not less than imprisonment if the least punishment for the completed crime is imprisonment for two years or more.

Section 2
A person who, with the intention of committing or promoting a crime, presents or receives money or anything else as pre-payment or payment for the crime or who procures, constructs, gives, receives, keeps, conveys or engages in any other similar activity with poison, explosive, weapon, picklock, falsification tool or other such means, shall, in cases where specific provisions exist for the purpose, be sentenced for preparation of crime unless he is guilty of a completed crime or attempt.

In specially designated cases a sentence shall also be imposed for conspiracy. By conspiracy is meant that someone decides on the act in collusion with another as well as that someone undertakes or offers to execute it or seeks to incite another to do so.

Punishment imposed for preparation or conspiracy shall be less than the highest and may be less than the lowest limit applicable to the completed crime. No greater punishment than imprisonment for two years may be imposed unless imprisonment for eight or more years can follow for the completed crime. Punishment shall not be imposed if the danger of the crime being completed was slight.

Section 3

Responsibility for attempting, preparing or conspiring to commit a crime shall not exist if a person voluntarily, by breaking off the execution of the crime or otherwise, has prevented its completion. Even if the crime was completed, a person who has unlawfully had to do with means to that end may not be held criminally responsible for that reason if he has voluntarily prevented the criminal use of the means.

Section 4

Punishment as provided for an act in this Code shall be imposed not only on the person who committed the act but also on anyone who furthered it by advice or deed. The same shall also apply to any other act punishable with imprisonment under another Law or statutory instrument.

A person who is not regarded as the perpetrator shall, if he induced another to commit the act, be sentenced for instigation of the crime and otherwise for aiding the crime.

Each accomplice shall be judged according to the intent or the negligence attributable to him. Punishments defined in law for the act of a manager, debtor or other person in a special position shall also be imposed on anyone who was an accomplice to the act of such person.

The provisions of this paragraph do not apply if the law provides otherwise in special cases. (Law 1994:458)

Section 5

If someone has been induced to be an accomplice to crime by coercion, deceit or misuse of his youth, innocence or dependent status or has been an accomplice only to a minor extent, the punishment imposed may be less than that otherwise provided for the crime. Punishment shall not be imposed in petty cases. This also applies where the issue is one of imposing a punishment provided for a person in a special position on an accomplice.

Section 6

A person who omits to report in time or otherwise to reveal a crime that is in process of being committed when this could have been done without danger to himself or to anyone in a close relationship to him, shall, in those cases where this has been covered by special provisions, be sentenced for failure to reveal the crime as is provided for a person who has been an accomplice to the crime to a minor extent only; however, in no case may a more severe punishment than imprisonment for two years be imposed. In cases subject to special provisions, the punishment for failure to reveal a crime in accordance with the present provision shall also be imposed on a person who did not realise that a crime was being committed but should have done so.

If parents, other persons bringing up a child, or guardians, in cases other than those described in the first paragraph, fail to prevent a person in their care or under their control from committing a crime when this could have been done without danger to themselves or to anyone in a close relationship to them and without reporting to some authority, punishment shall be imposed in accordance with the provisions of the first paragraph.

Failure to reveal or prevent a crime is not punishable unless the act in process of being committed has progressed so far that punishment can follow.

Section 7

Punishments provided in this Code for cases where someone procures a gain or appropriates something personally by crime shall be likewise imposed when someone intentionally procures a gain for or appropriates something for another person.

Chapter 24
On General Grounds for Exemption from Criminal Responsibility

Section 1

An act committed by a person in self-defence constitutes a crime only if, having regard to the nature of the aggression, the importance of its object and the circumstances in general, it is clearly unjustifiable.

A right to act in self-defence exists against,

1. an initiated or imminent criminal attack on a person or property,

2. a person who violently or by the threat of violence or in some other way obstructs the repossession of property when caught in the act,

3. a person who has unlawfully forced or is attempting to force entry into a room, house, yard or vessel, or

4. a person who refuses to leave a dwelling when ordered to do so. (Law 1994:458)

Section 2

If a person who is an inmate of a prison, is remanded in custody or is under arrest or otherwise deprived of liberty, escapes, or by violence or threat of violence offers resistance, or offers resistance in some other way to someone who is in charge of him and is responsible for seeing that he behaves, such force as is justifiable in view of the circumstances may be used to prevent the escape or to maintain order. This also applies if, in cases referred to in this paragraph, resistance is offered by someone other than those previously mentioned.

The right of a policeman and certain other personnel to use force is otherwise dealt with by provisions in the Police Act (1984:387).

(Law 1994:458)

Section 3

With mutiny or during combat, and also on occasions when a crime against military discipline results in a special danger, a military superior may, vis-à-vis a subordinate who is insubordinate, use the force necessary to secure obedience. (Law 1994:458)

Section 4

An act by a person, in cases other than those described previously in this Chapter, if committed out of necessity, constitutes a crime only if it is indefensible having regard to the nature of the danger, the injury caused to another and to the circumstances in general.

Necessity exists when a danger threatens life, health, property or some other important interest protected by the law. (Law 1994:458)

Section 5

If a person is empowered under Sections 1—4 of this Chapter or under Section 10 of the Police Act (1984:387) to commit an act which is otherwise subject to punishment, anyone who assists him is similarly entitled. (Law 1994:458)

Section 6

If a person who, in a case where Sections 1—5 of this Chapter or Section 10 of the Police Act (1984:387) apply, has done more than is permitted, he shall nevertheless not be held responsible if the circumstances were such that he had difficulty in stopping to think. (Law 1994:458)

Section 7

An act committed by a person with the consent of some other person towards whom it is directed, constitutes a crime only if the act, having regard to the injury, violation or danger which it involved, its purpose, and other circumstances, is indefensible. (Law 1994:458)

Section 8

An act committed by a person on the order of someone to whom he owes obedience shall not result in his being liable to punishment, if in view of the nature of the obedience due, the nature of the act and the circumstances in general, it was his duty to obey the order. (Law 1994:458)

Section 9

An act committed by a person labouring under a misapprehension concerning its permissibility shall not result in his being liable to punishment if the mistake arose by reason of an error in the proclamation of the criminal provision or if, for other reasons, it was manifestly excusable. (Law 1994:458)

PART THREE
ON SANCTIONS

Chapter 25
On Fines, etc.

Section 1

Fines shall be imposed according to the provisions laid down for the crime in question as day-fines, summary fines or standardised fines. If a particular form of fine is not prescribed for the crime, fines shall be imposed as day-fines or, if the crime is punishable with less than thirty day-fines, as summary fines. (Law 1993:201)

Section 2

Day-fines shall be determined in number to at least thirty and at most one hundred and fifty.

Each day-fine shall be imposed as a fixed amount from thirty up to and including one thousand Swedish crowns, having regard to what is judged to be reasonable with account taken of the income, wealth, obligations to dependants and other economic circumstances of the accused. If special reasons exist, the amount of the day-fine may be adjusted.

The lowest amount for a day-fine is four hundred and fifty Swedish crowns. (Law 1991:240)

Section 3

Summary fines shall be imposed to an amount of at least one hundred

Swedish crowns and at most two thousand Swedish crowns. However, if a lower maximum amount is specially provided for, it shall be applicable. (Law 1991:240)

Section 4

Standardised fines are fines that, in accordance with what is provided for the crime, shall be determined according to a special basis of computation.

The lowest amount for a standardised fine is one hundred Swedish crowns. (Law 1991:240)

Section 5

Fines may be used as a consolidated punishment for several crimes, if fines can be imposed for each and every one of the crimes.

If special reasons exist, the court may impose summary fines for one or more crimes for which such sanction is prescribed and at the same time impose another form of fine for other criminality. Consolidated fines may not be imposed for crime for which standardised fines or fines that may not be converted into imprisonment are prescribed. (Law 1991:240)

Section 6

Fines as a consolidated punishment for several crimes are imposed as day-fines, if any one of the crimes is punishable with a day-fine.

Day-fines as a consolidated punishment may be imposed up to a number of at most two hundred, and summary fines up to an amount of at most five thousand Swedish crowns.

If a certain minimum fine is prescribed for any one the crimes a lesser fine may not be imposed. (Law 1993:201)

Section 7

Fines accrue to the State. (Law 1991:240)

Section 8

The provisions of the Enforcement of Fines Act (Law 1979:189) regulate the collection and enforcement of fines.

Fines that are not paid may, unless otherwise provided, be converted into imprisonment for at least fourteen days and at most three months in accordance with the provisions of the Enforcement of Fines Act. (Law

1991:240)

Section 9

With regard to a conditional fine imposed upon a person in a particular case by decision of a court or other public authority, Sections 7 and 8 shall be correspondingly applicable. So far as other conditional fines are concerned, the provisions of this Chapter on fines shall be applicable. (Law 1991:240)

Chapter 26
On Imprisonment

Section 1

Imprisonment is imposed for a fixed term or for life in accordance with what is provided for the crime. A fixed term of imprisonment may not exceed ten years, unless otherwise provided in Section 2 or 3, nor be shorter than fourteen days. With a sentence to imprisonment combined with probation in accordance with Chapter 28, Section 3, the term of imprisonment shall be as there provided.

Separate provisions govern the use of imprisonment as a conversion punishment for the non-payment of fines. (Law 1981:331)

Section 2

Imprisonment may be imposed as a joint punishment for several crimes if imprisonment may be imposed for any one of the crimes.

Imprisonment for a fixed term may be imposed for longer than the severest of the punishments provided for the crimes but shall not exceed the sum total of the maximum terms that can be imposed for the individual crimes. Nor may it exceed the severest punishment that can be imposed by more than:

1. one year if the severest punishment provided is shorter than imprisonment for than four years,

2. two years if the severest punishment provided is imprisonment for four years or more but less than eight years; or

3. four years if the severest punishment provided is imprisonment for eight years or more.

With sentences imposed in accordance with the second paragraph, a fine shall be considered as corresponding to imprisonment for fourteen days.

Imprisonment for less than the longest of the minimum period provided for may not be imposed. (Law 1988:942)

Section 3

A person who has been sentenced to imprisonment for at least two years and who, after the judgement has acquired final legal force, commits a crime for which the punishment is imprisonment for more than six years, may be sentenced for such relapse to imprisonment for a term which exceeds by four years the maximum punishment that can be imposed for the crime or, in the case of several crimes, the maximum punishment that can be imposed for the crimes under Section 2.

A crime committed by a person who has not attained the age of twenty-one may not constitute a ground for such extension of the term of imprisonment as is provided in the first paragraph.

A foreign judgement may be given the same effect as a Swedish judgement. (Law 1981:211)

Section 4

Repealed (Law 1988:942)

Section 5

A person sentenced to imprisonment shall, for the enforcement of the punishment, be taken into a prison unless otherwise provided. (Law 1998:604)

Section 6

A person serving imprisonment for a fixed term shall, unless it follows otherwise from the second or third paragraph or by Section 7, be conditionally released when two-thirds of the sentence, but at least one month, has been served.

Conditional release may not, however, be granted with imprisonment imposed in accordance with the provisions of Chapter 28, Section

PART THREE ON SANCTIONS

3, nor from imprisonment in conversion of a fine.

At the request of a sentenced person, conditional release may be delayed to a later time than that which follows from the provisions of the first paragraph or by Section 7. (Law 1998:604)

Section 6a

Repealed (Law 1998:604)

Section 7

If the sentenced person seriously violates the conditions for the serving of the sentence in a prison, the date for conditional release may be postponed.

Such a postponement may amount to at most fifteen days on each occasion of use.

In deciding on the question of postponement consideration shall be given to whether the infringement may or can have other negative consequences for the sentenced person. (Law 1998:604)

Section 8

If several sentences of imprisonment are being served concurrently, the combined terms of imprisonment shall be taken into consideration in applying Section 6. However, this does not apply to imprisonment imposed under Chapter 28, Section 3 or conversion imprisonment for non-payment of fines.

Time served shall also include the time during which the punishment is considered to be under enforcement by reason of an order of the court referred to in Chapter 33, Sections 5 or 6. (Law 1993:201)

Section 9

The National Prison and Probation Administration decides on a delay in accordance with Section 6, third paragraph, and postponement of conditional release in accordance with Section 7.

The Government or an administration designated by the Government may provide that another prison and probation administration other than the National Prison and Probation Administration may decide on a delay or postponement of conditional release.

A decision on matters dealt with in the first paragraph shall take immediate effect unless otherwise provided. (Law 1998.604)

Section 10

After conditional release there shall follow a probationary period corresponding to the remaining portion of the sentence, but of at least one year. (Law 1998:604)

Section 11

In connection with a conditional release or at a later date, the decision may be taken that the conditionally released person shall be placed under supervision if this is considered necessary. Decisions concerning supervision are taken by a local prison and probation administration[①]. If such supervision has been ordered but found to be no longer required, a supervision board may decide that supervision be discontinued. Supervision shall cease without any special decision being taken after one year of the probationary period has elapsed unless other consequences follow from the provisions of Section 18. (Law 1998:604)

Section 12

Supervision and probation in general is carried out under the management of the local prison and probation administration. This administration also appoints a supervisor and, if necessary, may appoint one or more persons to assist in the supervision. (Law 1998:604)

Section 13

The conditionally released person, if under supervision, shall keep his supervisor informed of his residence, employment situation and other conditions of significance for the supervision, report to the supervisor when required to do so and in general maintain contact with the supervisor in conformity with the latter's instructions. To the extent that the local prison and probation administration so decides, the foregoing provisions on the supervisor shall also apply to an officer of the local prison and

---

① The Swedish Prison and Probation Service consists of the central administration, regional prison and probation administrations and local prison and probation administrations. Each local prison and probation administration has its own chief whose task is to manage unified prison and probation activities. There are no chiefs of individual prisons or probation offices (Translator's note).

PART THREE ON SANCTIONS

probation administration or other person. (Law 1998:604)

Section 14

During the probationary period the conditionally released person shall lead an orderly life, try to support himself to the best of his ability and otherwise observe what is required of him by this Code or through conditions made, or instructions given, with its support. He shall, when summoned, appear before the local prison and probation administration. If ordered to make compensation for damage caused by the crime, he shall make all possible efforts to meet this obligation.

When the conditionally released person is placed under supervision, the local prison and probation administration shall, through supervision and the provision of support and assistance, seek to ensure that he does not relapse into crime and that his general adjustment in the community is promoted. To this end the local prison and probation authority shall keep itself continuously informed about the conduct of his life and his circumstances in general. (Law 1998:604)

Section 15

If there is reason to suppose that, to facilitate his adjustment in the community, a conditionally released person needs the support of special conditions which must be observed during the probationary period, such conditions may be made for a stated period or until further notice. They may relate to:

1. place of residence or lodging for a stated period for at most one year at a time,

2. employment, other gainful occupation, education or training,

3. medical care, treatment for alcoholism or other care or treatment in or outside a hospital or other similar establishment.

If the conditionally released person is to undergo care or treatment under the first paragraph, point 3, it may be prescribed that he provide blood, urine and breath samples in order to monitor that he is not under the influence of dependency producing substances.

If the conditionally released person has been ordered to make compensation for damage caused by the crime, conditions may be made about the time and manner of meeting this obligation unless, in view of the conditionally released person's financial situation and other circumstances, such conditions may be presumed to counteract his adjustment in the community.

If the conditionally released person is under supervision, special instructions may be given about its conditions. They may specify the way in which and to what extent the conditionally released person shall maintain contact with the supervisor or the local prison and probation administration. They may also prescribe an obligation for the conditionally released person to notify the supervisor or the local prison and probation administration of absence from the place of work, school or other occupation or institution referred to in the conditions. (Law 1998:604)

Section 16

Instructions in accordance with Section 15 shall be given by a supervision board. The local prison and probation administration may give such instructions *pro tempore* until the board has made its decision on the matter.

If the progress and other personal circumstances of the conditionally released person warrant it, the supervision board may change or cancel a given condition or make a new condition. (Law 1998:604)

Section 17

Instructions concerning the carrying out of a condition referred to in Section 15 may be given by the supervisor, who may also allow a temporary easement of, and make any urgently needed adjustment.

Section 18

If the conditionally released person does not comply with what is required of him by this Code or with conditions or instructions issued with its support, the supervision board, in addition to making conditions in accordance with Section 15 or deciding on a matter described in Chapter 37, Section 7, first paragraph, may:

1. decide that a warning be given to the conditionally released person or

2. decide on supervision of the conditionally released person for a

PART THREE ON SANCTIONS

stated period after the one-year probationary period has elapsed, but at the most until the expiry of the probationary period. (Law 1983:240)

Section 19

If a conditionally released person has seriously disregarded his obligations and if it may be presumed that he will not allow himself be corrected by any measure that the supervision board may take, the board may declare the conditionally granted liberty forfeited for up to a period of fifteen days on each occasion. (Law 1998:604)

Section 20

A decision concerning a measure described in Section 18 may not be made after the expiry of the probationary period. A decision concerning a measure referred to in Section 19 may be made even after the expiry of the probationary period provided that the supervision board has taken up the question prior thereto. (Law 1973:918)

Section 21

The question of forfeiture of conditionally granted liberty and on the imposition of certain other measures when the person sentenced to imprisonment is found to have committed a further offence, is regulated by the provisions of Chapter 34.

Section 22

If the question arises of declaring a conditionally granted liberty forfeited or taking a measure described in Section 18 or a measure requiring the conditionally released person to go into care or treatment, or if the conditionally released person has eluded supervision, the supervision board may, if the circumstances warrant it, order that the conditionally released person be appropriately taken in charge until a further decision has been taken. Such a decision shall be reconsidered as often as there is reason to do so.

A person so detained may not be held longer than a week. However, if strong reasons so dictate, a new order for his detention for at most an additional week may be made. He may not be kept in detention after the expiry of the probationary period. (Law 1983:240)

Section 23

If conditionally granted liberty is declared wholly or partially forfeited, the period forfeited shall be regarded as a new punishment imposed by a sentence for the purpose of considering a further conditional release. (Law 1983:240)

Section 24

When conditionally granted liberty can no longer be declared forfeited, the punishment shall be considered fully served on expiration of the probationary period.

Chapter 27
On Conditional Sentence

Section 1

A conditional sentence may be imposed by a court for a crime for which the sanction of a fine is considered inadequate. (Law 1988:942)

Section 2

A conditional sentence may be combined with day-fines, at most two hundred, regardless of whether a fine is prescribed for the crime or not. (Law 1991:240).

Section 2a

A conditional sentence may, if the accused consents, be combined with a condition of community service. Such a condition shall prescribe an obligation to carry out unpaid work for at least forty hours and at most two hundred and forty hours.

When the court decides on a condition of community service it shall state in its judgement what length of imprisonment would have been imposed if imprisonment has been chosen as the sanction.

Where there is reason to do so, a condition of community service may be modified or ended at the request of a prosecutor. (Law 1998:604)

PART THREE ON SANCTIONS

Section 3

A person who receives a conditional sentence shall be subject to a probationary period of two years.

The probationary period begins on the day when the decision of the court on the sanction for the crime has acquired final legal force in respect of the sentenced person, whether by declaration of satisfaction with the decision or otherwise.

Section 4

During the probationary period the offender shall lead an orderly life and seek to support himself to the best of his ability.

If the conditional sentence has been combined with community service, the sentenced person shall carry out the community service in accordance with the plan of work that has been drawn up by the local prison and probation administration. (Law 1998:604)

Section 5

If the offender has been enjoined to make compensation for damage caused by his crime, he shall do what lies in his ability to meet this obligation. The court may direct that, during the probationary period, he shall, at times and in a manner stated in the sentence, seek to meet his obligation to pay damages in whole or in part.

If the crime has occasioned damage to property and it is considered suitable for the promotion of the offender's adjustment to society, the court may direct that the offender, at the times and in the manner stated in the judgement, assist the injured party in such work as may help to repair or contain the damage, or which, having regard to the nature of the crime and the damage caused, may otherwise appear suitable. Such a condition may be only be made with the consent of the injured party.

A condition made under the first or second paragraphs may be amended or cancelled following application by the prosecutor or offender. (Law 1987:761)

Section 6

If the offender does not comply with what is required of him by the conditional sentence, the court may, if the prosecutor proceeds in the matter before the expiry of the probationary period, and having regard to the circumstances;

1. decide that the offender be given a warning,

2. make a condition in accordance with Section 5 or change a condition previously issued,

3. revoke the conditional sentence and decide on another sanction for the crime.

A measure described in point 1 or 2 above may not be taken after the expiry of the probationary period.

If the conditional sentence is revoked, equitable consideration shall be given, in deciding on the sanction, to the fine which was imposed in accordance with Section 2 and Chapter 34, Section 5 together with what the sentenced person has undergone in consequence of the condition of community service. In this connection, imprisonment may be imposed for a shorter time than is prescribed for the crime. If the information referred to in Section 2a has been stated in the judgement, this shall be taken into consideration, if imprisonment is imposed, when deciding on the length of sentence. (Law 1998:604)

Section 7

Chapter 34 contains provisions concerning the revocation of a conditional sentence and certain other measures when the offender is found to have committed another crime.

Chapter 28

On Probation

Section 1

A sentence of probation may be imposed for a crime for which the sanction of a fine is considered inadequate. (Law 1988:942)

Section 2

Probation may be combined with day-fines, at most two hundred, regardless of whether a fine is prescribed for the crime or not. (Law

1991:240)

Section 2a

Probation may be combined, if the accused consents, with a condition of community service. Such a condition shall prescribe an obligation to carry out unpaid work for at least forty hours and at most two hundred and forty hours.

When the court decides on a condition of community service it shall state in its judgement what length of imprisonment would have been imposed if imprisonment has been chosen as the sanction.

Where there is reason to do so, a condition of community service may be modified or ended by a supervision board. (Law 1998:604)

Section 3

Probation may be combined with imprisonment for at least fourteen days and at most three months.

If the court imposes imprisonment and probation, it shall not impose a fine in accordance with Section 2 or a condition of community service.

The court may order the commencement of a sentence of imprisonment if the circumstances call for this course of action notwithstanding the fact that the judgement has not acquired final legal force. (Law 1998:604)

Section 4

Probation shall continue for a probationary period of three years from the date on which the implementation of the sanction commences. (Law 1983:240)

Section 5

Probation shall be combined with supervision from the date of the sentence. The court may, however, direct that the supervision be deferred until the sentence has acquired final legal force against the sentenced person. If the sentence is appealed against, a higher court may direct that further implementation shall not occur.

Supervision shall be discontinued without any special order after one year of the probationary period has elapsed unless another outcome is entailed as a consequence of the fourth paragraph or Section 5a, 7 or 9.

If implementation has been interrupted by decision of a higher court but the accused is nevertheless thereafter sentenced to probation, the period during which implementation did not take place shall not be counted in the probationary period or in the period stated in the second paragraph.

If probation has been combined with a planned treatment which the offender has undertaken to follow, the court, may order in the sentence that the period of supervision be longer than that prescribed in the second paragraph. Such a period shall not, however, be longer than the time required for completion of the treatment and shall not exceed the probationary period. (Law 1987:761)

Section 5a

If the conditional sentence has been combined with community service, the sentenced person shall carry out the community service in accordance with the plan of work that has been drawn up by the local prison and probation administration.

If it appears necessary that the sentenced person shall be under supervision until the community service has been completed, a supervision board may decide on such supervision for a certain period after one year of the probationary period has elapsed, but for not longer than the end of the probationary period. (Law 1998:604)

Section 6

The provisions of Chapter 26, Sections 12—17, shall be applicable in corresponding fashion to a person sentenced to probation. The court shall, however, appoint a supervisor in its judgement unless special reasons argue against. In addition, the court may also impose conditions in accordance with the provisions of Chapter 26, Section 15, first to third paragraphs and Chapter 27, Section 5, second paragraph. The supervision board may amend or terminate conditions of the latter kind if there are reasons for so doing. (Law 1993:209)

Section 6a

In cases covered by Chapter 30, Section 9, second paragraph, point 3, the court shall, if the planned treatment is of decisive importance for

PART THREE   ON SANCTIONS

the decision to sentence to probation, state in its judgement what would have been the length of imprisonment had imprisonment been chosen as the sanction.

In addition, in such cases, the judgement shall always state the conditions applicable to the treatment plan that the probationer has undertaken to follow.

In connection with such a treatment plan, a condition may be imposed that whoever is responsible for the treatment shall report to the local prison and probation administration and a public prosecutor if the probationer seriously neglects the obligations stated in. (Law 1998:604)

Section 6b

In a case falling under Section 6a, the court may order that the person sentenced, if remanded in custody in connection with the trial, shall instead be appropriately detained until he has been transferred to the treatment establishment or person providing the treatment stated in the treatment plan. The taking in charge may not last longer than one week. (Law 1992:373)

Section 7

If the probationer does not comply with the obligations entailed by the sentence to probation, the supervision board may, in addition to imposing conditions in accordance with Chapter 26, Section 15, or taking a decision on a matter described in Chapter 37, Section 7, first paragraph:

1. decide that a warning be given to the probationer or
2. decide that the probationer shall continue under supervision for a given period after one year of the probationary period has elapsed, but not for longer than at most the time for of the expiry of the probationary period.

If supervision has been ordered under the first paragraph, point 2, but is deemed to be no longer required, the supervision board may direct that supervision is to be discontinued. The same shall apply if the court, in accordance with the provisions of Chapter 34, Section 6, has ordered supervision and this has been in operation for a period of one year.

The supervision board may not order the measures mentioned in the first paragraph of this Section after the expiry of the probationary period. (Law 1988:942)

Section 8

If the sentenced person seriously neglects his obligations and it can be presumed that the measures which can be taken by the supervision board will have no effect, the board shall request the prosecutor to bring the matter before a court and demand that the probation order be revoked. The matter may also be brought before a court without a request from the board if the probationer, in a case subject to the provisions of Section 6a, first paragraph, seriously neglects the obligations incumbent upon him in accordance with the treatment plan.

The court proceedings mentioned in this Section shall be instituted before the expiry of the probationary period. (Law 1988:942)

Section 9

If the probation order is revoked, the court shall decide on another sanction for the crime, and in doing so shall take due account of what the sentence to probation has entailed for the probationer and to any fine or imprisonment imposed in accordance with the provisions of Sections 2 or 3 or Chapter 34, Section 6. In such cases, the court may impose a shorter imprisonment than that prescribed for the crime in question. If the information referred to in Section 2a, second paragraph or Section 6a, first paragraph, has been stated in the judgement, and if imprisonment is to be imposed, due account shall be taken of that information when deciding on its length.

If adequate reasons for the revocation of probation are not present, the court may instead decide on a measure described in Section 7. Such a measure may not be decided on after the expiry of the probationary period. (Law 1998:604)

Section 10

Chapter 34 contains provisions on the revocation of probation and certain other measures when the probationer is found to have committed another crime.

Section 11

If the question of revocation of probation arises, or the taking of a measure described in Section 7, or a measure so that the probationer may be taken into care or enter treatment, or if the probationer has eluded supervision, the supervision board or the court before which proceedings have been instituted in accordance with Section 8 may, if the circumstances warrant it, order that the probationer be appropriately detained while awaiting a further decision. Such a decision shall be reviewed as often as there is reason to do so.

No person thus detained may be held for longer than one week. If, however, there are exceptional grounds, he may be further detained for at most one week by a new decision.

If the probationer is detained when the court takes the decision to revoke the sentence of probation, it may order that he remain in such detention until its decision acquires final legal force.

The probationer may not be held after the expiry of the probationary period. (Law 1987:761)

Chapter 29
On the Determination of Punishment and Exemption from Sanction

Section 1

Punishments shall, with due regard to the need for consistency in sentencing, be determined within the scale of punishments according to the penal value of the crime or crimes taken.

In assessing the penal value, special consideration shall be given to the damage, wrong or danger occasioned by the criminal act, to what the accused realised or should have realised about this, and to the intentions or motives he may have had. (Law 1988:942)

Section 2

In assessing penal value, the following aggravating circumstances shall be given special consideration in addition to what is applicable to each and every type of crime:

1. whether the accused intended that the crime should have markedly more serious consequences than it in fact had,

2. whether the accused manifested especial ruthlessness,

3. whether the accused exploited some other person's vulnerable position or that person's special difficulties in protecting himself,

4. whether the accused grossly exploited his position or otherwise abused a special confidence or trust,

5. whether the accused induced another person to take part in the crime by coercion, deceit or misuse of that person's youthfulness, lack of understanding or dependent status, or

6. whether the crime was part of a criminal activity which was especially carefully planned or carried out on a large scale and in which the accused had a significant role, or

7. whether a motive for the crime was to aggrieve a person, ethnic group or some other similar group of people by reason of race, colour, national or ethnic origin, religious belief or other similar circumstance. (Law 1994:306)

Section 3

In assessing penal value, the following mitigating circumstances shall be given special consideration in addition to what is prescribed elsewhere, if, in a particular case:

1. the crime was occasioned by the grossly offensive behaviour of some other person,

2. the accused, in consequence of a mental disturbance or emotional excitement, or for some other cause, had a markedly diminished capacity to control his actions,

3. the actions of the accused were connected with his manifestly deficient development, experience or capacity for judgement,

4. the crime was occasioned by strong human compassion or

5. the act, without being free from criminal responsibility, was such as is covered by Chapter 24.

PART THREE   ON SANCTIONS

The sentence imposed may be less severe than that prescribed for the crime in question if this is called for having regard to the penal value of the crime. (Law 1994:458)

Section 4

In determining the appropriate punishment, the court, if sufficient consideration cannot be given to the circumstances through choice of sanction or forfeiture of conditionally granted liberty, shall, besides the penal value of the crime, take reasonable account of whether the accused has previously been guilty of crime. In this connection, special consideration shall be given to the extent of any previous criminality, to the time that has elapsed between the crimes, and to whether the previous and the new criminality are similar in nature or whether in both cases they are of an especially serious character.

Section 5

In determining the appropriate punishment, the court shall, besides the penal value of the crime, give reasonable consideration to:

1. whether the accused has suffered severe bodily harm as a result of the crime,

2. whether the accused to the best of his ability has attempted to prevent, remedy or limit the harmful consequences of the crime,

3. whether the accused gave himself up,

4. whether the accused would suffer harm through expulsion by reason of the crime from the Realm,

5. whether the accused, as a result of the crime, has suffered, or there is good reason to suppose that he will suffer, dismissal from, or termination of, employment, or will encounter any other obstacle or special difficulty in the pursuit of his occupation or business,

6. whether the accused, in consequence of advanced age or ill health, would suffer unreasonable hardship by a punishment imposed in accordance with the penal value of the crime,

7. whether, having regard to the nature of the crime, an unusually long time has elapsed since its commission or

8. whether there exists any other circumstance that calls for a lesser

punishment than that warranted by the penal value of the crime.

If any circumstance covered by the first paragraph exists, the court may, if there are special grounds for so doing, impose a less severe punishment than that prescribed for the crime.

Section 6

If, in view of a circumstance described in Section 5 it is manifestly unreasonable to impose a sanction, the court shall grant exemption from sanction.

Section 7

If a person commits a crime before attaining the age of twenty-one, special consideration shall be given to his youth in determining the punishment. A milder punishment than that prescribed for the crime may be imposed in such cases. No person shall be sentenced to life imprisonment for a crime committed before attaining the age of twenty-one.

Chapter 30
On Choice of Sanction

Section 1

In choosing a sanction, imprisonment shall be considered a more severe sanction than conditional sentence or probation.

Provisions on the sanction of special care are set out in Chapter 31.

Section 2

Unless other provisions are applicable, no person shall be sentenced to more than one sanction for the same crime. (Law 1988:942)

Section 3

If a person is sentenced for more than one crime, the court shall impose a joint sanction for the crimes in question unless other provisions are applicable.

If there are special grounds for so doing, the court may impose a sentence of a fine for one or more crimes and, at the same time, impose another sanction for any remaining crime or crimes. In addition, the

PART THREE   ON SANCTIONS

court may impose imprisonment for one or more crimes at the same time as it imposes a conditional sentence or probation for any remaining crime or crimes. (Law 1988:942)

Section 4

In choosing a sanction, the court shall pay special attention to any circumstance or circumstances that argue for the imposition of a less severe punishment than imprisonment. In this connection, the court shall consider such circumstances as are mentioned in Chapter 29, Section 5.

As a reason for imprisonment, the court may take into account, besides the penal value and nature of the crime or crimes, the fact that the accused has previously been guilty of committing a crime or crimes. (Law 1988:942)

Section 5

If a crime has been committed by a person who has not attained the age of eighteen, the court may impose imprisonment only if there are extraordinary reasons for so doing. It follows from the provisions of Chapter 31, Section 1a, that the court shall in the first place sentence to closed juvenile care[1].

If a person who has attained the age of eighteen but not twentyone has committed a crime, the court may impose imprisonment only if, in view of the penal value of the crime or other special reasons, this course of action is justified. (Law 1998:604)

Section 6

A person who commits a crime under the influence of a serious mental disturbance may not be sentenced to imprisonment. If, in such a case the court also considers that no other sanction should be imposed, the accused shall go free from sanction. (Law 1991:1138)

Section 7

In choosing a sanction, the court shall consider, as a motive for imposing a conditional sentence, whether there is an absence of reason to

---

[1] Closed juvenile care has elsewhere been translated as "institutional treatment for young offenders" (Translator's note).

fear that the accused will be guilty of continued criminality.

As a special reason for imposing a conditional sentence instead of imprisonment, the court may consider that the sentence shall be combined with a condition of community service if the accused is willing to accept such a condition, and that such a condition is appropriate having regard to the accused as person and the circumstances in general. (Law 1988: 942)

Section 8

A conditional sentence shall be combined with a day-fine unless a fine, having regard to an obligation to undertake community service or other consequences of the crime, would occasion the accused undue hardship, or unless there are other special grounds for not imposing a fine. (Law 1998:604)

Section 9

In choosing a sanction, the court shall, as a reason for imposing probation, give consideration to whether such a sanction can contribute to the accused refraining from continued criminality.

As special grounds for probation, the court may consider:

1. whether a manifest improvement has occurred in the personal or social situation of the accused in some respect that may be presumed to have a bearing on his criminality,

2. whether the accused is undergoing treatment for misuse of a dependency producing substance or other condition that may be presumed to have a bearing on his criminality, or

3. whether the misuse of a dependency producing substance, or some other special circumstance necessitating essential care or other treatment, contributed to the commission of the crime and the accused declares himself willing to undertake treatment in accordance with a personal plan that can be realised in conjunction with the implementation of the sanction, or

4. whether the accused is willing for the probation to be combined with a condition of community service, and that such a condition is appropriate having regard to the accused as person and the circumstances in

PART THREE   ON SANCTIONS

general. (Law 1998:604)

Section 10

In assessing whether probation should be combined with day-fines, the court shall consider whether this is called for having regard to the penal value or nature of the crime or the previous criminality of the accused. (Law 1988:942)

Section 11

Probation may be combined with imprisonment only if this is unavoidably called for having regard to the penal value of the crime or the previous criminality of the accused. (Law 1988:942)

Chapter 31
On Committal to Special Care

Section 1

If a person being under the age of twenty-one and having committed a criminal act, can be made subject to treatment or other measure under the Social Services Act (Law 1980:620) or the Care of Young Persons Special Provisions Act (Law 1990:52), the court may commit the case to the social welfare board to make arrangements for the necessary treatment by the social welfare services in accordance with a treatment plan prepared by the board for the accused. Committal may only take place if the planned measures of the social welfare services, combined if necessary with a fine or youth service in accordance with the third paragraph below, can be considered sufficiently interventional having regard to the penal value and nature of the crime and the previous criminality of the accused. If it appears from the treatment plan that the accused shall be subject to treatment or some other measure based on the provisions of the law on social welfare service, the court shall issue an order that he shall undertake such treatment or be subject to the measure.

If the penal value or nature of the criminal act, or the previous criminality of the accused, so requires, the court may combine committal for treatment by the social welfare services, with:

1. day-fines up to a maximum of two hundred regardless of whether a fine is the punishment provided for the crime in question or not.

2. a special condition that the accused shall carry out unpaid work or take part in some other specially arranged activity (youth service) for at least twenty hours and at most one hundred hours providing that the accused agrees.

Where there is reason to do so, a condition of youth service may be modified or ended at the request of a prosecutor.

If the crime has occasioned damage to property, the court, in connection with committal to treatment in accordance with the first paragraph, may direct, if it is suitable for the promotion of the sentenced person's adjustment in the community, that he shall, at times and in the manner stated in the sentence, assist the injured party with such work as may help to repair or limit the damage or otherwise appears appropriate having regard to the nature of the crime and the damage caused. Such an order may be made only with the consent of the injured party. (Law 1998:604)

Section 1a

If a person has committed crime before attaining the age of eighteen, and if the court finds in application of Chapter 30 that the sanction should be imprisonment, it shall instead decide on the sanction of closed juvenile care for a certain period. This shall not apply, however, if, having regard to the age of the accused at the time of prosecution or other circumstance, special reasons argue against this course of action.

The court may impose closed juvenile care for at least fourteen days and at most four years.

Provisions on the enforcement of closed juvenile care are contained in the Act (Law 1998:603) on the Enforcement of Closed Juvenile Care. (Law 1998:604)

Section 2

If a person who has committed a crime can be made subject to treatment under the Act on the Treatment of Drug Misusers (Law 1988:

870), the court may hand the case over to the social welfare committee or, if the person in question has already been admitted to an institution where such treatment is provided, to the board of such an institution, to arrange the necessary treatment. The social welfare committee or institutional board shall be consulted before the court takes its decision.

If the punishment provided for the crime is more severe than imprisonment for one year, a committal for institutional treatment in accordance with the first paragraph shall be ordered only if there are special grounds for so doing. (Law 1994:97)

Section 3

If a person who has committed a crime for which the sanction cannot be limited to a fine, suffers from a serious mental disturbance, the court may commit him for forensic psychiatric care if, having regard to his mental condition and personal circumstances, admission to an institution for psychiatric care combined with deprivation of liberty and other coercive measures, is called for.

If the crime has been committed under the influence of a serious mental disturbance, the court may decide that a special release inquiry under the Act on Forensic Psychiatric Care (Law 1991:1129) shall be conducted during the time in care if there is risk for relapse into serious criminality of a serious kind by reason of the mental disturbance.

The court may, in conjunction with a committal to forensic psychiatric care impose another sanction, but not imprisonment or committal for other special care, if this is called for having regard to the previous criminality of the accused or for other special reasons. (Law 1991:1138)

Section 4

Repealed (Law 1991:1138)

Chapter 32
Repealed (Law 1986:645)

Chapter 33
On Deduction of Period of Arrest and Remand in Custody

Section 1
Repealed (Law 1988:42)

Section 2
Repealed (Law 1988:942)

Section 3
Repealed (Law 1973:43)

Section 4
Repealed (Law 1988:942)

Section 5

If a person sentenced to imprisonment for a fixed term or to closed juvenile care, or if the court orders, in conformity with Chapter 34, Section 1, that such sanction shall cover further crimes, and if the sentenced person has been deprived of liberty through arrest, remand in custody or admission to a forensic psychiatry unit under Section 10 of the Forensic Psychiatric Examinations Act (1991:1137) for at least twenty-four hours by reason of being suspected of a crime that has been tried and subject to sentence, the period of such deprivation of liberty, insofar as enforcement of another sentence has not proceeded simultaneously, shall be considered as time served in prison or in a special youth institution in consequence of the sentence imposed. The court shall state the number of days to be considered as served in its judgement. If the time by which the sentence of imprisonment exceeds the period of deprivation of liberty is small, the court may direct that the term of imprisonment shall be considered to have been served in full as a result of the deprivation of liberty.

PART THREE   ON SANCTIONS

If a conditional sentence or a sentence of probation is revoked and imprisonment for a fixed period is imposed instead, then insofar as the deduction provided for in the first or third paragraphs has not been made, the provisions of the first paragraph shall also be applicable to:

1. deprivation of liberty preceding the conditional sentence or the sentence to probation,

2. deprivation of liberty preceding a judgement directing that the conditional sentence or sentence to imprisonment shall include further crimes, and to

3. any detention provided for in Chapter 28, Section 6 b or Section 11, third paragraph.

If a person is sentenced to a fine and has been deprived of liberty in the manner described in the first paragraph by reason of being suspected of a crime that has been subject to sentence, the court may direct that the sentence has been enforced in full or in part as a result of the deprivation of liberty. (Law 1998:604)

Section 6

The provisions of Section 5 on taking account of a period of deprivation of liberty as time reckoned for the enforcement of a sentence may also be applied to the extent found to be reasonable to a deprivation of liberty which took place outside the Realm.

Section 7

Repealed (Law 1987:761)

Section 8

In trial by a higher court of an appeal concerning the imposition of a sanction, a decision on a question dealt with in Sections 5 and 6 may be amended even though no appeal has been lodged against such decision. (Law 1988:942)

Section 9

Repealed (Law 1988:942)

Chapter 34
Certain Provisions on Concurrence of Crimes and Change of Sanction

Section 1

If a person who has been sentenced for a crime to imprisonment, conditional sentence, probation or closed juvenile care is found to have committed another crime prior to the sentence, or commits a new crime subsequent to the sentence but before the sanction has been fully implemented or has been otherwise terminated, the court may, with due regard to what is provided in Sections 2—7 concerning certain cases, and the particular circumstances:

1. order that the earlier sanction imposed shall also apply to the second crime,

2. sentence separately to a sanction for that crime, or,

3. if the earlier sentence has acquired final legal force, revoke the sanction imposed by it and impose a different kind of sanction for the crimes.

If probation has been combined with imprisonment in accordance with the provisions of Chapter 28, Section 3, the imprisonment so imposed shall be considered to be a part of the probation when applying the provisions of this Chapter. (Law 1998:604)

Section 2

If the offender is serving life imprisonment, only an order in accordance with Section 1, point 1 may be made.

Section 3

If the prior sentence to imprisonment is for a fixed term, an order in accordance with Section 1, point 1 may be made only if it is obvious that, so far as a sanction is concerned, the new crime compared with the earlier one is of no appreciable importance, or else that there are extraordinary reasons for so doing.

PART THREE ON SANCTIONS

If in applying Section 1, point 2 a punishment is imposed for a crime committed before the implementation of the earlier sentence has begun, all possible care shall be taken when determining the punishment that the combined punishments do not exceed what could have been imposed for the two crimes under the provisions of Chapter 26, Section 2, and in so doing a less severe punishment than that provided for the crime may be imposed.

The revocation of imprisonment in conformity with Section 1 point 3 may occur only if judgement is pronounced before the punishment has been fully enforced.

Section 4

If Section 1, points 1 or 2 are applied with respect to a person conditionally released from imprisonment, the conditionally granted liberty or part thereof shall be declared forfeited if the crime was committed during the probationary period if no special reasons argue against. The court may consider as special reasons for not declaring the conditionally granted liberty forfeited or declaring only a portion forfeited:

1. whether the new criminality when compared with the earlier criminality is of lesser character;

2. whether a long time has elapsed between the crimes, or

3. whether a forfeiture appears unreasonable.

Should forfeiture not be declared in accordance with the first paragraph, the court may decide on a measure provided for under Chapter 26, Section 18 or prolong the probationary period by at most one year beyond the time that follows from the provisions of Chapter 26, Section 10.

A measure in accordance with the third paragraph may be decided on only before the end of the probationary period. Forfeiture may be decided on only where the question arises in connection with a case in which the conditionally released person has been remanded in custody or received notice of prosecution within one year from the end of the probationary period. (Law 1998:604)

Section 5

If the sanction previously imposed is a conditional sentence, an order in accordance with Section 1, point 1, may be made only for crime committed before the beginning of the probationary period.

If an order is made under Section 1, point 1, the court may, if the penal value or nature of the new crime or crimes so requires, also impose day-fines, at most two hundred, whether a fine is provided for the crime or not.

If it is necessary for the court to be able to make use of Section 1, point 1 instead of revoking the conditional sentence in accordance with Section 1, point 3 and sentence to imprisonment, the court may, if such special reasons exist as are given in Chapter 30, Section 7, decide that the conditional sentence shall be combined with an order on community service. If such a condition is ordered, the court shall apply the provisions of Chapter 27, Section 2 a, second paragraph.

If Section 1 point 1 or 2 is applied, the court may decide on a measure in accordance with Chapter 27, Section 6, point 1 or 2, or prolong the probationary period to three years, although this can only be done if the sentenced person has been remanded in custody or received notice of prosecution before the end of the probationary period.

If a conditional sentence is revoked in accordance in accordance with the provisions of Section 1, point 3, the court, when deciding on a new sanction, shall take reasonable account of any fines that have been imposed in accordance with the second paragraph or Chapter 27, Section 2, as well as the consequences for the sentenced person as a result of the order on community service. In consequence thereof the court may sentence to a shorter imprisonment than is prescribed for the crime. If the information provided for in Chapter 27, Section 2, second paragraph has been given, the court shall take this into consideration when the length of sentence is decided upon.

A conditional sentence may be revoked in accordance with Section 1, point 3 only if the question arises in connection with a case in which the sentenced person has been remanded in custody or received notice of prosecution within one year from the end of the probationary period. (Law 1998: 604).

PART THREE ON SANCTIONS

Section 6

If the sanction previously imposed was probation, the court may, in applying the provisions of Section 1, point 1, and if the penal value or nature of the new crime, or the offender's previous criminality so require, also sentence to day-fines, at most two hundred, regardless of whether a fine is the prescribed punishment for the crime in question or not.

If it is necessary for the court to be able to make use of Section 1, point 1 instead of revoking the probation in accordance with Section 1, point 3 and sentence to imprisonment, the court may, if such special reasons exist as are given in Chapter 30, Section 9, second paragraph point 4, decide that the probation shall be combined with an order on community service. If such a condition is ordered, the court shall apply the provisions of Chapter 28, Section 2a, second paragraph.

If imprisonment is the punishment provided for the new crime, and if, having regard to the provisions of Chapter 30, Section 11, the provisions of Section 1, point 1 cannot be applied unless such an order be combined with deprivation of liberty, the court may, instead of sentencing to a fine, impose imprisonment in accordance with the provisions of Chapter 28, Section 3.

If the provisions of Section 1, point 1 or 2 are applied, the court may decide on a measure provided for in Chapter 28, Section 9, or prolong the probationary period for at most five years. If the sentenced person has undertaken to follow a treatment plan in accordance with the provisions of Chapter 30, Section 9, second paragraph, point 3, the provisions of Chapter 28, Section 6a, shall be applied.

If the accused is sentenced to imprisonment under the provisions of Section 1, point 3, the court, when deciding on the length of the punishment, shall make reasonable allowance for what he may have undergone in consequence of the sentence to probation and to the time served of any imprisonment to which he was sentenced under the first paragraph of this Section or Chapter 28, Section 3, and to any fine to which he may have been sentenced under the provisions of the first paragraph of this Section or of Chapter 28, Section 2. In cases here described, imprisonment may be imposed for a shorter period than is provided for the crime. If the information described in Chapter 28, Section 6 a, first paragraph, has been stated in the sentence, due regard shall be paid to this when deciding on the length of the punishment if imprisonment is imposed.

A sentence to imprisonment under the provisions of the third paragraph may not be imposed, nor may a decision under the provisions of the second paragraph, a decision under the provisions of the fourth paragraph or a decision on revocation of probation, be taken other than in a case in which the sentenced person has been remanded in custody or received notice of prosecution before the end of the probationary period. (Law 1998: 604)

Section 7

If the sanction previously imposed was closed juvenile care, an order in accordance with the provisions of Section 1, point 1 may be made only if it is manifest that the new crime by comparison with the earlier crime is, so far as the sanction is concerned, without any particular significance, or if there are other special reasons for so doing.

If a sanction has been imposed under the provisions of Section 1, point 2 for a crime committed before enforcement of the earlier sentence has been started, the court, when deciding on the sanction shall ensure that the sanction taken together do not exceed what could have been imposed for both crimes. The court may therewith sentence to a lesser punishment than that prescribed for the crime.

If the accused is sentenced to imprisonment under the provisions of Section 1, point 3, the court, when deciding on the length of the punishment, shall make reasonable allowance for what he may have undergone in consequence of the sentence to closed juvenile care. A decision on the revocation of closed juvenile care may only be made if the sentence is passed before the fixed period of enforcement has expired. (Law 1998: 604)

Section 8

Repealed (Law 1979:680)

PART THREE ON SANCTIONS

Section 9

Repealed (Law 1981:211)

Section 10

If in application of Section 1, point 1, by a sentence which has acquired final legal force, imprisonment, a conditional sentence, probation or closed juvenile care imposed in an earlier sentence has been deemed to cover further crime and, if the earlier sentence is changed by a higher court by a judgement which acquires final legal force, the question of a sanction for the said crime shall, following notification by a prosecutor, be reconsidered by the court. This also applies when a sanction has been decided on under the provisions of Section 3, second paragraph or Section 7, second paragraph and the earlier sanction has been changed.

If it is found when a sentence to imprisonment for a fixed term or closed juvenile care is to be enforced that the sentenced person committed the crime before the enforcement of a sanction to which he was sentenced for another crime has begun and if it does not appear from the judgements that the latter sanction has been taken into consideration, the court, once the sentences have acquired final legal force, shall, following notification by the prosecutor and in application of the provisions of Section 3, second paragraph or Section 7, second paragraph, determine the punishment the sentenced person shall undergo as a result of the sentence which is the last to be implemented. (Law 1998:604).

Section 11

If a sentence to life imprisonment is to be enforced concurrently with a sentence to a fine, imprisonment as conversion of a fine, imprisonment for a fixed period, a conditional sentence, probation or closed juvenile care, the sentence to life imprisonment shall supplant the other sanction.

If a sentence to imprisonment for a fixed term of at least two years or to closed juvenile care for at least two years is to be enforced concurrently with a sentence to a fine or imprisonment as conversion of a fine imposed before the enforcement of the aforementioned sanctions has been commenced, the aforementioned imprisonment or sentence to closed juvenile care shall supplant the other sanction. (Law 1998:604).

Section 12

Repealed (Law 1979:680)

Section 13

Repealed (Law 1981:211)

Sections 14—17

Repealed (Law 1975:667)

Section 18

If the question arises of extradition to Sweden for enforcement of a sentence under which a person has been sentenced to imprisonment as a joint sanction for two or more crimes and if, under the legislation of the foreign state, extradition may not take place for all the crimes, the court shall, following notification by a prosecutor, revoke the joint sanction imposed earlier and impose a sanction for the criminality for which extradition may take place.

The provisions of the first paragraph shall also apply when a sentence in a Swedish criminal case, relating to two or more crimes, is to be enforced abroad in accordance with the Act on International Collaboration in the Enforcement of Sentence in Criminal Cases (1972:260) or the Act on International Collaboration on the Supervision of Conditionally Sentenced or Conditionally Released Offenders (1978:801) and an impediment to enforcement exists under the Laws of the foreign state in respect of one or more of the crimes. (Law 1981:211)

Chapter 35

On Limitations on Sanctions

Section 1

No sanction may be imposed unless the suspect has been remanded in custody or received notice of prosecution for the crime within:

1. two years, if the crime is punishable by at most imprisonment for one year,

2. five years, if the most severe punishment is imprisonment for

more than one but no more than two years imprisonment,

3. ten years, if the most severe punishment is imprisonment for more than two but no more than eight years,

4. fifteen years, if the most severe punishment is imprisonment for a fixed term of more than eight years,

5. twenty-five years, if life imprisonment can be imposed for the crime.

If an act includes several crimes, then, regardless of what is stated above, a sanction may be imposed for all of the crimes, provided that a sanction can be imposed for any one of them.

Section 2

Repealed (Law 1975:667)

Section 3

If a person remanded in custody is released without having received notice of prosecution for the crime or if the case against someone is rejected or dismissed after he has received such notice, the remand in custody or service of notice shall be considered as never having occurred if the possibility of imposing a sanction arises.

Section 4

The times specified in Section 1 shall be reckoned from the date when the crime was committed. If the occurrence of a certain effect of the act is a prerequisite for the imposition of a sanction, time shall be reckoned from the date when such effect occurred.

If a crime described in Chapter 6, Sections 1—4 and 6 or an attempt to commit such a crime has been committed against a child under fifteen years of age, the times stated in Section 1 shall be reckoned from the date on which the injured party attains or would have attained fifteen years of age.

If, in a bookkeeping crime which is not petty, the person responsible for bookkeeping has been declared bankrupt, has been granted or has offered a composition or has suspended payments within five years of the crime, the time shall be reckoned from the date when this occurred. If the person responsible for bookkeeping has been the subject of a tax audit or tax assessment audit within five years of the crime, the time shall be reckoned from the day when the audit was decided. (Law 1996:659)

Section 5

Repealed (Law 1971:964)

Section 6

In no case may a sanction be imposed when, from the date mentioned in Section 4, the following periods have elapsed:

1. five years, if the crime is not subject to a punishment of more than a fine and the time for the imposition of a sanction for the crime is determined under Section 1, point 1,

2. fifteen years if, in cases other than those falling under the first paragraph, the crime is not subject to imprisonment for more than two years,

3. thirty years in other cases. (Law 1971:964)

Section 7

Sentences to fines lapse after five years have expired from the date when the judgement acquired final legal force. This does not apply if, at the expiry of the stated period, the sentenced person has been notified of an application for conversion of the fine and this application has not been finally determined. If the application does not lead to conversion of the fine, it shall lapse when the court's final decision in the case acquires final legal force. Special provisions govern the lapse of a sentence imposing conversion of a fine.

If the sentenced person dies, an imposed fine lapses. If the sentence acquired final legal force during the sentenced person's lifetime and moveable property has been distrained or placed in public custody in order to secure payment of the fine, it shall, however, be payable out of such property.

The previous sections concerning fines apply equally to a conditional fine subject to an order for payment. (Law 1983:351)

Section 8

A sentence to imprisonment lapses if its enforcement has not begun before the period stated below has elapsed from the time the sentence ac-

PART THREE ON SANCTIONS

quired final legal force:

1. five years, if imprisonment for not more than one year was imposed,

2. ten years, if imprisonment for more than one year but not more than four years was imposed,

3. fifteen years, if imprisonment for more than four years but not more than eight years was imposed,

4. twenty years, if imprisonment for a fixed term of more than eight years was imposed,

5. thirty years, if life imprisonment was imposed. (Law 1971:964)

Section 9

If the serving of imprisonment for a fixed term is interrupted, the provisions of Section 8 shall be correspondingly applicable concerning the continuation of enforcement and therewith time shall be computed having regard to what remains of the imposed punishment. The time shall be reckoned from the date when the interruption occurred or, if conditional release has been granted but declared revoked, from the date when the revocation decision acquired final legal force.

Section 10

A sentence to closed juvenile care lapses if its enforcement has not begun within five years from the time the sentence acquired final legal force.

If enforcement of the sentence has been interrupted then what is provided in the first paragraph shall be applicable in the matter of the continued enforcement. The time shall be reckoned from the day of the interruption. (Law 1998:604)

Section 11

Repealed (Law 1986:645)

Chapter 36
On Forfeiture of Property, Corporate Fines and Other Special Legal Effects of Crime

Section 1

The proceeds of a crime as defined in this Code shall be declared forfeited unless this is manifestly unreasonable. The same shall apply to anything a person has received as payment for costs incurred in conjunction with a crime, provided that such receipt constitutes a crime under this Code. The value of the article received may be declared forfeited instead of the article itself.

In determining whether it would be manifestly unreasonable to declare the proceeds of a crime forfeited under the provisions of the first paragraph, consideration shall be given inter alia, to whether there is reason to believe that liability to pay damages in consequence of the crime will be imposed or otherwise discharged. (Law 1986:1007)

Section 2

Property which has been used as an auxiliary means in the commission of a crime under this Code or which is the product of such a crime may be declared forfeited if this is called for in order to prevent crime or for other special reasons. This also applies to property the use of which constitutes a crime under this Code or which is otherwise used in a manner which constitutes such a crime.

The value of property may be declared forfeited instead of the property itself. (Law 1968:165)

Section 3

Forfeiture may also be decided on in cases other than those described in Section 2 in respect of objects which:

1. by reason of their special nature and other circumstances, give rise to a fear that they may be put to criminal use,

2. are intended for use as a weapon in a crime against human life or

PART THREE   ON SANCTIONS

health and which have been discovered in circumstances which give rise to a fear that they would be put to such use, or

3. are intended for use as an auxiliary aid in a crime entailing damage to property and have been discovered in circumstances which clearly give rise to a fear that they would be put to such use. (Law 1989:136)

Section 4

If, as a result of a crime committed in the course of business, the entrepreneur has derived financial advantages, the value thereof shall be declared forfeited, even if this is not so provided for in Section 1 or 2 or otherwise specially provided for.

The provisions of the first paragraph shall not apply if forfeiture is unreasonable. In assessing whether such is the case, consideration shall be given inter alia to whether there is reason to believe that some other obligation to pay a sum corresponding to the financial gain derived from the crime will be imposed upon the entrepreneur or will be otherwise discharged by him.

If proof of what is to be declared forfeited cannot, or can only with difficulty, be presented, the value may be estimated to be an amount that is reasonable in view of the circumstances. (Law 1986:1007)

Section 5

Forfeiture of property or its worth in consequence of crime may, if no provision is otherwise made, be exacted of:

a) the offender or an accomplice in the crime,

b) the person whose position was occupied by the offender or an accomplice,

c) the person who profited from the crime or the entrepreneur described in Section 4,

d) any person who after the crime acquired the property through the division of jointly held marital property, or through inheritance, will or gift, or who after the crime acquired the property in some other manner and, in so doing, knew or had reasonable grounds to suspect that the property was connected with the crime.

If the property did not belong to any of the persons in the categories (a)—(c) in the first paragraph, it may not be declared forfeited.

Any special right to property that has been declared forfeited remains if the special right is not also declared to be forfeited.

Such a right gained by distraint or security for payment ceases if the property is declared forfeited unless for some special reason it is ordered that the right shall remain. (Law 1987:791)

Section 6

Instead of forfeiture, the court may prescribe a measure for the prevention of misuse. (Law 1986:118)

Corporate fines

Section 7

For a crime committed in the exercise of business activities the entrepreneur shall, at the instance of a public prosecutor, be ordered to pay a corporate fine if:

1. the crime has entailed gross disregard for the special obligations associated with the business activities or is otherwise of a serious kind, and

2. the entrepreneur has not done what could reasonably be required of him for prevention of the crime.

The provisions of the first paragraph shall not apply if the crime was directed against the entrepreneur or if it would otherwise be manifestly unreasonable to impose a corporate fine. (Law 1986:1007)

Section 8

A corporate fine shall consist of at least ten thousand Swedish crowns and at most three million Swedish crowns. (Law 1986:118)

Section 9

In determining the amount of a corporate fine, special consideration shall be given to the nature and extent of the crime and to its relation to the business activity. (Law 1986:118)

Section 10

A corporate fine may be remitted or set at less than it should have

PART THREE ON SANCTIONS

been under the provisions of Section 9:

1. if a sanction for the crime is imposed on the entrepreneur or a representative of the entrepreneur,

2. if the crime involves some other payment liability or a special legal effect for the entrepreneur,

3. if this is otherwise called for on special grounds. (Law 1986: 118)

Common provisions

Section 11

The provisions of an act or statutory instrument concerning a special legal effect arising from the fact that someone is sentenced to punishment shall also apply when some other sanction stated in Chapter 1, Section 3, is imposed.

In the application of the first paragraph, a conditional sentence and probation, and also, unless the sentence otherwise states, committal for special care, shall be considered equivalent to imprisonment. In that connection, if so ordered, probation and committal for special care shall be considered as corresponding to imprisonment for at least six months. (Law 1986:118)

Section 12

If sentencing someone to a sanction is a prerequisite for the forfeiture of property or other special legal effect which may follow upon crime, the court may, if the sanction for the crime is remitted, order, insofar as circumstances give cause, that such legal effect shall ensue. (Law 1986: 118)

Section 13

If a crime has been committed by someone who has not attained fifteen years of age or who has acted under the influence of serious mental disturbance, the court may order forfeiture of property or other special legal effect that may follow upon the crime only if, and to the extent that, this may be regarded as reasonable having regard to his mental state, the nature of the act, and other circumstances. (Law 1986:118)

Section 14

If a sanction can no longer be imposed because of the death of the offender or for other cause, property may be declared forfeited or a corporate fine imposed by reason of the crime or a measure be prescribed to avert misuse only if, in proceedings pertaining thereto, a summons has been served within five years from the time when the crime was committed. In such a case the prosecutor may institute proceedings only if called for in the public interest.

In a case falling under the present description the provisions of Chapter 35, Section 3 shall be correspondingly applicable. (Law 1986:118)

Section 15

A decision concerning forfeiture or measure to avert misuse or concerning a corporate fine is null and void if its implementation has not occurred within ten years from the date when the decision acquired final legal force. (Law 1986:118)

Section 16

If an act or statutory instrument prescribes that a declaration be made concerning forfeiture or other special legal consequence of a crime, the declaration may nevertheless be dispensed with if such a legal consequence is manifestly unreasonable. (Law 1986:1007)

Section 17

Forfeited property and corporate fines accrue to the State unless otherwise prescribed.

If the proceeds of crime described in Section 1, corresponding to the damage occasioned to an individual, are declared forfeited from some person, the State shall in that person's stead pay compensation to the injured party to an amount corresponding to the value that has accrued to the State as a consequence of the decision on forfeiture. In the enforcement of this decision, the party subject to the forfeiture shall be entitled to make a deduction for any amount he shows himself to have already paid in compensation to the injured party. (Law 1986:1007)

PART THREE ON SANCTIONS

Chapter 37
On Supervision Boards

Section 1

The Government determines the division of the country into supervision board areas.

A supervision board consists of chairman, vice-chairman and three other members, unless the Government decrees that a given board shall have more members. The chairman and two members constitute a quorum. In urgent cases and also in matters of less importance the chairman alone may decide on behalf of the board. Such decisions shall be reported at the next meeting of the board.

The Government may order that a supervision board shall work in sections. For such sections the applicable parts of the Law governing the board shall apply. (Law 1983:240)

Section 2

The Government or an administration designated by the Government appoints the chairman and vice-chairman of the supervision boards. In the absence of the chairman, the vicechairman acts as chairman. When both the chairman and vicechairman are absent, a temporary deputy is appointed by the National Prison and Probation Administration. The chairman, vicechairman and deputy shall be legally qualified and have experience of service as judges.

The other members are appointed by election. An equivalent number of deputies for them are elected. Elections are conducted by the municipal council if the supervision board's area comprises a single municipality and, otherwise, by the county council. If, in the supervision board's area, there is also a municipality not included in a county council region, the election is administered by the county council and the local council in the proportions between them that are decided by the county administrative board on the basis of the population figures. If a supervision board's area includes several counties or parts of counties, the Government, using the same principles, decides the number of members and deputies for each county or part of a county.

Proportional representation of members or deputies in county council or municipal elections shall be adopted, if requested by at least as many members of the county council or local council as correspond to the quotient obtained if the number of members present is divided by the number of persons to be elected, increased by 1. If the quotient is a fraction, it shall be rounded off to the next higher integer. Provisions governing the procedure for such proportional representation exist in the law (1992: 339) on proportional election procedures. If the deputies are not elected proportionally, the order in which they shall be summoned to serve shall also be decided in the election.

Members and non-temporary deputies are appointed for terms of four years. If a member who has been appointed in a proportional election resigns before the expiry of his term, a deputy is appointed in accordance with the order between deputies decided in the election. If a member or deputy who has not been appointed in a proportional-representation election resigns, a new member or deputy is appointed for the remainder of the term. Temporary deputies shall be appointed for at most six months.

When a member or deputy is to be appointed, the supervision board shall notify the fact to the body which is to appoint him. (Law 1998: 598)

Section 3

Any person entitled to vote in municipal elections, who is officially registered in a parish within the jurisdiction of the board and has not attained the age of seventy, and who will not attain that age during the term of office envisaged, is eligible for election as a member or deputy member of a supervision board. No person with a guardian under the terms of Chapter 11, Section 7, of the Code on Parents and Children may be elected as a member or deputy member of a supervision board. Nor shall legally qualified judges, public prosecutors, police officers, officials of the prisons and probation service, attorneys, or persons whose profes-

PART THREE ON SANCTIONS

sion is to plead the cause of others before a court of Law be elected as a member or deputy member of such board. The supervision board shall determine the eligibility of an elected member or deputy member on its own motion.

If a member ceases to be eligible for office, his duties in that capacity shall be regarded as terminated. (Law 1991:510)

Section 4

The National Parole Board shall consist of one member, who occupies or has occupied a judicial office and who shall be chairman of the Board, together with four other members. Deputies are appointed in a number determined by the Government. The Government appoints the chairman, other members and deputies. In the absence of the chairman, his function shall be exercised by a member or deputy designated by the Government and qualified for appointment as chairman.

In urgent cases and in matters of minor importance the chairman alone may take decisions on behalf of the Board. Such decisions shall be notified at the next meeting of the Board.

The chairman, other members and deputies are appointed for terms of five years. If a member or deputy leaves before the expiry of his term, a new member or deputy is appointed to serve for the balance of the term. (Law 1983:240)

Section 5

A member or deputy of a supervision board and the National Parole Board shall have taken a judge's oath. The same grounds for disqualification that apply to a judge shall apply to a member or deputy, but the provisions of Chapter 4, Section 13, point 7 of the Code of Judicial Procedure shall not be applicable to a member or deputy of a supervision board.

With respect to decisions by a board referred to in the first paragraph, applicable parts of the provisions governing voting in criminal cases in a superior court shall be observed. (Law 1981:211)

Section 6

If a sentenced person requests an oral hearing on a matter dealt with by a supervision board, he shall be granted the opportunity.

In a matter before the National Parole Board an opportunity to be heard in person shall be granted to a sentenced person if this can be assumed to be useful and can be conveniently arranged. (Law 1981:211)

Section 7

A person sentenced to imprisonment may request review of a decision of a local prison and probation administration taken in accordance with Chapter 26, Section 11, Section 12, second sentence, or Section 13, second sentence by the supervision board in whose area a local prison and probation administration is active. The board may also, on its own initiative, take up such a decision for review and in other respects decide on a matter the resolution of which is incumbent upon the probation authority in accordance with any of the provisions aforesaid. The local prison and probation administration may refer such a matter to the board for decision.

Any person sentenced to imprisonment and dissatisfied with a decision of a supervision board made in accordance with the provisions of Chapter 26, Section 11, 15, 18, 19 or 22, shall be entitled to require a review of the decision by the National Parole Board. (Law 1998:604)

Section 8

The provisions of Section 7, first paragraph, are correspondingly applicable to a person sentenced to probation.

A person sentenced to probation may appeal to a court of appeal against a supervision board's decision in matters described in Chapter 26, Section 15, or Chapter 28, Section 7 or 11. The document shall be handed in to the supervision board. The time allowed for making the appeal is to be reckoned from the date when he received notice of the decision. The courts of appeal shall apply the provisions of the Code of Judicial Procedure concerning appeals from the decisions of district courts. (Law 1994:1037)

Section 9

In a matter concerning the revocation of conditionally granted release from prison in accordance with the provisions of Chapter 26, a public defence counsel shall be appointed to assist the person affected by the measure unless it must be assumed that there exists no need for such assistance. (Law 1996:1623)

Section 10

A decision taken by a local prison and probation administration and a supervision board under Sections 7 and 8 is immediately applicable unless otherwise provided. (Law 1998:604)

Section 11

An appeal may only be lodged against a decision made in accordance with this Code by a supervision board concerning matters other than those covered by Sections 7 and 8, to a court of appeal in accordance with Section 8 or to the National Parole Board. (Law 1981:211)

Chapter 38
Certain Procedural Provisions, etc.

Section 1

A person receiving a conditional sentence may, before the time for appeal has expired, make a declaration stating that he is satisfied with the judgement as to the sanction imposed. Such a declaration shall also relate to fines imposed under Chapter 27, Section 2. The declaration shall be made in the manner prescribed by the Government.

A declaration once made in the prescribed manner is not retractable. If the offender has appealed against the judgement, his appeal shall be considered withdrawn by the declaration so far as the sanction for the crime is concerned.

Special provisions exist on the declaration of satisfaction in connection with a sentence to imprisonment and a sentence to closed juvenile care. (Law 1998:604)

Section 2

If a court has committed someone for care within the social welfare services in accordance with Chapter 31, Section 1, and the sentenced person thereafter substantially violates an order made in accordance with the provisions of Chapter 31, Section 1 second or third paragraph, the court may, following an application by a prosecutor, revoke the order on committal to care and sentence to another sanction for the crime. Reasonable account shall be taken of any fine that has been imposed in accordance with Chapter 31, Section 1 third paragraph, point 1 and to what the sentenced person has undergone in consequence of an order on youth service in accordance with Chapter 31, Section 1 third paragraph, point 2.

The court may decide to issue a warning to the sentenced person instead revoking the order in accordance with the first paragraph if this is a sufficient measure.

Even in cases which do not fall under the first paragraph, its provisions shall be correspondingly applicable if the planned care or measures that the social welfare board presented in its report in accordance with Section 11 of the law (1964:167) containing special provisions on young offenders do not come about or if the planned care differs essentially from the plan presented in the report. The same shall apply correspondingly when the court has committed someone for care in accordance with Chapter 31, Section 2, and the care which the social welfare board, in a report to the court, declared its intention to provide, proves impossible to arrange. (Law 1998:604)

Section 2a

If, in the determination of the quantum of punishment or choosing a sanction, it is apparent from the judgement that special consideration was given to whether the accused, in consequence of the crime, might be dismissed from or be served with notice of termination of an employment and, if that assumption, in respect off which the judgement was based, is found to have been wrong, the court which first passed judgement in the case may on application by a prosecutor or the sentenced person, revoke the sanction and impose a new sanction for the crime. This shall apply, however, only insofar as the earlier sanction has not been implemented in full. If such application is made, the court may order that the sanction previously imposed shall not be implemented until further no-

PART THREE ON SANCTIONS

tice.

If the sanction previously imposed was a conditional sentence or probation and if the new sanction upon is imprisonment, the court, in establishing the length of the prison sentence, shall pay due regard to what the offender may have undergone in consequence of conditional sentence or probation. In this connection, the court may impose imprisonment for a shorter period than that prescribed for the crime. If a sentence of imprisonment or closed juvenile care is set aside and the court imposes a new sentence of the same character, the term served of the earlier sanction shall be considered as an enforcement of the new sanction. The court in its judgement shall state the length of the term already served. (Law 1998:604)

Section 3

Questions concerning measures to be taken under Chapter 27, Section 2a, third paragraph, Section 5 third paragraph or Section 6, shall be considered by the court that first adjudged the case in which a conditional sentence was imposed. The question of a measure ordered under Chapter 31, Section 1 fourth paragraph shall be considered by the court that first adjudged the case in which the sentence to committal to the care of the social welfare services was passed.

Proceedings under Chapter 28, Section 8, shall be brought before the district court within whose area the supervision board which has raised the matter in question operates, or before the court which first adjudged the case in which the sentence of probation was imposed.

Cases referred to in this Section may also be brought before a court in which a criminal charge lies against the sentenced person, or before the court in the locality where the sentenced person mainly resides, if, having regard to the inquiries to be made and also to costs and other circumstances, the court considers it appropriate. (Law 1998:604)

Section 4

Notification under Chapter 34, Section 10, shall be addressed to the first court in any one of the cases.

Application under Chapter 34, Section 18, shall be made to the court which first adjudged the case. (Law 1981:211)

Section 5

Proceedings to which reference is made in Chapter 27, Section 6, or Chapter 28, Section 8, shall be considered instituted when the offender was informed of the application to take up the case. (Law 1981:211)

Section 6

Lay assessors shall participate in the decision-making of a court of first instance on matters described in Sections 2 or 2a or in Chapter 27, Section 6, Chapter 28, Section 9, or Chapter 34, Section 10, second paragraph, or Section 18. This also applies to the revocation of a sanction under Chapter 34, Section 1, point 3, forfeiture of conditionally granted liberty or other measure taken under Chapter 34, Section 4, and to measures taken under Chapter 34, Section 5, third paragraph or Chapter 34, Section 5, third paragraph or Section 6, second paragraph.

A court of first instance sitting with one qualified judge shall be considered competent to decide on matters described in Chapter 27, Section 2a, third paragraph, or Section 5, third paragraph, Chapter 28, Section 11, first and second paragraphs or Chapter 31, Section 1, fourth paragraph. (Law 1998:604)

Section 7

Repealed (Law 1981:211)

Section 8

In cases concerning measures taken under Section 2 or 2a, or Chapter 27, Section 2a third paragraph, Section 5 third paragraph, or Section 6, or Chapter 28, Section 9, Chapter 31, Section 1 fourth paragraph or Chapter 34, Section 10, second paragraph, a court of the first instance shall provide the sentenced person with an opportunity of making his views known. If he desires to be heard orally, he shall be afforded an appropriate opportunity. In cases concerning measures to be taken under Chapter 34, Section 18, the sentenced person shall be afforded an opportunity of making his views known if this be possible. The court's settlement of the matter shall be made by decision.

Measures taken under Chapter 28, Section 11, first and second paragraphs may be decided without affording the offender the opportunity of making his views known. (Law 1998:604)

Section 9

The court's decision on a measure to be taken in accordance with Chapter 27, Section 2a, third paragraph or Section 5, third paragraph, Chapter 28, Section 11, first and second paragraphs, Chapter 31, Section 1, fourth paragraph or Chapter 34, Section 10, second paragraph, or Section 18, shall take immediate effect unless otherwise ordered. This also applies to decisions on conditions, supervision or probationary periods in accordance with the provisions of Chapter 27, Section 6, Chapter 28, Section 9, or Chapter 34, Section 4, 5 or 6. (Law 1998:604)

Section 10

A warning decided upon by a court or a supervision board shall be promptly delivered to the offender in person. If the warning cannot be delivered in connection with the decision, another court or supervision board may be requested to deliver it.

Section 11

Repealed (Law 1973:918)

Section 12

Police authorities shall assist the court, the supervision boards, the National Parole Board and local prison and probation administrations to secure the offender's appearance in a proceeding or in a matter dealt with in accordance with this Code or his detention under Chapter 26, Section 22 or Chapter 28, Section 6b or Section 11. (Law 1998:604)

Section 13

The National Prison and Probation Administration or, if empowered by the Administration, a director of a regional prison and probation administration, may alter what a local prison and probation administration has decided in accordance with this Code. The Administration's decision in such a matter cannot be appealed. This also applies to a decision by the director of a region, which can, however, be amended by the Administration.

The first paragraph does not apply to decisions referred to in Chapter

26, Section 6, third paragraph, Section 7, Section 11, Section 12, second sentence, Section 13, second sentence, or Section 16 first paragraph, second sentence. (Law 1998:604))

Section 14

The National Prison and Probation Administration may alter a decision concerning the delay or postponement of conditional release which in accordance with the empowerment provided for in Chapter 26, Section 9, second paragraph has been decided on by another prison and probation administration. The person concerned by such a decision may request the National Prison and Probation Administration to review the decision if it has gone against him.

A decision of the National Prison and Probation Administration taken in accordance with the provisions of Chapter 26, Section 6, third paragraph and Section 7 may be appealed to an administrative court.

Leave to appeal is required with an appeal to the administrative court of appeal. (Law 1998:604)

Section 15

The National Prison and Probation Administration may, in accordance with Section 7 a of the law (1971:291) on administrative procedure, present the official case in a county administrative court and an administrative court of appeal. (Law 1998:604)

The National Prison and Probation Administration presents the official case in the Supreme Administrative Court.

Section 16

The Government or an administration designated by the Government may order State compensation for damage that has been caused by a sentenced person in the course of the unpaid work performed in accordance with Chapter 27, Section 2a, first paragraph, Chapter 28, Section 2a, first paragraph and Chapter 31, Section 1, third paragraph, point 2. (Law 1998:604)

后　记

　　记得有位学者说过，翻译与评论之间或许有些天然的不和谐。大致意思是说，翻译是精细的活，可以见木不见林，而评论却可以由林及木，或宏大或细微。译者自知才疏学浅，只敢研习揣摩，从没有翻译乃至评论一国法典的念头。承蒙我的导师谢望原教授不弃，嘱我翻译《瑞典刑法典》，我即忐忑不安地开始了这项艰难的翻译工作。一方面，我认为借此可以提升自己阅读理解英文专业论著的能力；另一方面，我也感到世事皆在人为，翻译法典也许确实能为我国刑法学研究略尽我的绵力。

　　从翻译初始直至结束，译者深切体会到了翻译法典之难。既要准确传达原本之刑法条文的含义，还要切实符合译本之广大读者的思维。译者总在二者之间徘徊，不断选择条文的用语或表述，力求平衡和完满。尽管经译者和审校者再三斟酌，译者仍不能确信语言的转换没有变更条文的原意，希望读者不吝赐教，对翻译中的谬误多予批评指正。

　　此外要说明的是，我体会到仅仅根据制定法的条文对一国法律制度予以分析乃至评判，可能会曲解它在实践中所产生的实际效果。对刑法典的解释，不能单纯依赖其字面的含义，更应当了解刑法典背后制定、修改以及适用的背景。所以，译者也恳请读者，不要简单依照条文的含义断定条文所包含的刑法制度以及适用效果。要深入了解一国之刑法制度，所需要的不仅是一部刑法典，还有很多此外的东西。

　　本刑法典的翻译是在译者攻读博士期间完成的，现在能将其交付北京大学出版社出版，得益于身边很多老师和同学以及责任编辑陈新旺先生的鼓励和帮助。虽然我还并未完成学业，但在读书期间，深感于自己以及身边的同学一面寻求精神的家园一面渴求物质的享受，总在不停的踟蹰和挣扎，但是最后总能说服自己前方就是希望所在，正所谓

"路漫漫其修远兮,吾将上下而求索"。

  要特别指出的是,我的导师谢望原教授作为本丛书的总编译,为本法典的翻译和出版作了大量指导和审校工作,谨致诚挚谢意!

陈　琴

2004 年 11 月 5 日

于中国人民大学